I10793183

IMAGES
of America

BEVERLY REVISITED

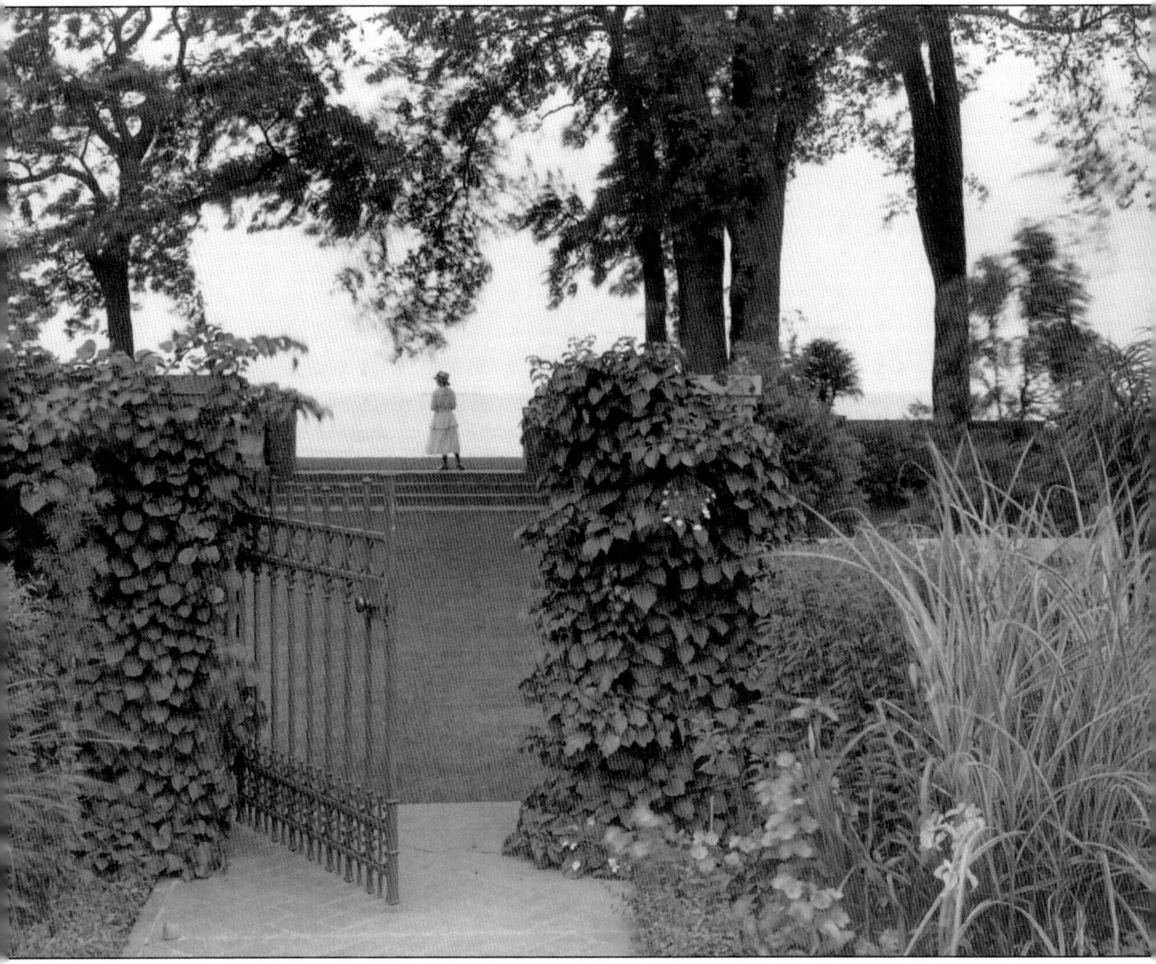

An unidentified woman takes in an early-20th-century view of the Atlantic Ocean from the Italian garden at the estate of Robert and Marie Antoinette Evans, now known as the David S. Lynch Memorial Park. Beverly has long been known to many as the "Garden City," although the derivation of that term is unknown. (Courtesy of the Beverly Historical Society.)

ON THE COVER: This *c.* 1875 image of Green's Field in Ryal Side shows the Bass River and River Street in the background. The First Parish Church and First Baptist Church on Cabot Street can be seen in the distance at middle left. The Gray's Moroccan Factory smokestack, the B. E. Cole and Company Shoe Factory, and the LeFavour Shoe Factory are visible on Rantoul Street. (Courtesy of the Beverly Historical Society.)

IMAGES
of America

BEVERLY REVISITED

Beverly Historical Society

ARCADIA
PUBLISHING

ISBN 978-0-7385-7358-8

Published by Arcadia Publishing
Charleston, South Carolina

Printed in the United States of America

Library of Congress Control Number: 2010922844

For all general information contact Arcadia Publishing at:
Telephone 843-853-2070
Fax 843-853-0044
E-mail sales@arcadiapublishing.com
For customer service and orders:
Toll-Free 1-888-313-2665

Visit us on the Internet at www.arcadiapublishing.com

CONTENTS

ACKNOWLEDGMENTS

The Beverly Historical Society is very grateful to the trustees, staff, and volunteers who worked so hard on this project. Historians love to spend time looking through old photographs and documents, but limiting the number possible for this book meant making some painful choices and eliminating many favorite stories. Curator of collections Darren Brown worked tirelessly to find just the right images and to make sure we got the history right. Research assistant Terri McFadden brought many stories to life through her expressive writing. We are lucky to have such a talented and knowledgeable staff. Ed Brown, Virginia Currier, Jeff Dauzat, Dave Fletcher, Fred Hammond, Adrienne Howard, Babette Loring, and Tina Torsey put many thoughtful hours into this project. Kay Curran, Paul Larcom, Erich and Scott O'Neil, and Amy Whelan made valuable contributions. And, of course, many thanks to those donors who have helped us to acquire such an extraordinary collection of images and documents. We are very grateful for their generosity and their stewardship of Beverly history.

Unless otherwise noted, all images appear courtesy of the Beverly Historical Society.

—Susan Goganian, director

INTRODUCTION

Originally a part of Salem known as the Bass River Side (or sometimes Cape Ann Side), Beverly became a town in 1668. It was named for the minster town of Beverley, England. It changed from a town to a city government in 1894. Originally it was in the territory of the Agawam Indians, who were decimated in a plague before the first white settlers arrived. Beverly's colonial history began with the Thousand Acre Grant of 1635 to five men: Roger Conant, who had founded Salem in 1626; John Woodberry; William Trask; John Balch; and Peter Palfrey, who transferred his 200 acres to William Dodge. John Balch built a house near the Bass River that year. That house, or one which had replaced it by 1680, remained in the family until the 20th century. It is now owned by the Beverly Historical Society. Other settlers quickly followed them, and Bass River was allowed to build its own meeting house in 1656. The Reverend John Hale became minister of the first church established there in 1667, and political independence was gained the following year. Colonial Beverly, along with other Essex County towns, suffered heavily in 1675 during King Philip's War, when the military company commanded by Capt. Thomas Lothrop of Beverly was ambushed and wiped out by Native Americans near present South Deerfield. Reverend Hale became a figure in the 1692 witchcraft delusion and later wrote an important book, *A Modest Inquiry on the Nature of Witchcraft*, to analyze the mistakes that had been made. Controversial Beverly resident Dorcas Hoar came within a day of being hanged as a witch before saving herself with a "confession."

Beverly played an important role during the Revolutionary War. In addition to sending many men into the army, the town's harbor became a strategic base for the many privateer vessels that preyed on British shipping. Hugh Hill was the most famous of the privateer captains. After George Washington took command of the Continental Army in the summer of 1775, he made Beverly the base of what became known as Washington's Navy. The first armed vessel to sail from Beverly was the schooner *Hannah*. During the clash between the *Hannah* and HMS *Nautilus* on October 10, 1775, Beverly came under enemy fire for the only time in its history. Early in the war, when merchants began hoarding supplies, Beverly women broke into a warehouse in what became known as the Sugar Riot and seized stocks of sugar and sold it for the colonial currency, which some merchants refused to accept.

The railroad came to Beverly in 1839 when the Eastern Railroad extended its line north from Salem; the Gloucester Branch, which runs through Beverly Farms, was added in 1847. During the period from around 1850 to the 1920s, Beverly became the heart of the Gold Coast when the summer estates of many rich and famous Americans were constructed here, including such family names as Frick, Moore, Ayer, Loring, and Sears. Many immigrant families came to work on the estates and stayed on to enhance Beverly's cultural diversity.

The Civil War came at a high price to the town. In 1860, Beverly had a population of just over 6,000. More than 700 Beverly men served in the war; 74 died of battle wounds or disease, with some of the sickness contracted in POW camps. Beverly resident Hannah Rantoul was a founding member of U.S. president Abraham Lincoln's Sanitary Commission, which tried to improve conditions for the troops. After the war, Beverly's Grand Army of the Republic Chipman Post No. 89, one of the most active in the state, contributed to the Civil War memorial that stands at Monument Square, which was dedicated in October 1882.

Beverly enjoyed a great distinction from 1909 until 1912, when it became the nation's "Summer White House." U.S. president William Howard Taft chose this community for a summer seaside getaway for himself and his family. For the first two summers he occupied the Stetson Cottage on the shorefront estate of Robert and Marie Antoinette Evans, at what today is Beverly's prized Lynch Park. Unfortunately, Robert Evans died from injuries sustained in a fall from a horse just before the president and his family moved in, and after two summers, his widow Marie Antoinette tired of the U.S. Secret Service, reporters, and nosy tourists tramping about her grounds. She evicted the president, and to make sure nobody could change her mind, she had Stetson Cottage cut in half and floated on a barge to Marblehead, after which she built the beautiful Italian garden on the site. For the last two summers, President Taft stayed at Parramatta, the Corning Street estate of the late Henry W. Peabody.

The most significant time in the city's industrial history began in 1903, when the massive United Shoe Machinery Corporation complex, locally known as "the Shoe," was constructed between Elliott and Balch Streets. The business drew many Italian immigrants to its construction jobs. The Shoe became Beverly's largest employer for generations of workers, both blue and white collar. In addition to providing jobs, the company provided for its workers by building an 18-hole golf course (now municipally owned), tennis courts, a clubhouse, and other amenities. After antitrust laws forced the company to break up in the 1980s, the former Shoe complex was refurbished and reborn as the Cummings Center, the site for a number of thriving firms.

Today this city is home to Montserrat College of Art, Endicott College, and what may be the most extraordinary magic show in America, Le Grand David and His Own Spectacular Magic Company. For more than 30 years it has performed to sold-out audiences at two restored downtown theaters, the Cabot Street Cinema (originally the Ware) and the Larcom, named for Beverly native Lucy Larcom, a renowned author and poet. The North Shore Music Theater, a popular summer attraction, opened in 1955. Sports have long been a part of Beverly's heritage. Its high school teams have a long history of excellence, and the first Little League Baseball game in Massachusetts was played at Bessie Baker Park in 1950. In the 1990s, the Beverly Little League constructed its home complex at Harry Ball Field, which is considered the finest youth sports facility in the area. Two of Beverly's star athletes, Stu Irving and Roger Norris, were members or alternates of a U.S. Olympic Team, and the fascinating Eleo Sears was one of the best tennis and squash players of her day.

One

Early Beverly

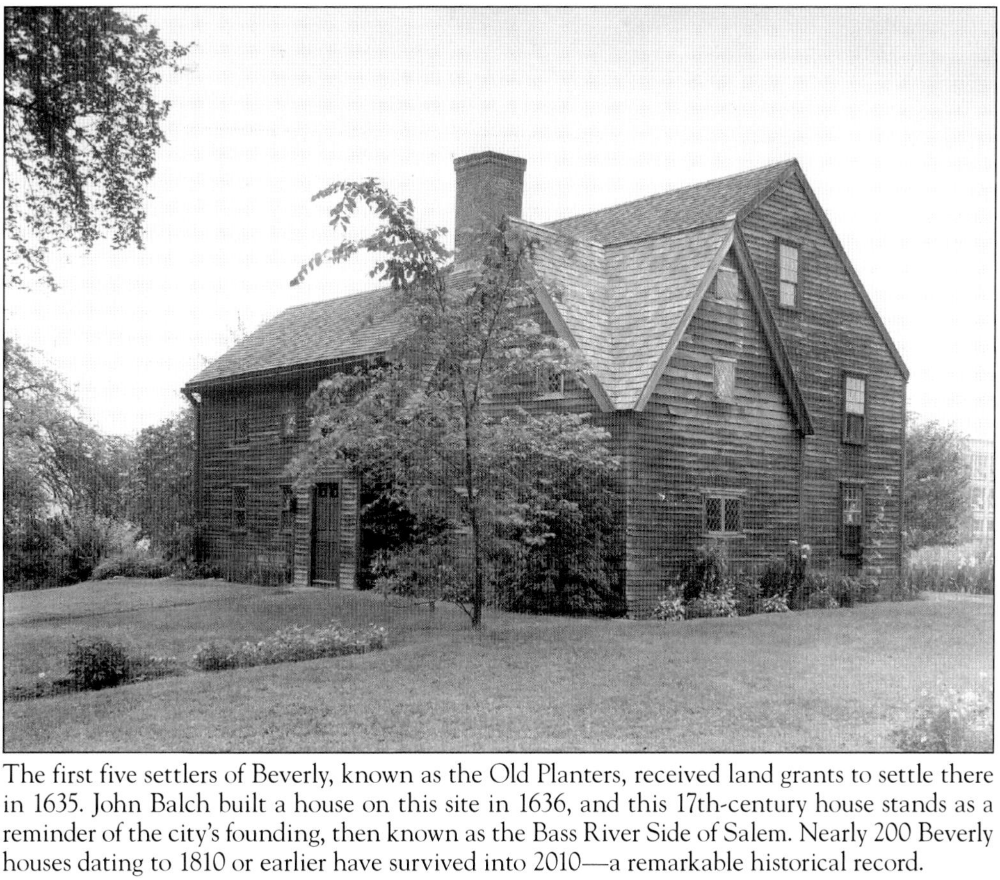

The first five settlers of Beverly, known as the Old Planters, received land grants to settle there in 1635. John Balch built a house on this site in 1636, and this 17th-century house stands as a reminder of the city's founding, then known as the Bass River Side of Salem. Nearly 200 Beverly houses dating to 1810 or earlier have survived into 2010—a remarkable historical record.

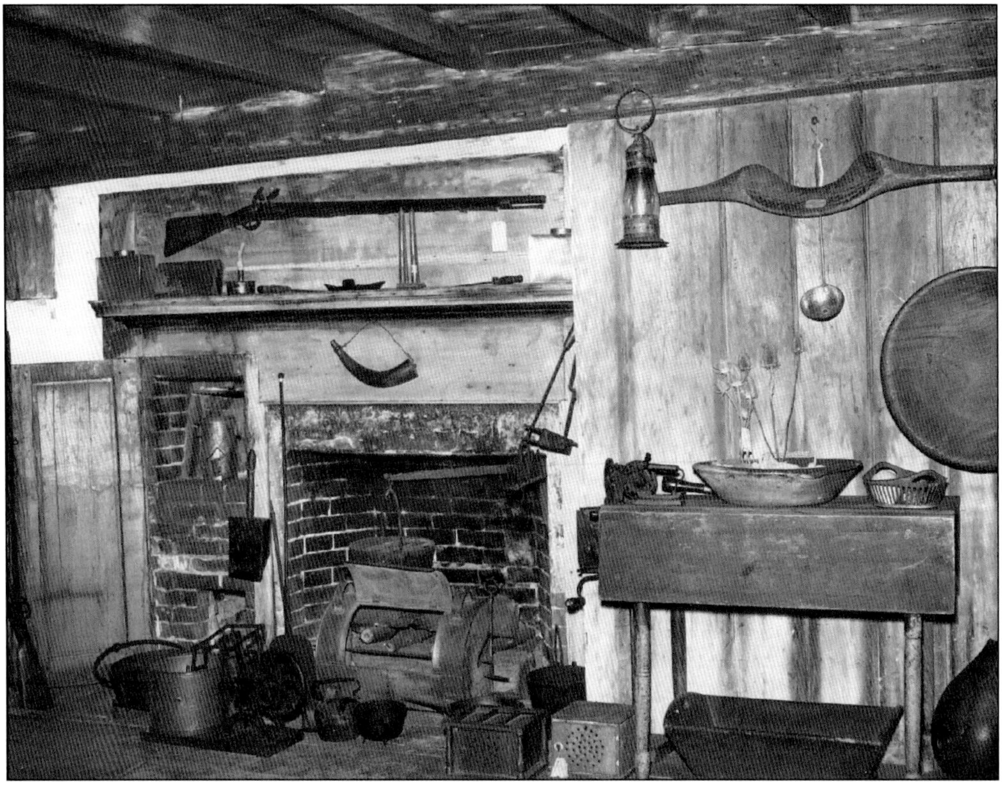

Long thought to date to 1636, recent testing indicates that the earliest part of the Balch House may date to 1680. The original structure consisted of one room with a sleeping loft above. Later the kitchen (shown here) was added onto the first floor and an additional bedroom added to the loft, which was enclosed. The kitchen fireplace with its side oven is an 18th-century alteration.

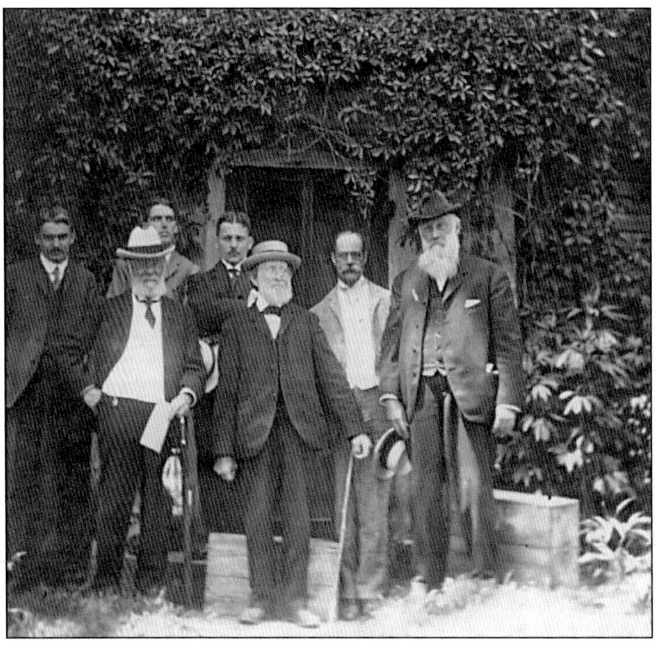

The Balch family history in this country began when John Balch arrived in Massachusetts in 1623. Descendants, now found throughout the United States, began the practice of biennial reunions here in 1905. Shown at that first event are, from left to right, William H. Balch, John Balch, George Balch, Alfred Balch, Benjamin Balch, William L. Balch, and Dr. Galusha Balch, who wrote an extensive genealogy of the family, which was first published in 1897.

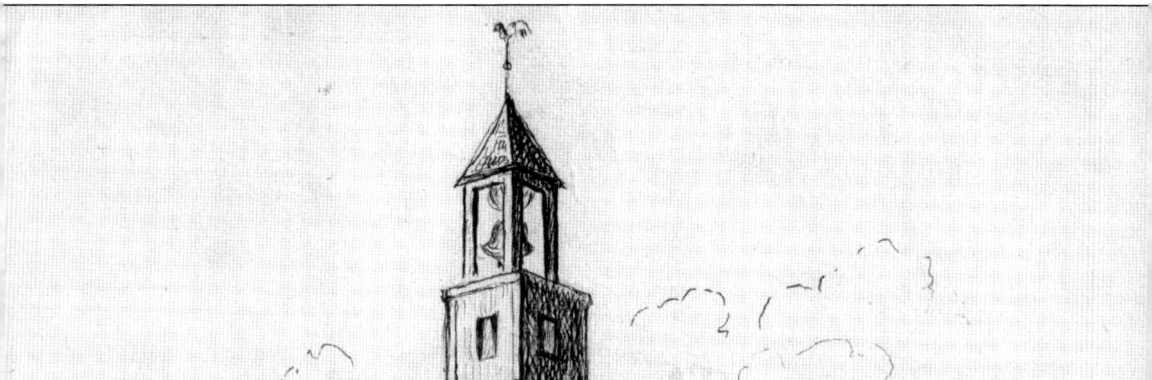

The residents of early Beverly, citizens of Salem, worshipped there rather than in their own neighborhood. This required men, women, and children to travel across the river in boats or to make the long journey around by land. This inconvenience prompted a request to establish a separate meeting house on the Bass River Side. Permission was granted to hire a teacher in 1650, and by 1664, the Reverend John Hale was serving in that capacity. In 1667, Beverly formally separated from the Salem church, acquiring the ability to perform all religious and parish functions, and Hale became the first minister. A year later, the Town of Beverly was established, completing the separation from Salem. This drawing shows the second First Parish structure, the first at the current Cabot Street location, which was built about 1682. The current (third) church building was constructed in 1770.

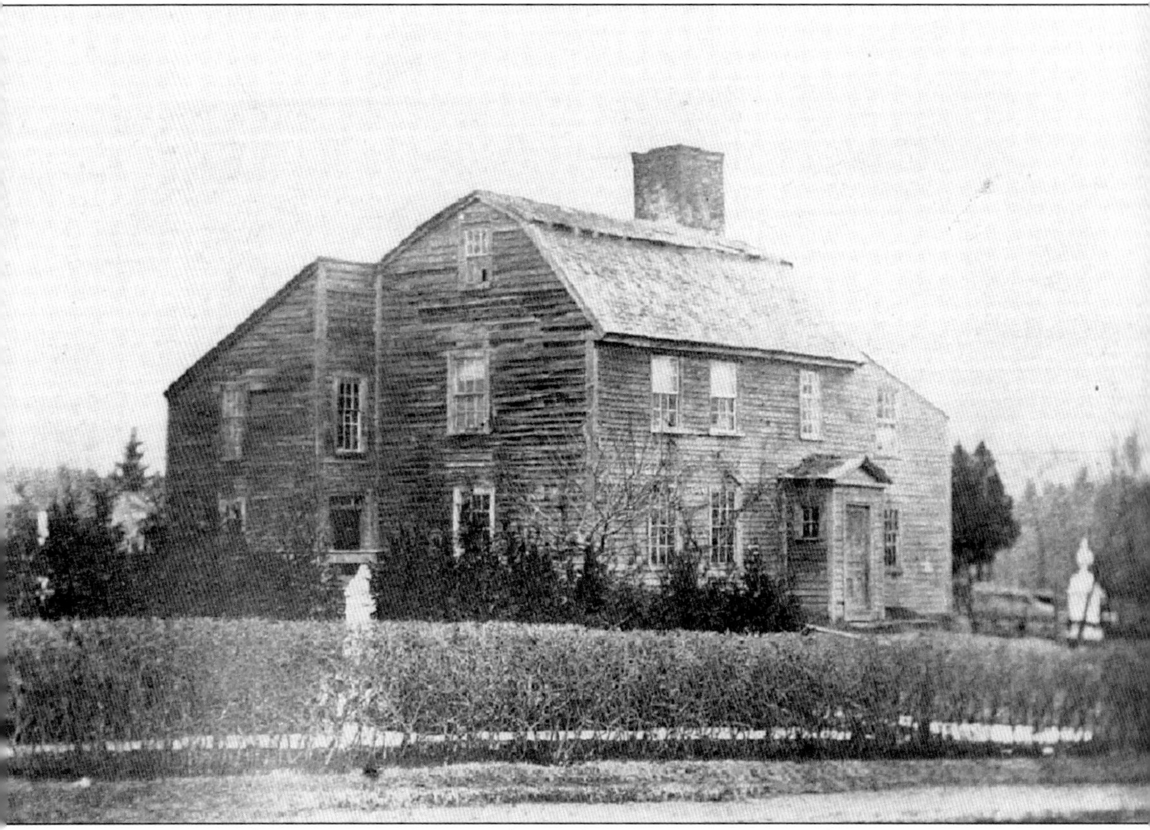

This long-gone house at 66 Hale Street, located on the current Central Cemetery property, was the home of Dorcas Hoar, Beverly's most infamous 17th-century "witch." She came within a day of hanging during the witch fervor in 1692 before saving herself with a "confession." A fortune-teller, she was prosecuted in 1678 for receiving stolen goods from the home of her neighbor and employer, the Reverend John Hale, where she had frightened his children into silence by threatening to bewitch them. She was identified as a witch by David Balch in 1690 and was hours away from execution in September 1692 when she earned a reprieve, as others had, by relating tales that fit the testimony of her accusers. As the witchcraft hysteria subsided, the trials that took place were less susceptible to wild accusations, and Hoar was released from jail several months later.

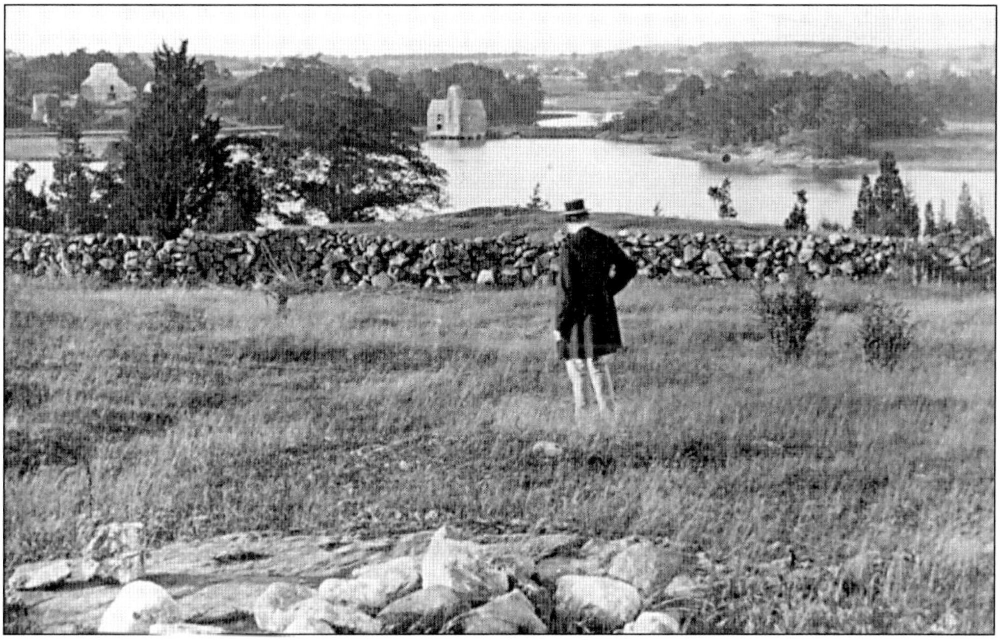

Built around 1647 near what is now the junction of McKay and Elliott Streets in the Ryal Side neighborhood, John Friend's corn mill was in use for about 225 years; it burned in 1889. The region remained part of Salem until 1753. The first half of the 20th century saw a surge of building in the area as a result of the factory constructed by the United Shoe Machinery Corporation.

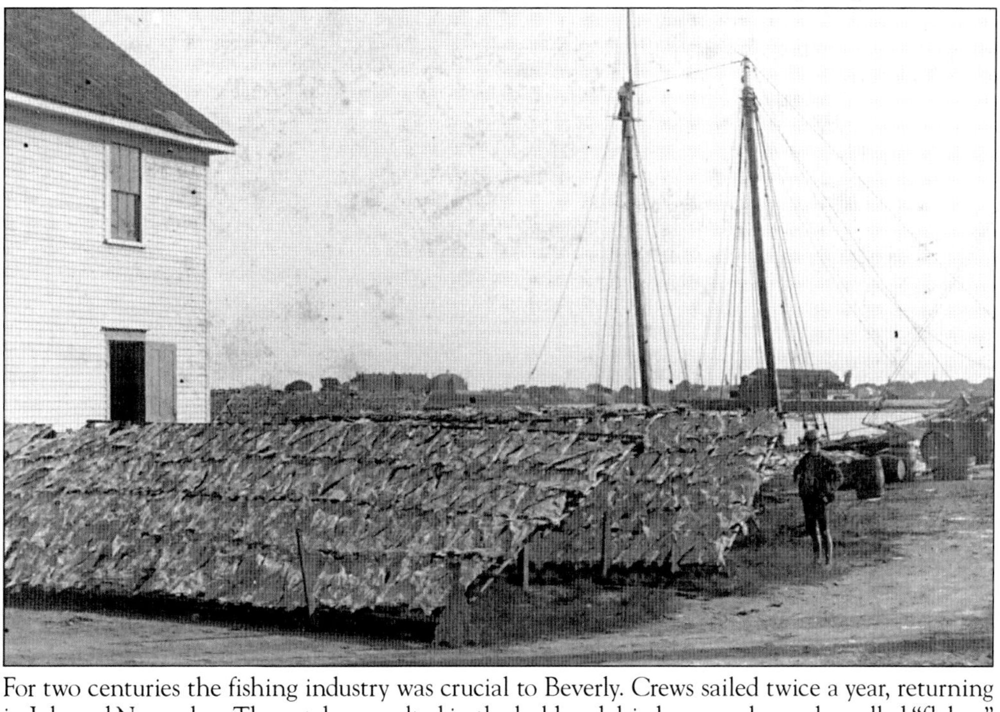

For two centuries the fishing industry was crucial to Beverly. Crews sailed twice a year, returning in July and November. The catch was salted in the hold and dried on wooden racks, called "flakes," along the waterfront. Fish were shipped to Europe and to feed the slaves in the Caribbean. In the 19th century one quarter of Beverly men were fishermen, and others worked in related businesses.

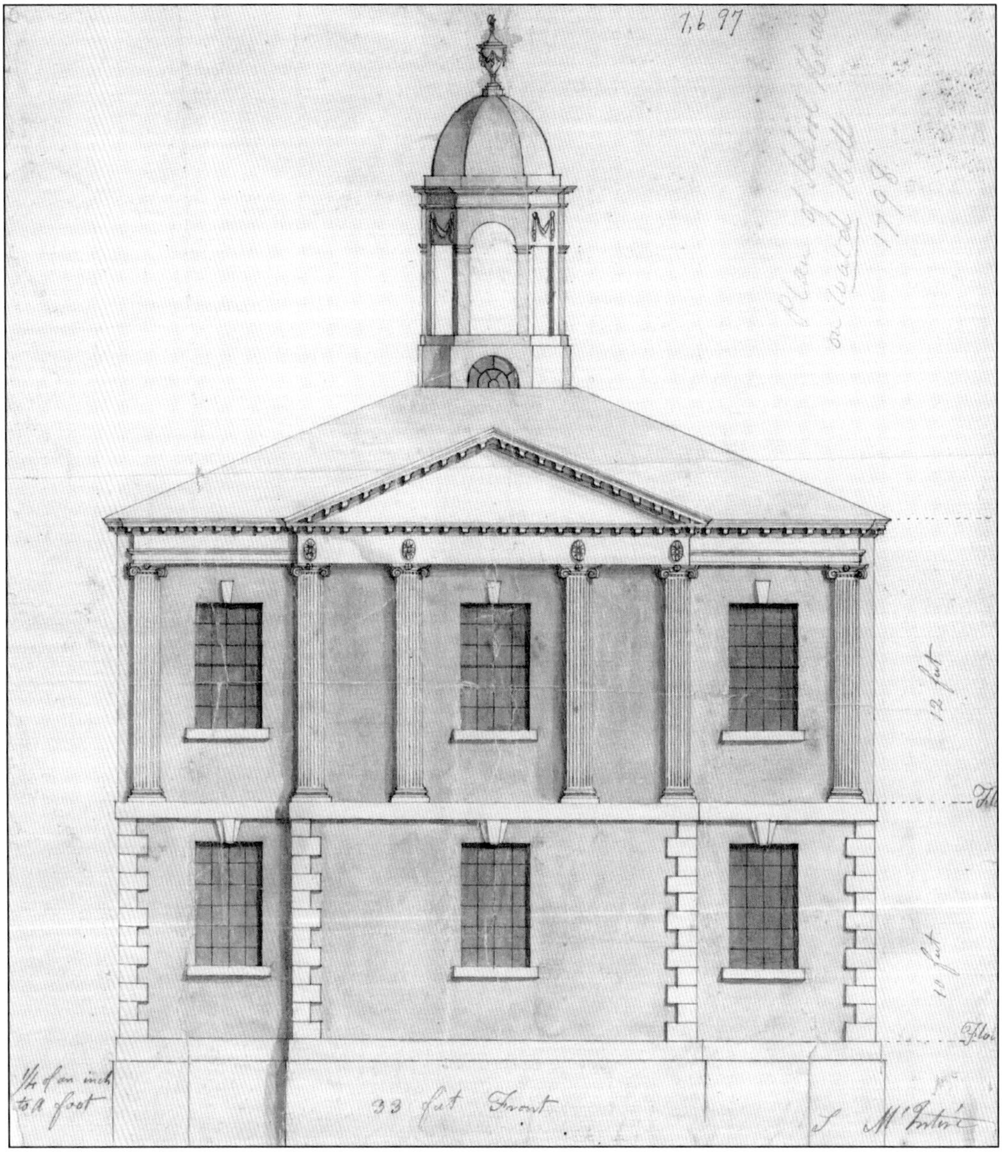

Samuel McIntire called himself a woodcarver, but he was also renowned for his architectural achievements. Born in Salem in 1757, he learned from his father, Joseph (a housewright), and from available books. Much of McIntire's architectural accomplishments can be seen in his hometown, where he built or renovated a number of buildings for Elias Hasket Derby and other Salem merchants. One of the town's historic districts is named for him. He also built the former Salem Courthouse and Hamilton Hall, which still stands on Chestnut Street. McIntire is widely known for woodcarvings on buildings and furniture along with for ships' figureheads. This beautiful architectural drawing was for a commission that came to McIntire in 1798 for the original Hardie School on Essex Street. Later the building was moved to Watch Hill, where, much altered, it still stands. McIntire died in 1811.

Privateers were permitted by law to prey on the enemies of the United States. Many Beverly men, including the well-known Hugh Hill, sailed on the vessels that disrupted British trade, intercepted messages, and provided captured goods to the Colonial Army and the home market. The Cabot family controlled most of the Beverly vessels, but it was a risky business, and fortunes were lost as well as made.

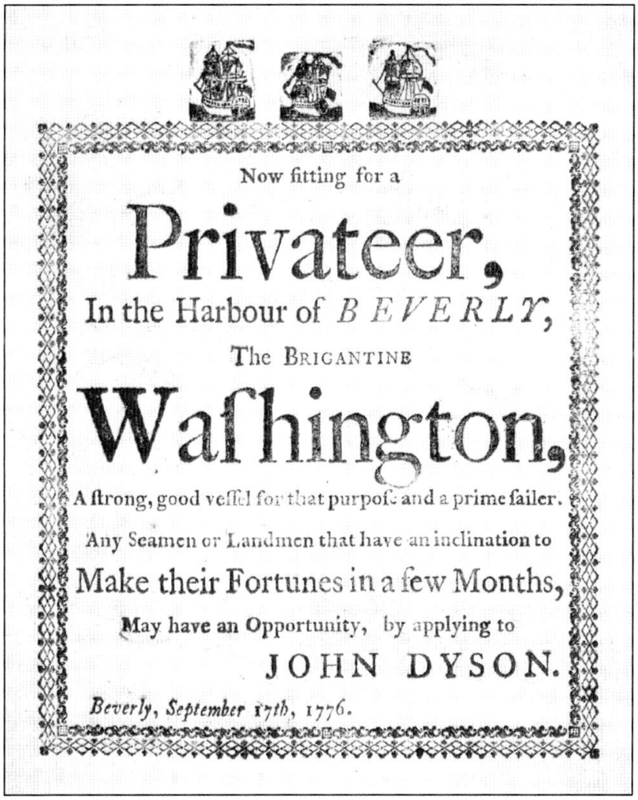

Now fitting for a

Privateer,

In the Harbour of *BEVERLY,*

The BRIGANTINE

Washington,

A strong, good vessel for that purpose and a prime sailer.

Any Seamen or Landmen that have an inclination to

Make their Fortunes in a few Months,

May have an Opportunity, by applying to

JOHN DYSON.

Beverly, September 17th, 1776.

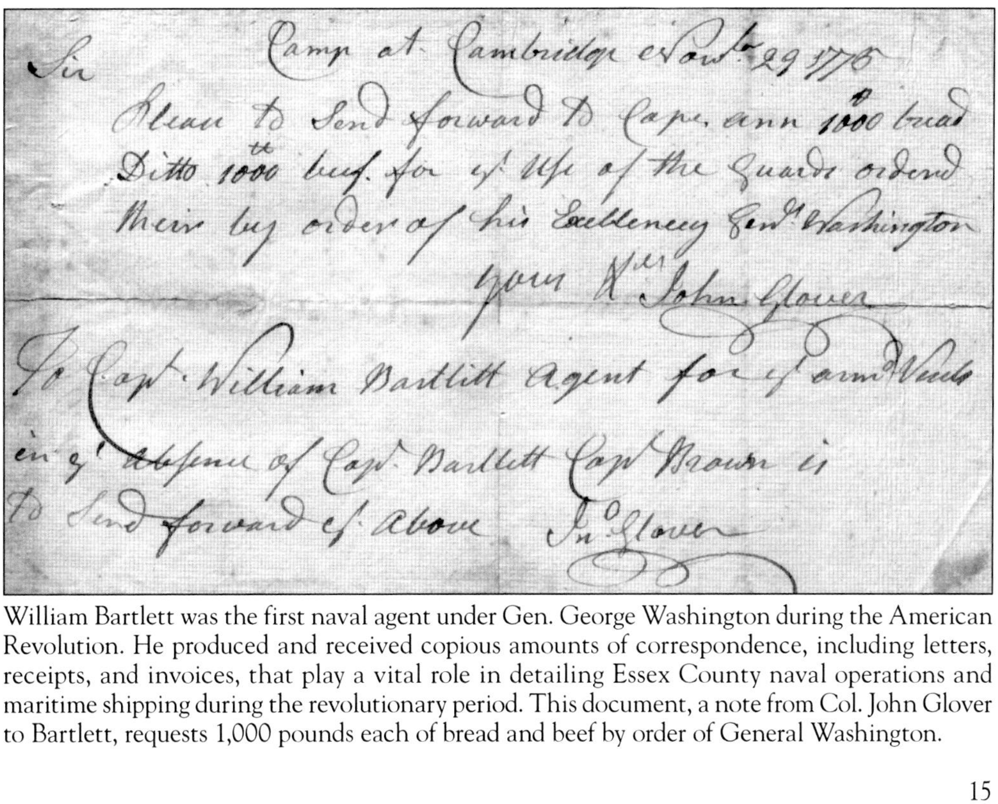

Camp at Cambridge Novr 29 1775

Sir

Please to Send forward to Cape ann 1000 bread
Ditto 1000 beef for ye Use of the Guards ordered
their by order of his Excellency Genl Washington

Your Hr Sr John Glover

To Capt William Bartlett Agent for ye armd Vessels
in ye absence of Capt Bartlett Capt Brown is
to Send forward ye above Jno Glover

William Bartlett was the first naval agent under Gen. George Washington during the American Revolution. He produced and received copious amounts of correspondence, including letters, receipts, and invoices, that play a vital role in detailing Essex County naval operations and maritime shipping during the revolutionary period. This document, a note from Col. John Glover to Bartlett, requests 1,000 pounds each of bread and beef by order of General Washington.

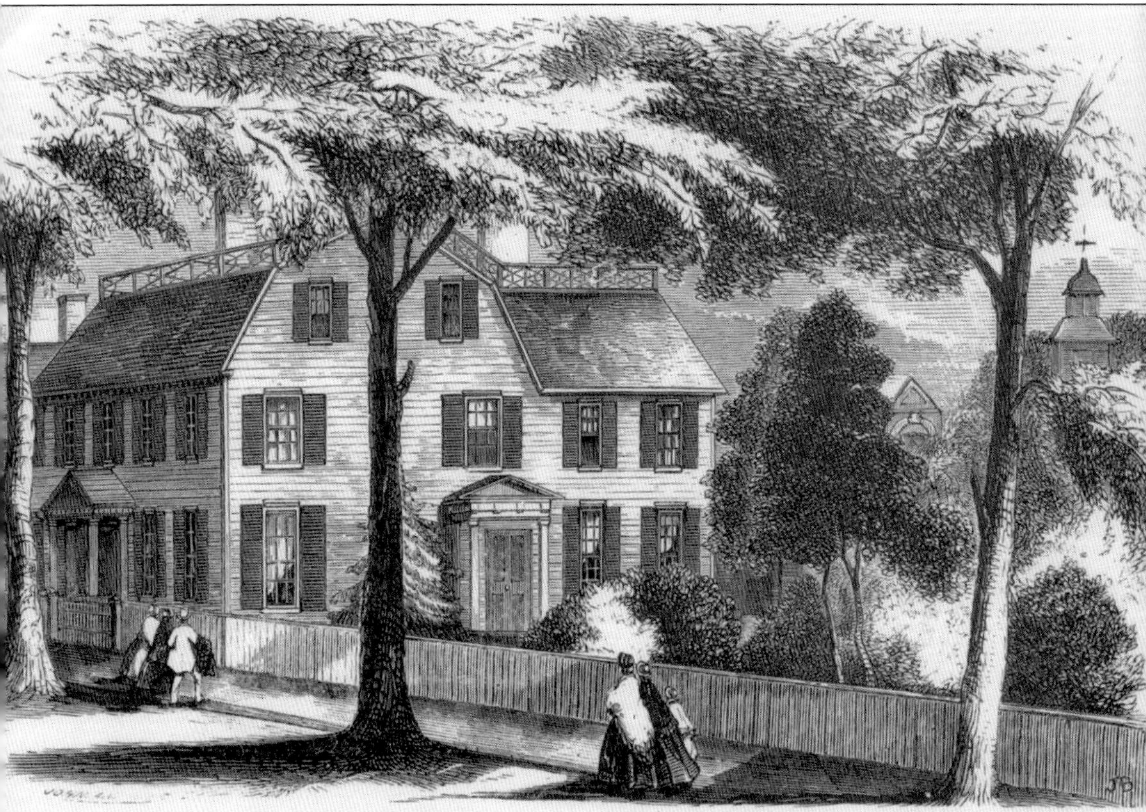

THE RESIDENCE OF MOSES BROWN. Esq.
BEVERLY MASS.

Moses Brown was a graduate of Harvard College and began his business life in Beverly as a merchant before the Revolutionary War. In 1775, he raised a company and joined Col. John Glover's regiment as a captain the following year. He took part in ferrying the Continental Army at Brooklyn Heights and was active in the action at Trenton. On his return to Beverly, Brown began a successful business partnership with Israel Thorndike, his brother-in-law. The two men were involved in shipping, building the Essex Bridge, and were among the founders of Beverly Bank in 1802. Brown was painted by Gilbert Stuart toward the end of his career; that painting is on display at the John Cabot House.

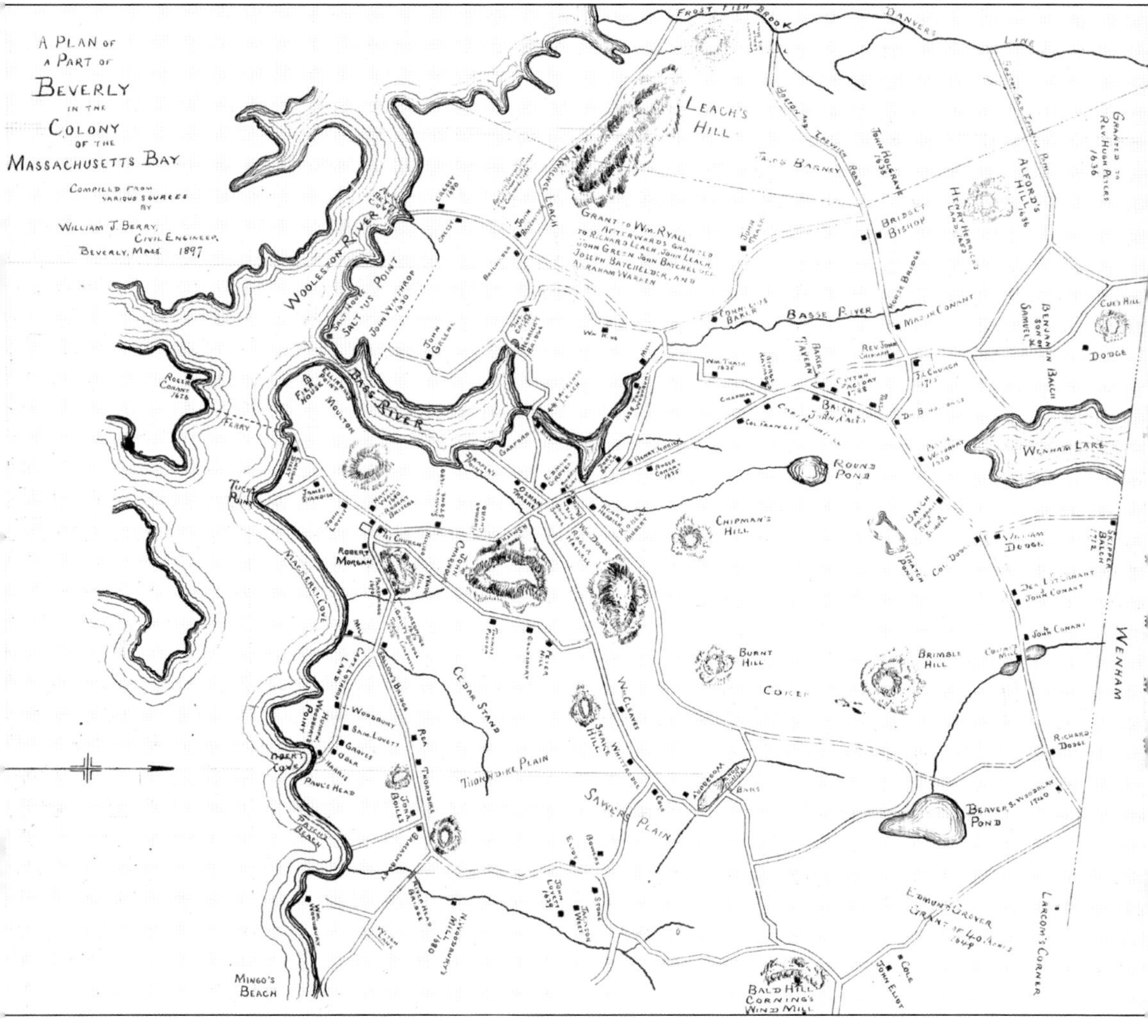

This compilation map, created in 1897 and amended in 1927, provides an illustration of early Beverly. Beverly Harbor is seen on the left, with the Bass River also at left in the middle of the map. Wenham Lake is seen at right. The properties of many of Beverly's 17th- and 18th-century residents are shown. Of particular note, moving clockwise from the harbor, are the following: Mingo and Patch's Beaches, where Beverly's Gold Coast would emerge; the ferry crossing, approximately located where a bridge now connects Beverly and Salem; the land granted originally to William Ryal in what is now the neighborhood of Ryal Side; the home of Edward and Sarah Bishop, who were accused of witchcraft; the first cotton factory in America, located within a triangle of roads below the Bass River; and various Conant properties, originally given to Roger Conant, one of Beverly's Old Planters.

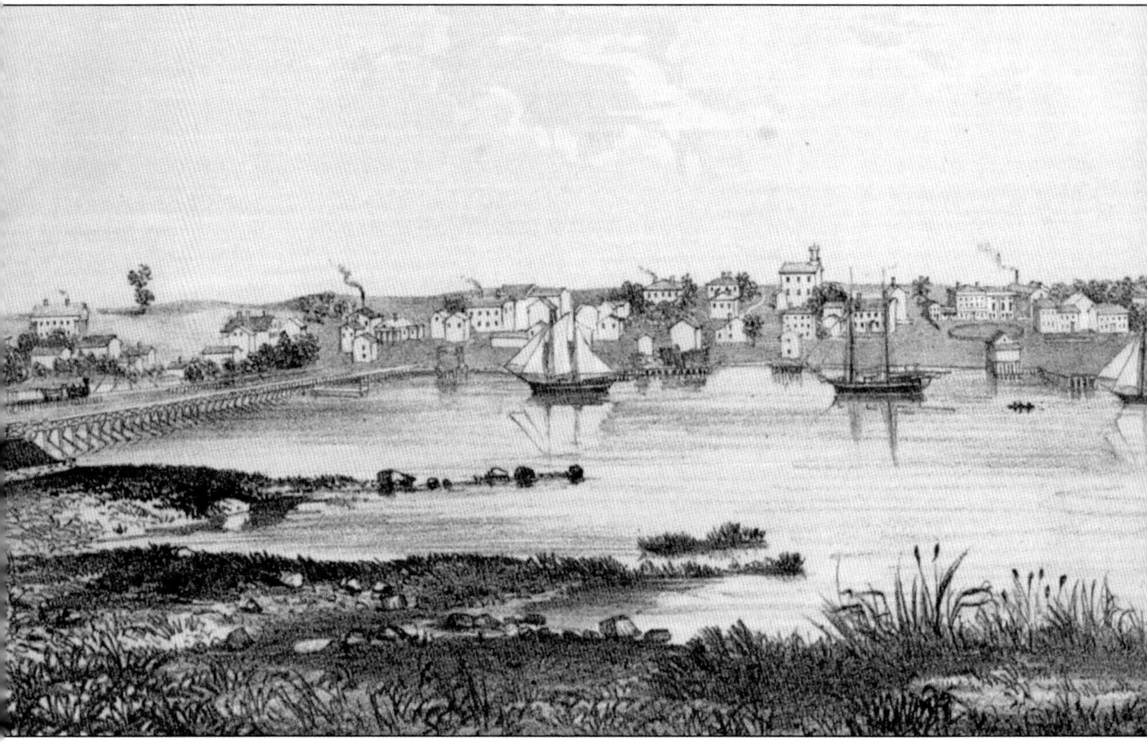

Although the earliest English settlers were farmers, soon many Beverly residents turned to the sea. By the time this view was printed around 1850, fishing and maritime trade provided employment for a large segment of the community, both at sea and in trades supporting the mariners. Fortunes were made by the men who owned the wharves and ships. The coming of the railroad in 1839 was the beginning of a long period of community growth. Up until this time the town had clung to

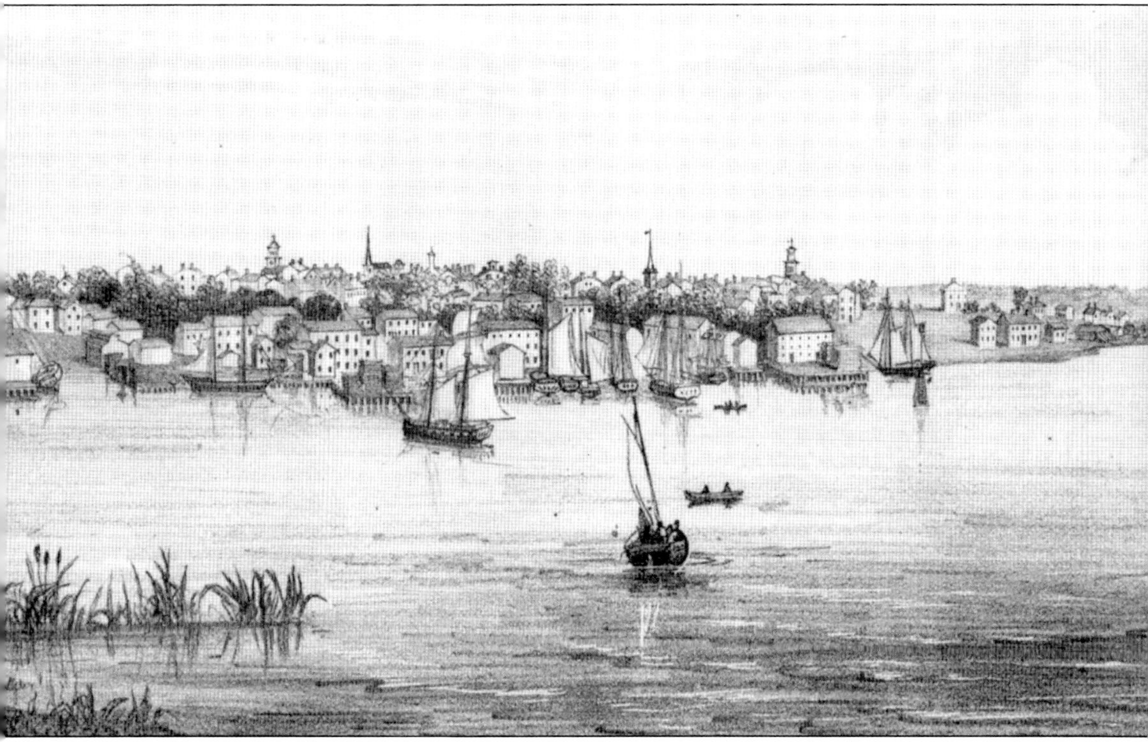

the coastline, but now building began along the Bass River and up on Goat Hill. Tanneries and shoemaking factories were built on Rantoul and Park Streets. Neighborhoods sprang up in the areas around these streets for the immigrant workers from Italy, Ireland, and French Canada who arrived to take jobs provided by the new industries.

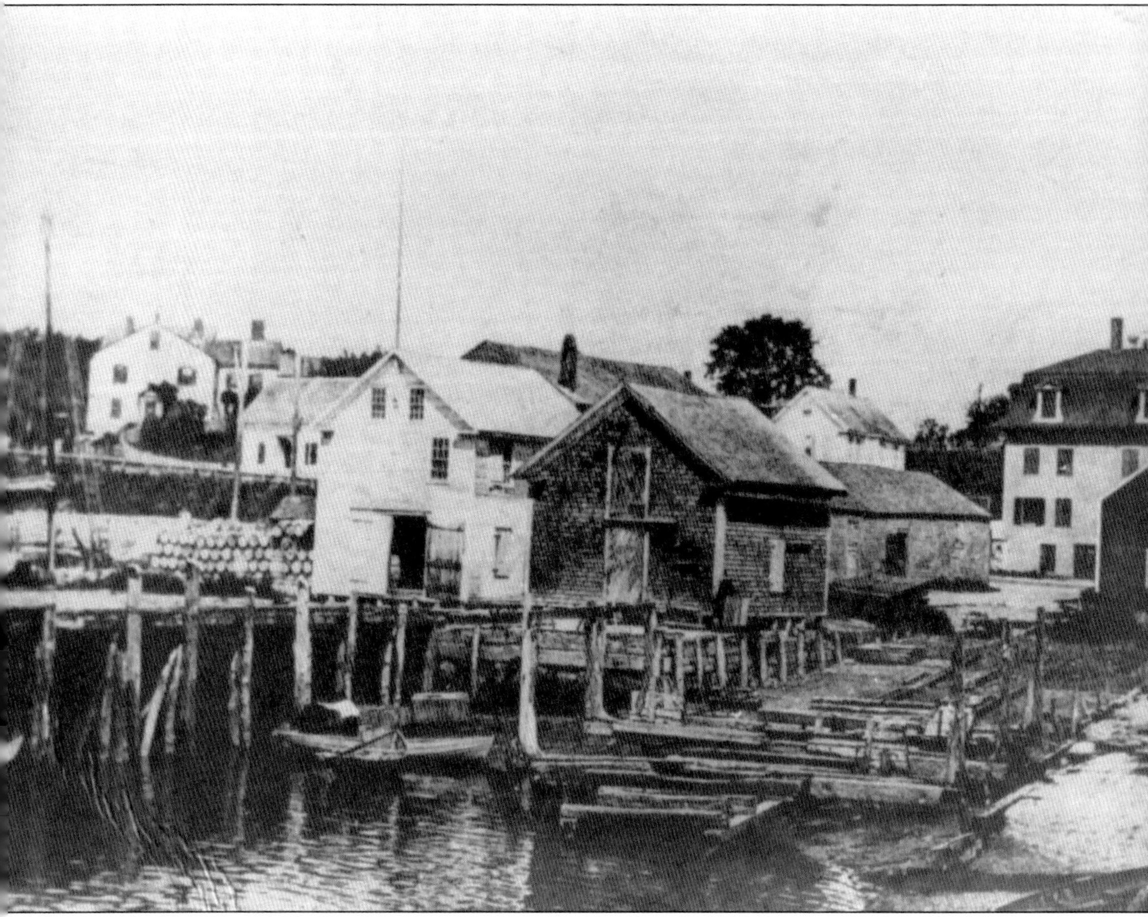

By 1777, the American Revolution had brought severe shortages, skyrocketing prices, and nearly worthless paper money to Massachusetts. The frustration and deprivation was widespread and sparked a female protest directed against Beverly merchants who were suspected of hoarding. Privateer vessels patrolling the Atlantic coastline had captured so much sugar from enemy ships that they were exporting it, yet it was not available to locals at reasonable prices because the merchants would not accept currency of dubious value. As was the case in other American communities, the combination of shortages and suspected price-gouging inflamed residents. In November 1777, approximately 60 women marched to the Cabot distillery on Water Street; upon breaking in they confiscated two large barrels. The sugar was sold in a local shop owned by one of the female participants, and the merchants were compensated for the loss of their goods.

Two

Coastal Life

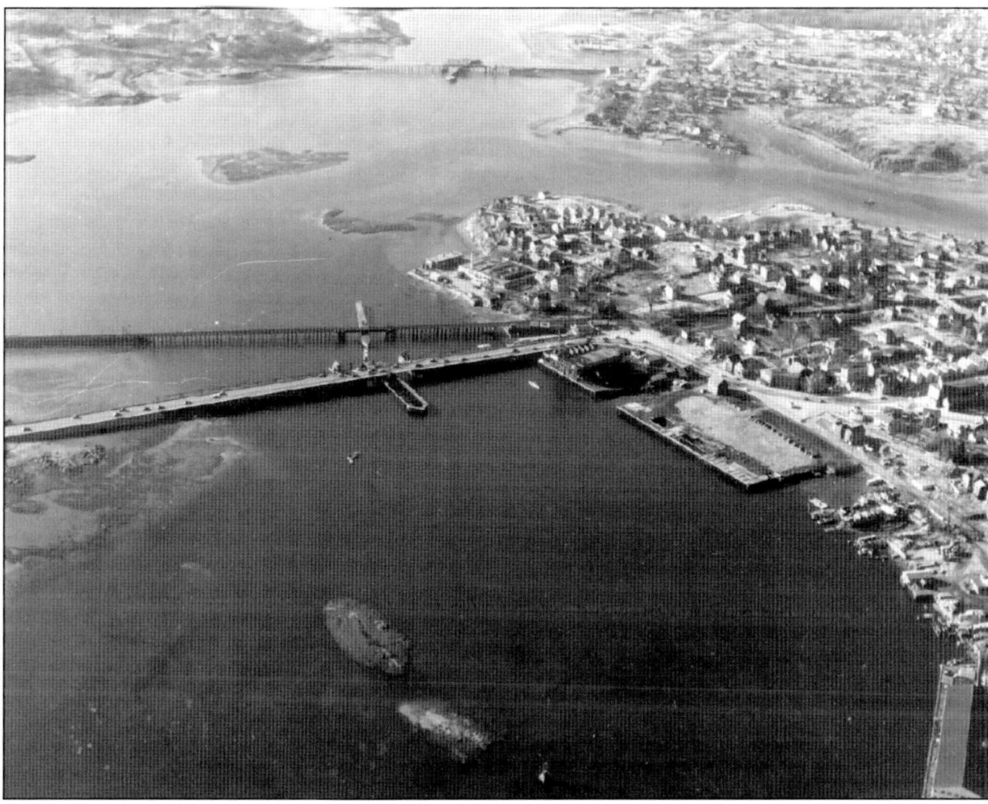

From its earliest days, Beverly was tied to the Atlantic Ocean by the fishing industry and worldwide maritime trade. By the 19th century, the local beaches and parks had become popular with residents and visitors alike. This aerial view, taken in 1950, shows the old Beverly/Salem Bridge with the Bass River in the background. The original bridge was built in 1788.

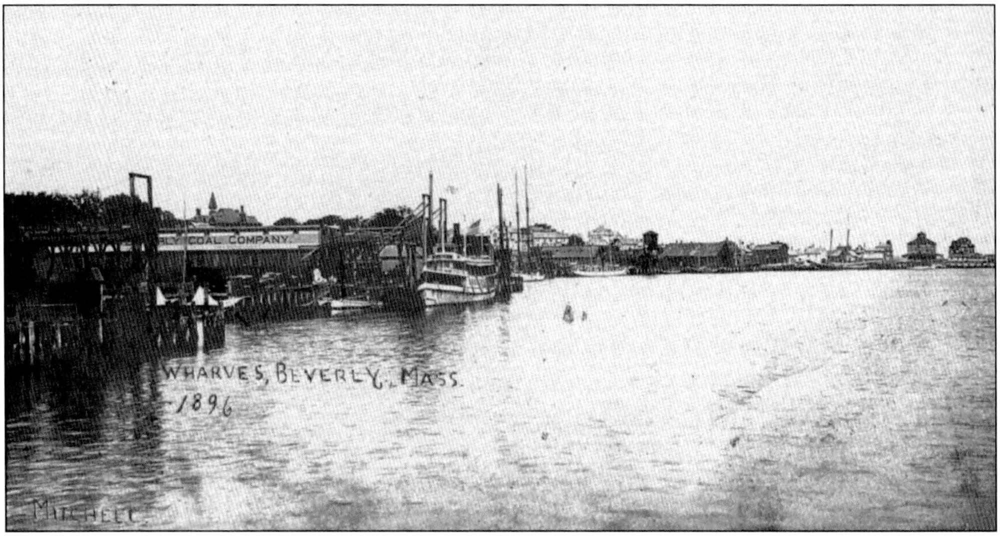

The first commercial wharf in Beverly was Briscoe Wharf, built about 1699, followed by Union Wharf (originally known as Coaster's Wharf). The ship *Hannah,* involved in the first naval battle of the American Revolution, sailed from Glover's Wharf. William Bartlett, George Washington's naval agent, had a warehouse on his wharf, later known as the Old Pickett Warehouse, which was the center of activity for the sale of prize ships and their goods. The Lee, Cabot, Brown, and Thorndike families owned a significant wharf as well. The Cabot family alone owned parts of more than 70 privateers that sailed from Beverly, and the *Pilgrim*, under the command of Capt. Hugh Hill, was credited with capturing 50 prizes (enemy ships). In the photograph above, Beverly Coal Company and Foster's Wharf are visible along this busy commercial section of the waterfront in 1896. The image below is a close-up of the Essex Bridge railing around 1910, with the Sprague, Breed, and Brown Company and the Pickett Coal Company running along the waterfront.

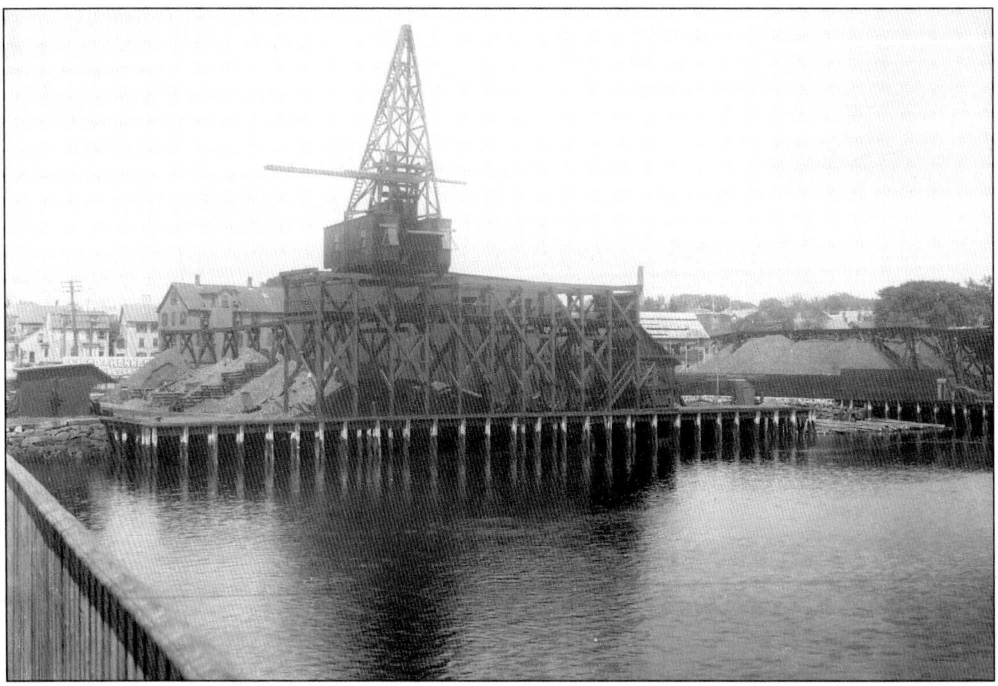

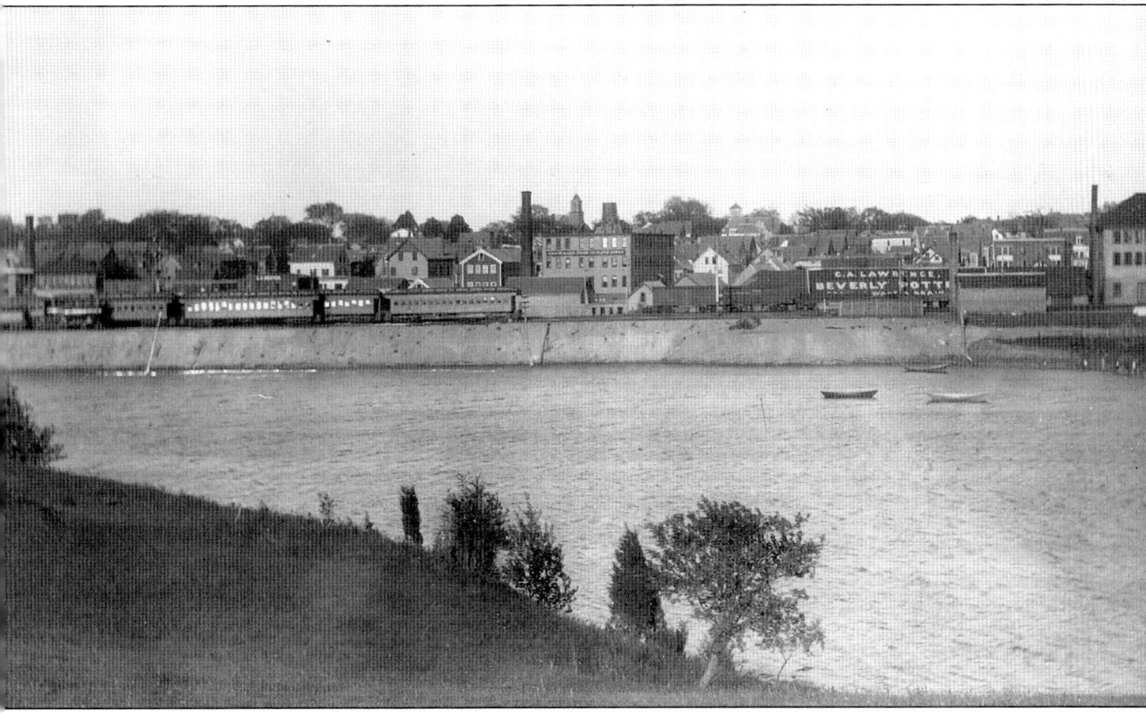

Many of the businesses along River and Park Streets can be seen in this scenic view across the Bass River, taken from Green's Field in Ryal Side around 1870. Beverly Pottery, which was famous for its redware and bean pots, was largely responsible for Boston being nicknamed "Beantown." Beverly Pottery was commissioned by the state department of the Grand Army of the Republic, the largest Union veteran organization, to create souvenir bean pots for the 1890 national encampment in Boston. These were given to all of the veterans, who proudly returned home with their souvenir from Beantown. Beverly Pottery was operated by Charles A. Lawrence, who was of Portuguese descent and had changed his surname from Solares. The Solon Lovett Shoe Factory, to the immediate right of the pottery, and the George H. Allen Box Factory, a total loss in an 1891 fire, are also visible.

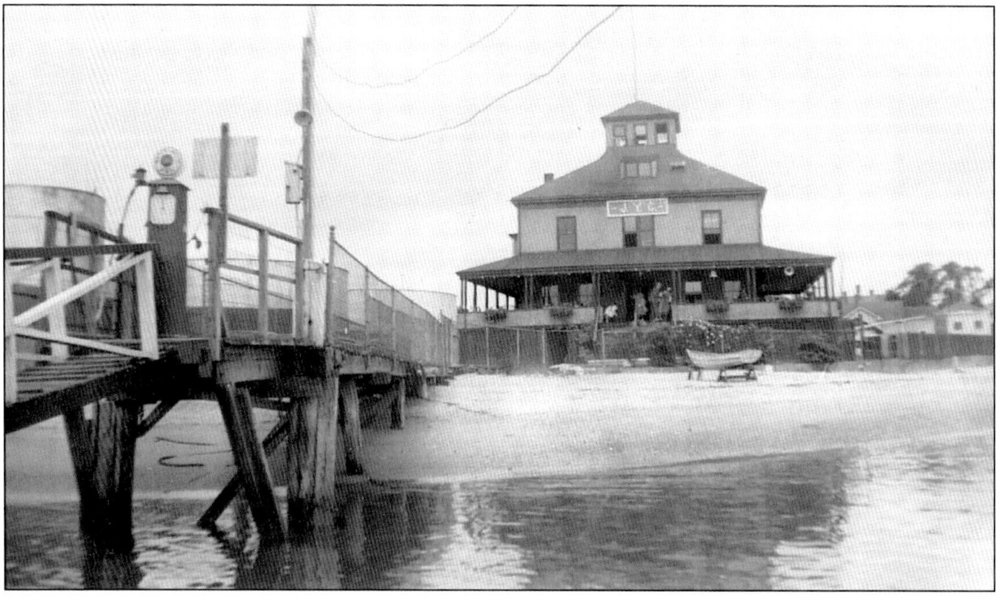

The Jubilee Yacht Club at Tuck's Point grew out of the need for old sailors to have a place to congregate. It was incorporated in 1896 and named after the America's Cup contender of 1893. As pleasure sailing became a popular pastime, the club expanded its membership. The former Oceana House (seen above) became the Jubilee's home after its second season and remained so until it was destroyed in a 1963 fire. The Oceana House was a summer hotel with a long piazza providing impressive views of the harbor. The adjoining property, seen below around 1950, became the home of the Gulf Oil Corporation in the early 20th century. It was the former location of the Pickett Coal Company's Wharf and Kilham's Wharf. Later it became the Beverly Chemical Terminal Company and is now the site of Tuck's Point Condominiums.

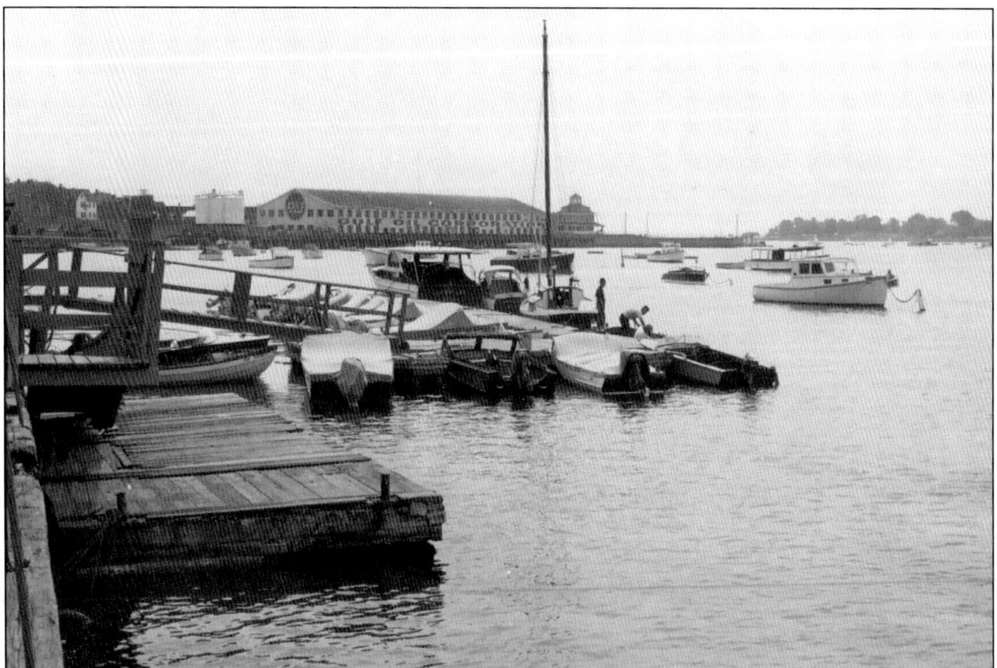

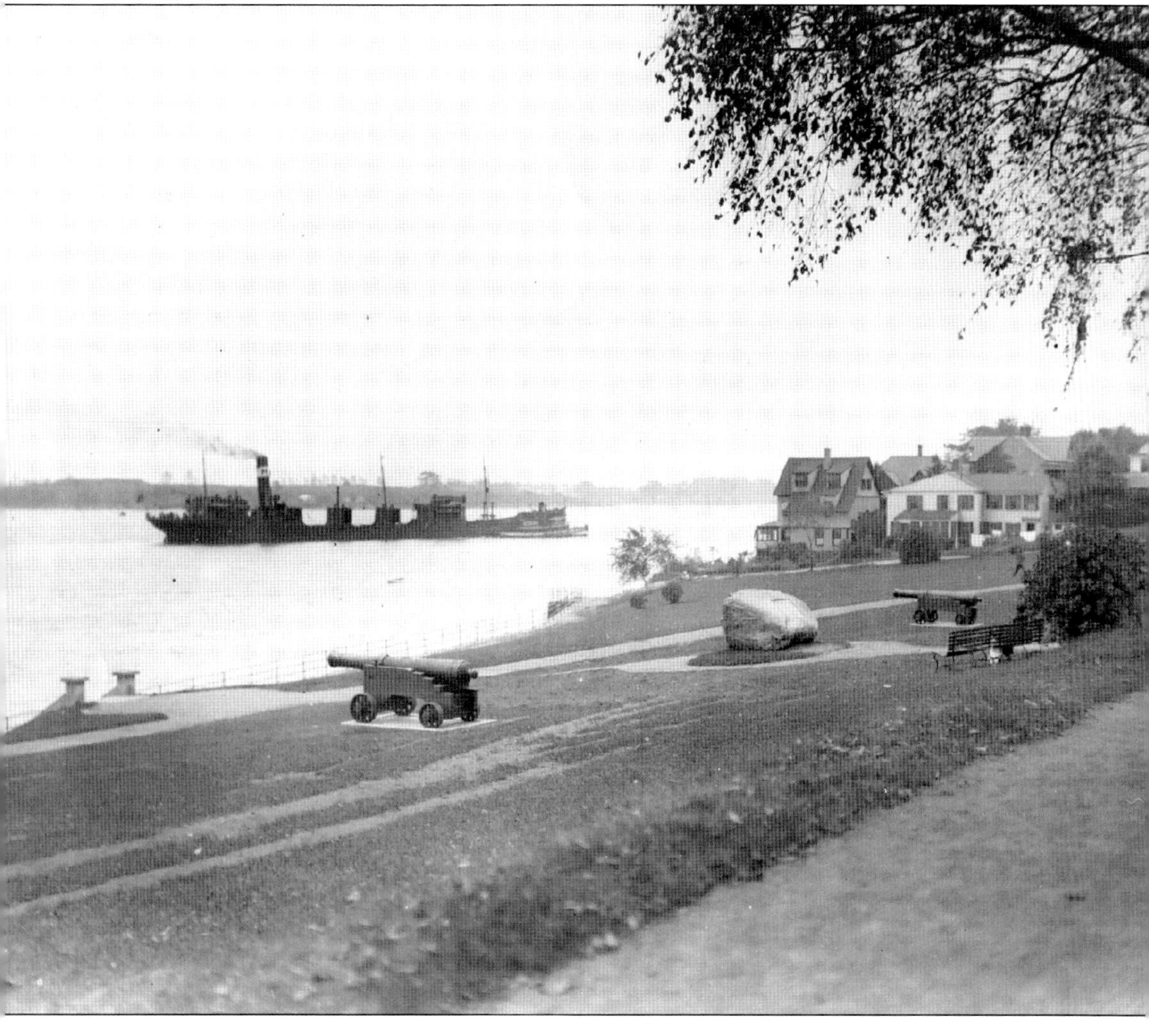

Beverly citizens were actively involved in the quest for independence, founding a Committee of Correspondence to state the rights of colonists in 1772. In 1775, Gen. George Washington chose Beverly Harbor as his base for naval operations. The 78-ton schooner *Hannah*, leased and operated by Marblehead men, sailed out of Beverly to harass enemy ships. The British vessel *Nautilus*, larger and better armed, was dispatched after her. A battle just off today's Independence Park commenced. The tides helped the Americans, and local citizens fired on the grounded British ship. She floated free that evening after taking damage. On July 17, 1776, Col. John Glover gathered his regiment on the parade ground of this same spot, joined by Beverly townspeople. The colonel read the Declaration of Independence, followed by the salute of cannon and the ringing of church bells.

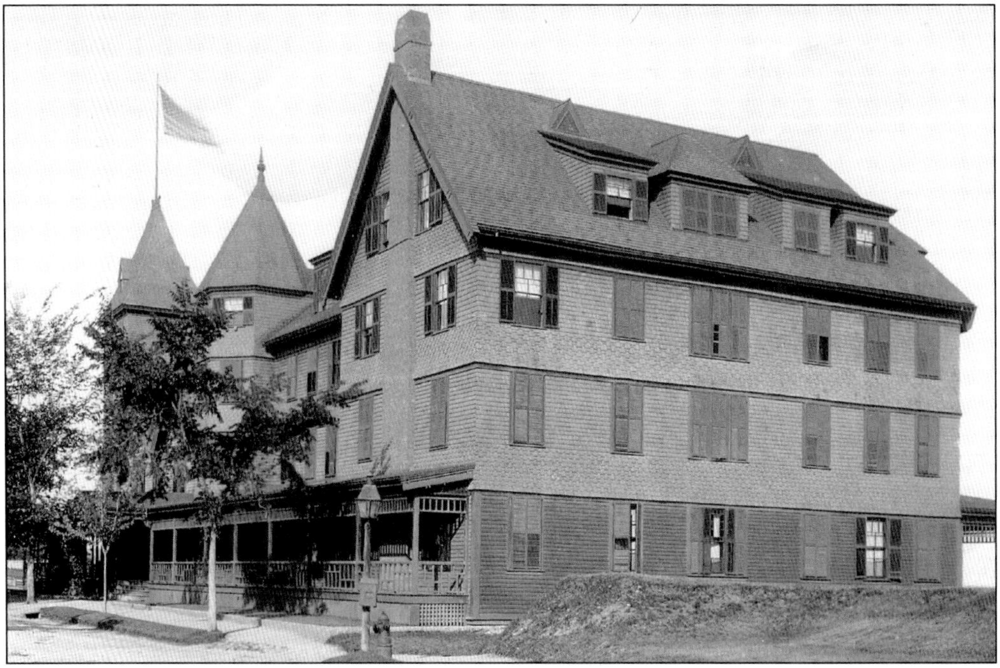

In the 19th century, city dwellers began trekking to the coast to enjoy the ocean breezes and seaside recreation. To satisfy these visitors, Beverly businessman and realtor Israel LeFavour built the Queen Hotel on Lothrop Street in 1889 at a cost of $73,000. Just two and half years later, the five-story building caught fire and burned to the ground in a spectacular blaze seen for miles around. Oceana House on Maple Avenue also provided a home-away-from-home for summer boarders. The Beverly City Directory promised visitors who stayed there good boating, bathing, and fishing at three nearby waterfronts and the "coolest place on the coast."

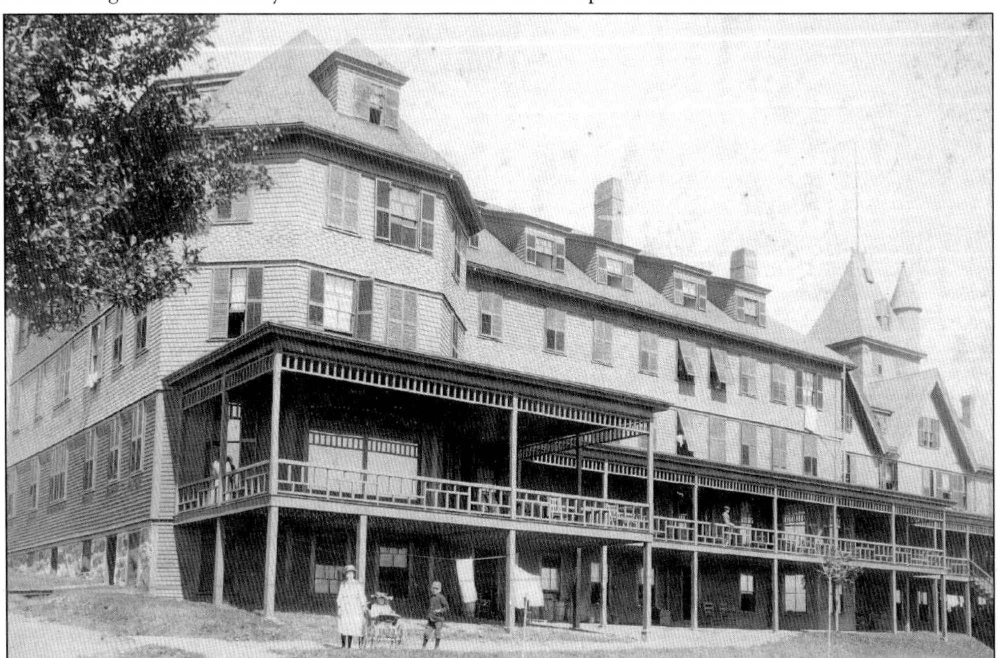

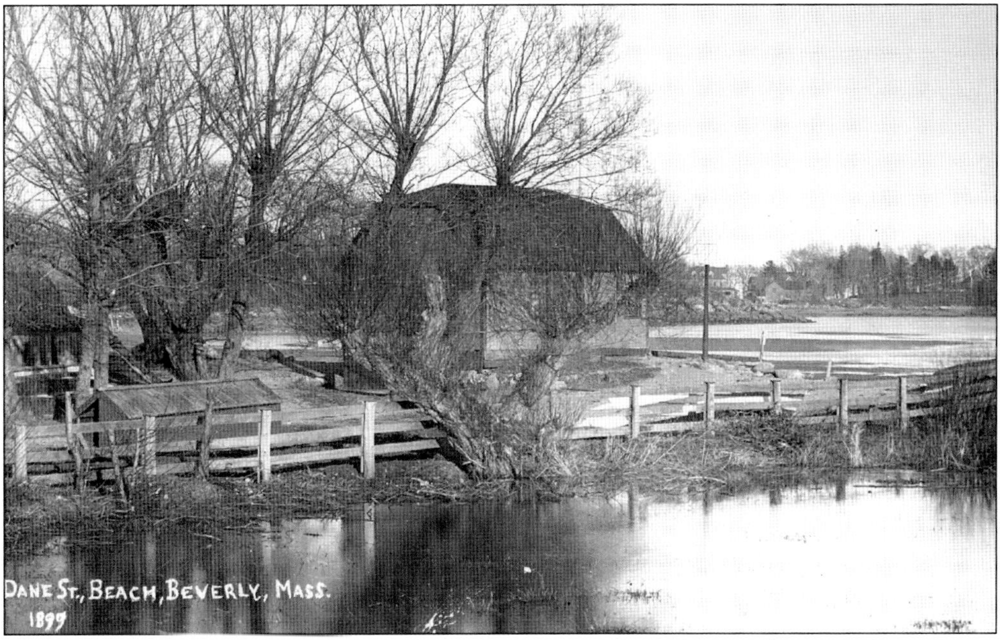

The beach and grassy area at the foot of Dane Street at Lothrop Street is known as Dane Street Beach and Percy F. Lyons Park. Lyons was a Beverly serviceman who lost his life during World War I. The city began purchasing parcels of land for the beach in the early 20th century. The southern side of Dane Street was known as the frog pond. It was filled, and the first bathhouse was constructed. City records show that as many as 2,000 people used the beach on a single summer day. This popular recreational area has been used for a variety of activities, including band concerts, fireworks, exhibitions, and fire musters, and it remains one of the most popular parks in the city for beachgoers, dog walkers, and all who appreciate the beauty of the Beverly coast.

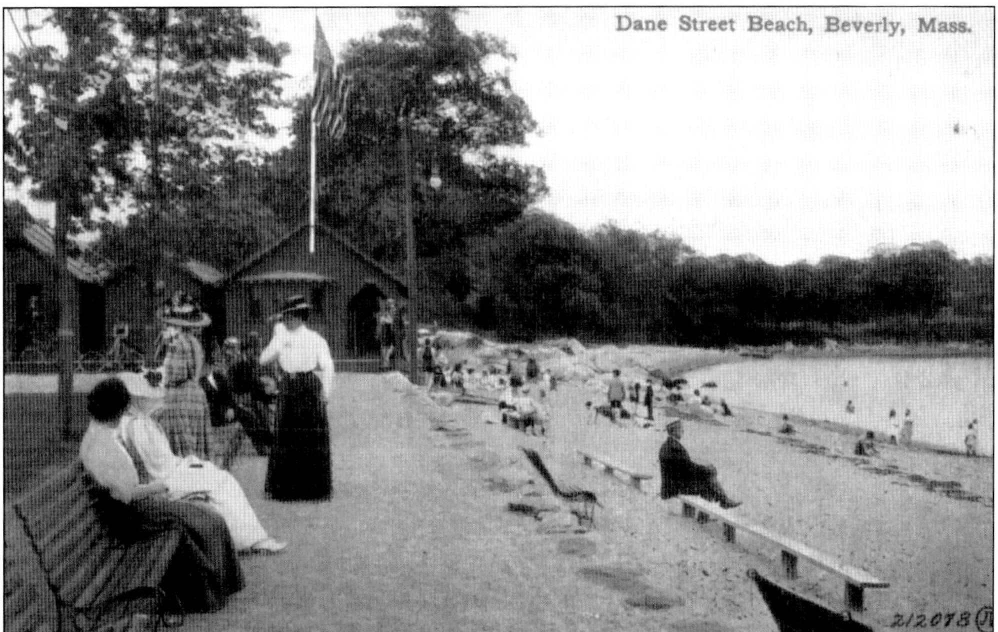

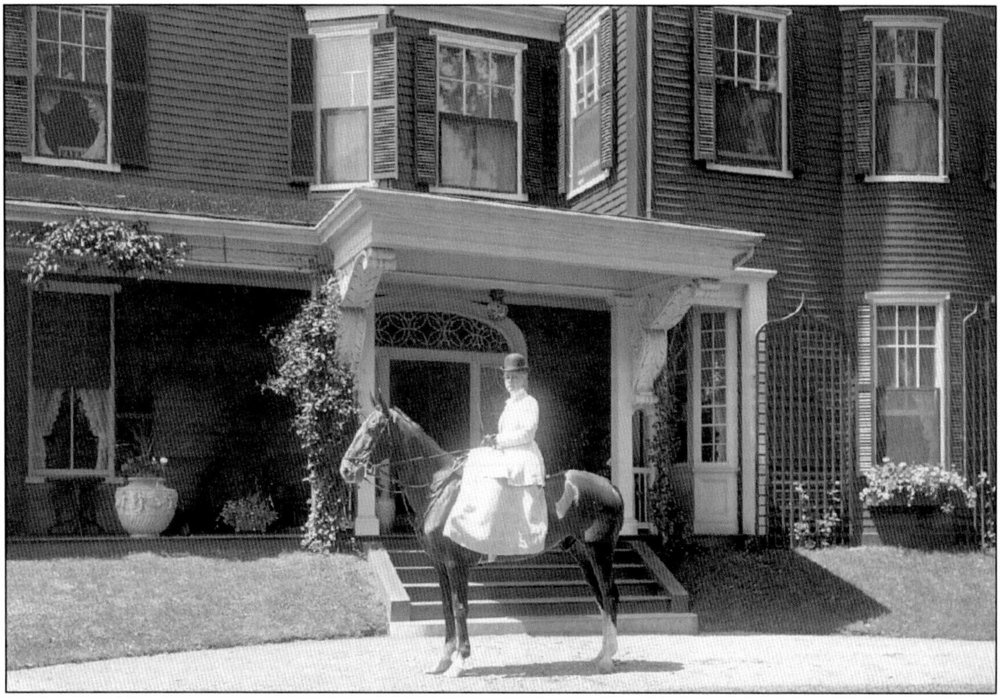

Following the presidential election of 1908, William Howard Taft was in need of a summer residence and narrowed the search to Essex County. He eventually chose Stetson Cottage, a home on the property of Robert Dawson Evans and his wife, Marie Antoinette Evans. Robert Evans died from injuries sustained in an equestrian accident shortly before the president's arrival. Souvenir hunters had already descended upon the Evans property and began ripping shingles from the Summer White House. The grieving widow, seen here around 1913, decided after the second summer of trespassers, U.S. Secret Service, and a total lack of privacy that she had had enough and was going to evict the president. The easiest way to do this was to sell the house with the caveat that it had to be moved. Here it is seen en route to Marblehead.

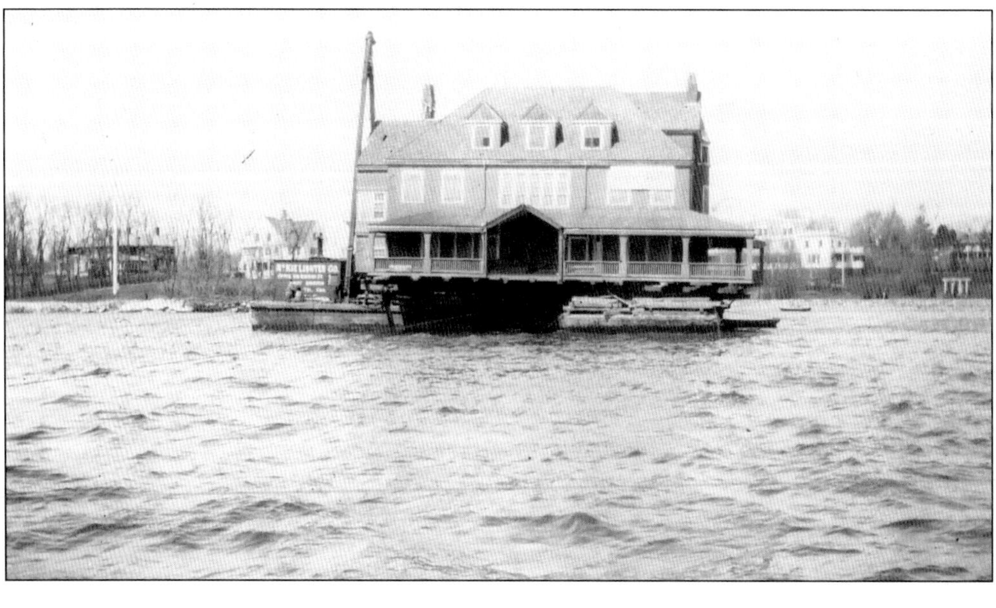

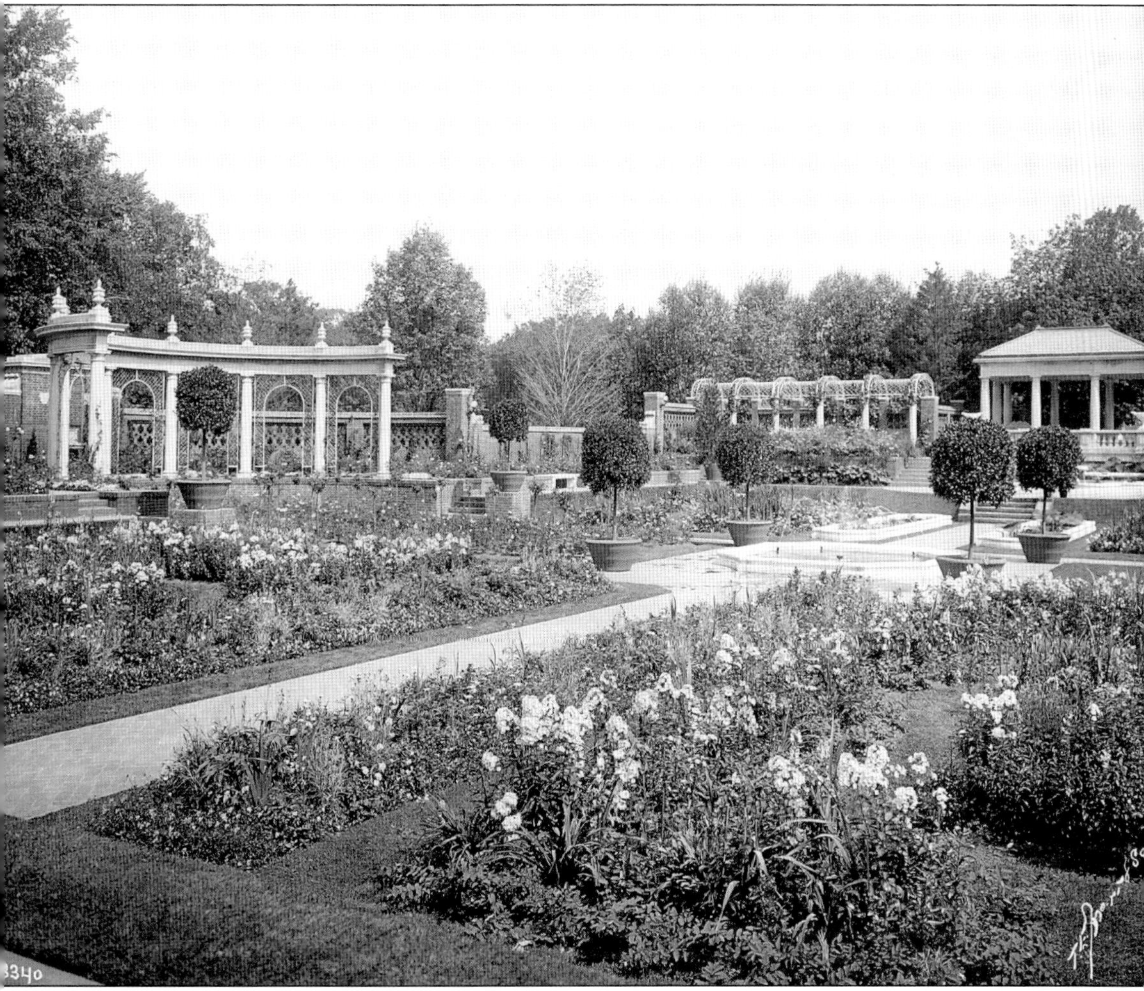

Having rid herself of the nuisance of having the president of the United States living in her guest cottage, Marie Antoinette Evans decided to construct a sunken Italian garden in its foundation. Following her death, the property was left to her two sisters and was eventually bequeathed to Beverly Hospital in 1936. David S. Lynch, a Beverly resident and owner of a leather company in Salem, left money upon his death in 1942 to the City of Beverly to create a public park for the residents of the community. The following year the property was purchased by the City of Beverly, and Lynch Park was born. The former Evans estate has changed during the past half century, but it is still considered one of the most beautiful spots along the North Shore. The Italian garden, now the Lynch Park Rose Garden, has been the site of countless weddings. Band concerts, fund-raisers, picnics, and children running through the park are all commonplace, with the picturesque backdrop of the Evans-era carriage house and Beverly Harbor.

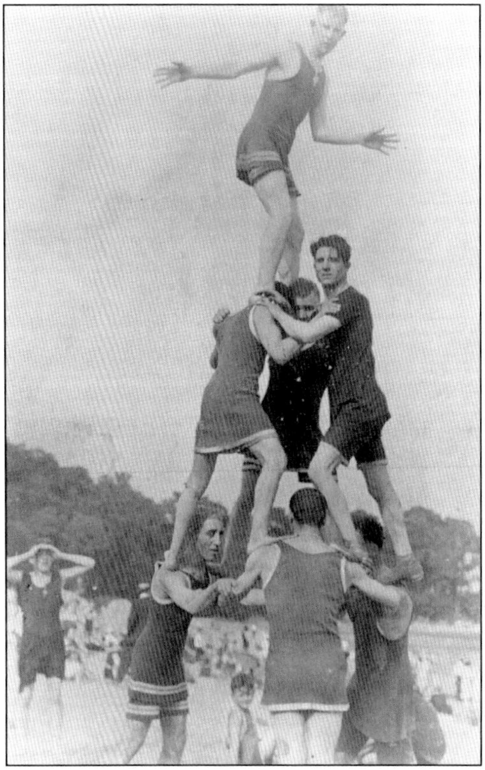

Over the years, people of all ages have enjoyed good times along Beverly's coast. The young men forming this human pyramid at Dane Street Beach were photographed around 1920. Only one is identified, Amos Pinciaro, who is standing at bottom left. Generations of Beverly children have attended summer camp at Lynch Park. The programs are run by the Beverly Recreation Department, and preschool kids to middle school youth enjoy crafts, games, and athletics. In addition to camp programs, the recreation department offers classes in many outdoor activities for adults. In the 1990s, a teenage fad was playing in the mud pit. Below, Julie Sullivan and Dan McGrath cavort in the pit.

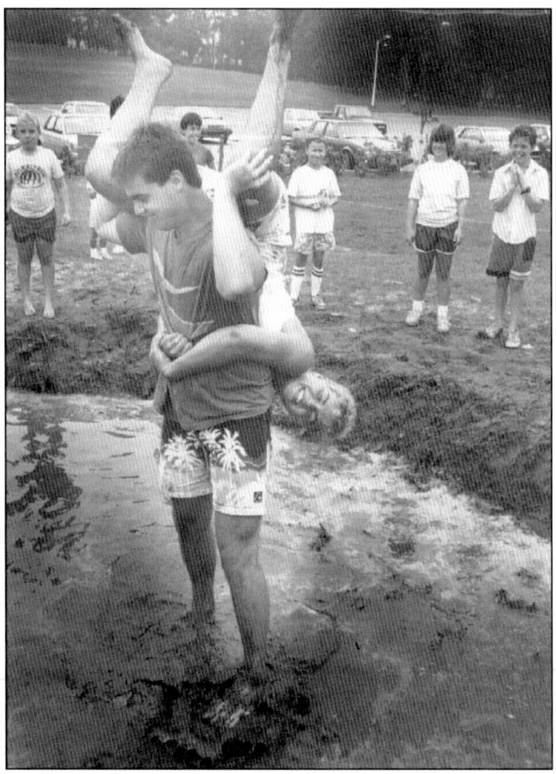

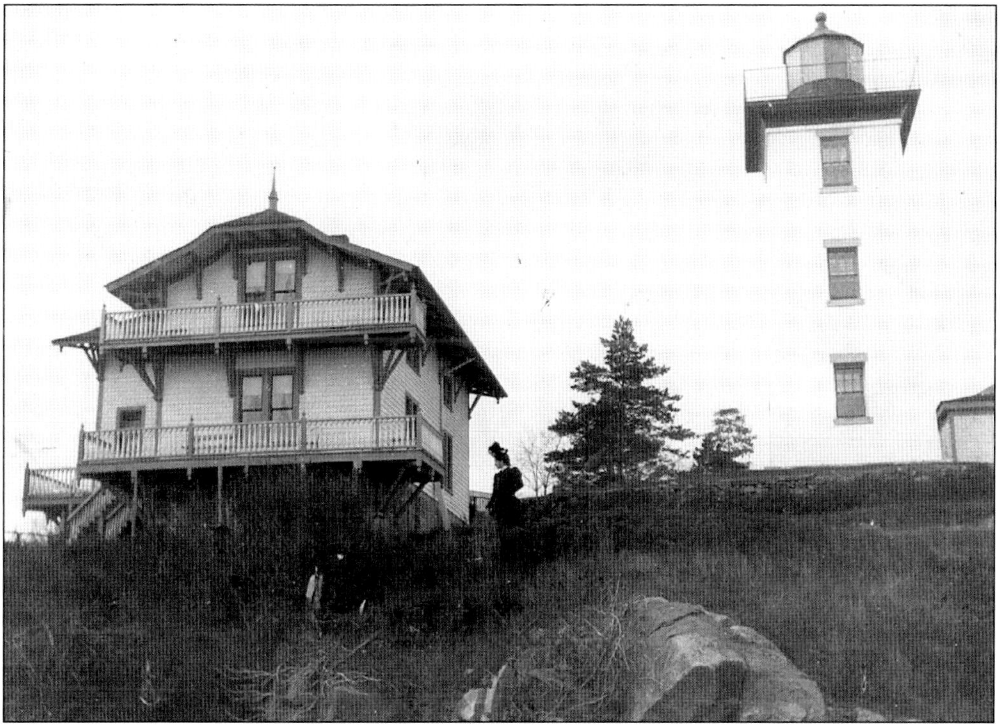

Hospital Point was originally known as Paul's Head or Thorndike's Point for 17th-century owner Paul Thorndike. In 1775, an artillery battery was established there shortly after the encounter between the HMS *Nautilus* and General Washington's vessel *Hannah*. Its current name was acquired after 1801, when a smallpox hospital was built there during an epidemic. The U.S. Lighthouse Service installed the lighthouse and keeper's house in 1872. An electric light beam was installed in 1927 in the steeple of the First Baptist Church and was designated as the Hospital Point Rear Range Light. The lighthouse is formally known as the Hospital Point Front Range Light. The light was automated in 1947, and the last keeper departed the station. The above image is from around 1900; local commercial photographer Lizzie Mitchell took the one below around 1910.

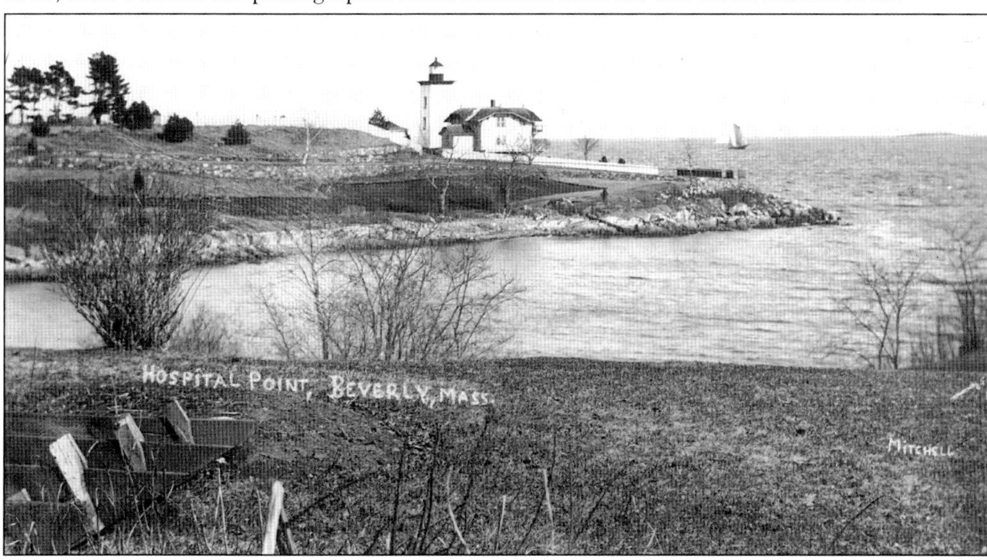

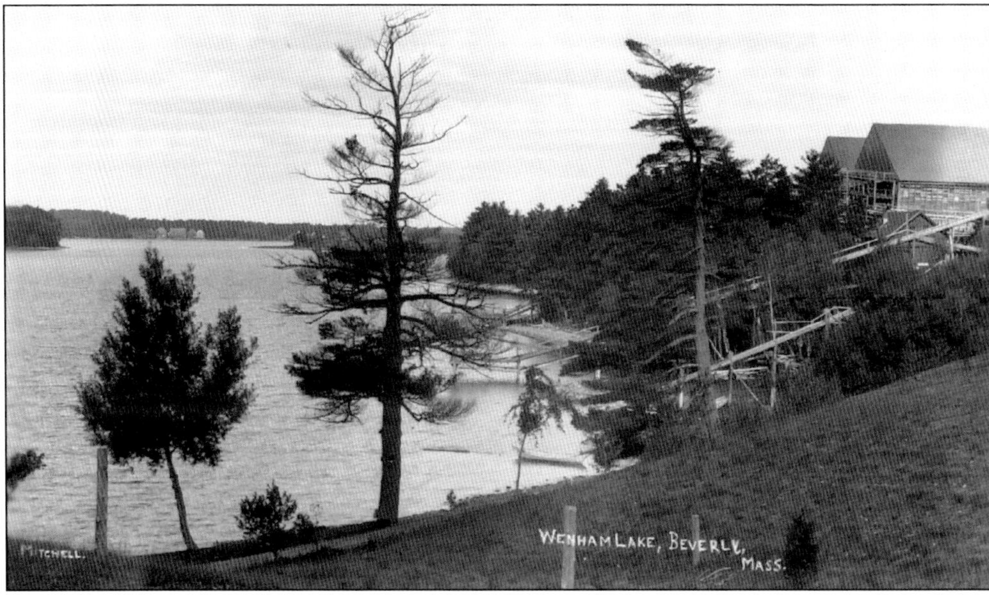

Wenham Lake is a natural body of water defined as a Great Pond (one larger than 10 acres) in early Massachusetts law. No doubt Naumkeag peoples (Native Americans) made use of the natural resources there, like the schools of alewife fish that swam from the sea up the Ipswich River to spawn. Fish were both an important source of food and fertilizer. Recreational fishermen are known to have caught bass, white and yellow perch, pickerel, and horned pout. For many years, people enjoyed unrestricted use of the lake, canoeing, boating, swimming, sailing, and shooting. In the winter, skaters, ice fishermen, and horse-drawn sleighs used the nearly 320 acres of frozen surface. In the 1860s, the water supply for larger communities, like Beverly and Salem, was deemed inadequate. Eventually Wenham Lake was closed to recreational activities to protect the water supply.

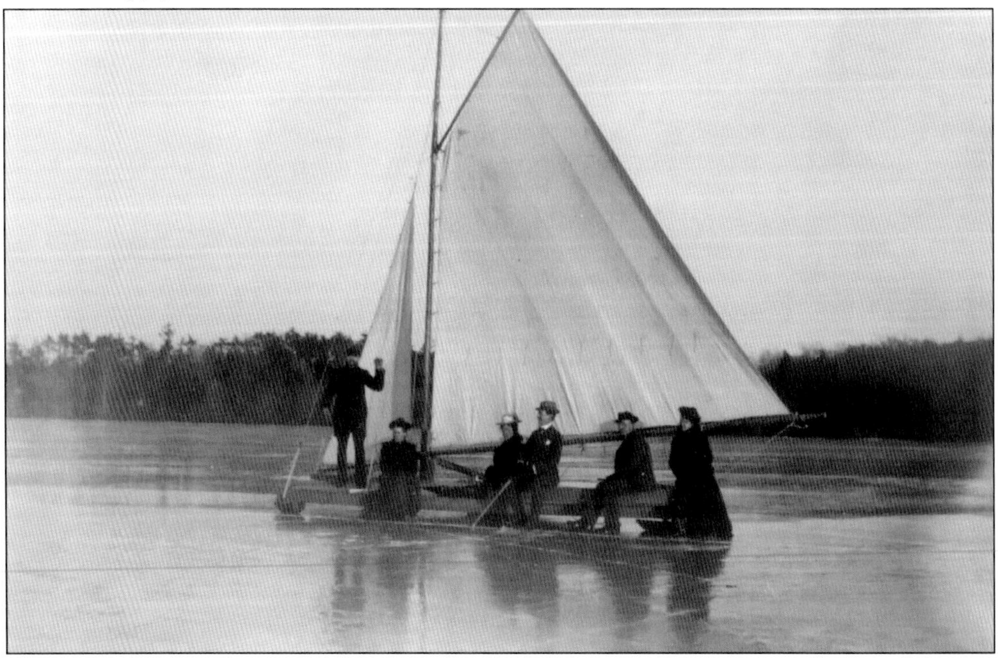

Three

PEOPLE

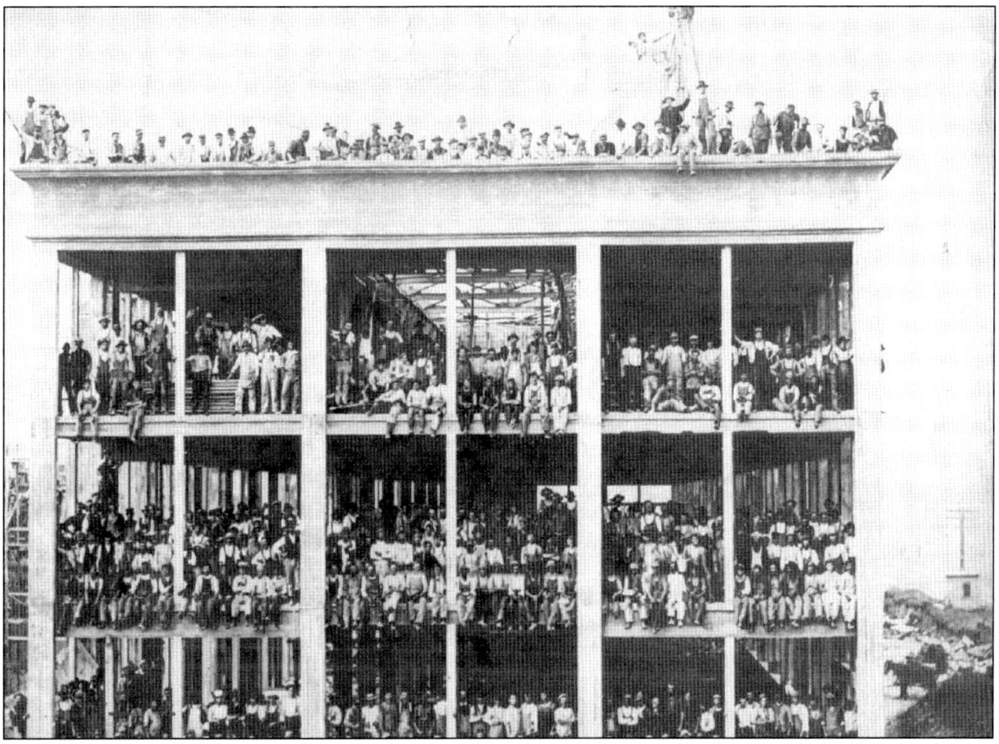

Some of the four million Italian immigrants who came to this country in the 19th and 20th centuries found their way to Beverly. They worked as laborers, stonemasons, and gardeners on the coastal estates and along the Bass River and helped build the massive factory for the United Shoe Machinery Corporation, which opened in 1905. Through hard work, mutual support, and determination they became a vital part of the city's life.

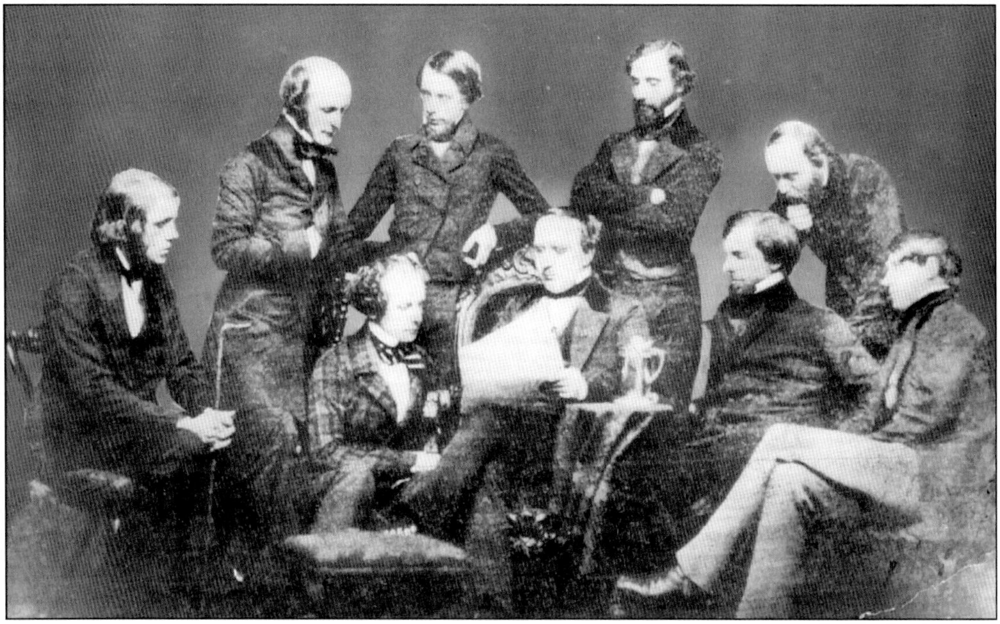

A very early photograph in the Beverly Historical Society archives shows members of the Harvard Dinner Club around 1860. From left to right are Dr. David H. Lyman, Henry Kidder, Dr. George Hayward, John Cunningham, Rev. Edward Everett Hale, Samuel Eliot, Francis Hayes, Caleb William Loring, and Samuel Eliot Guild. Rev. Edward Everett Hale was a descendant of Rev. John Hale. He wrote *The Man Without a Country* at the home of William Sohier in Beverly.

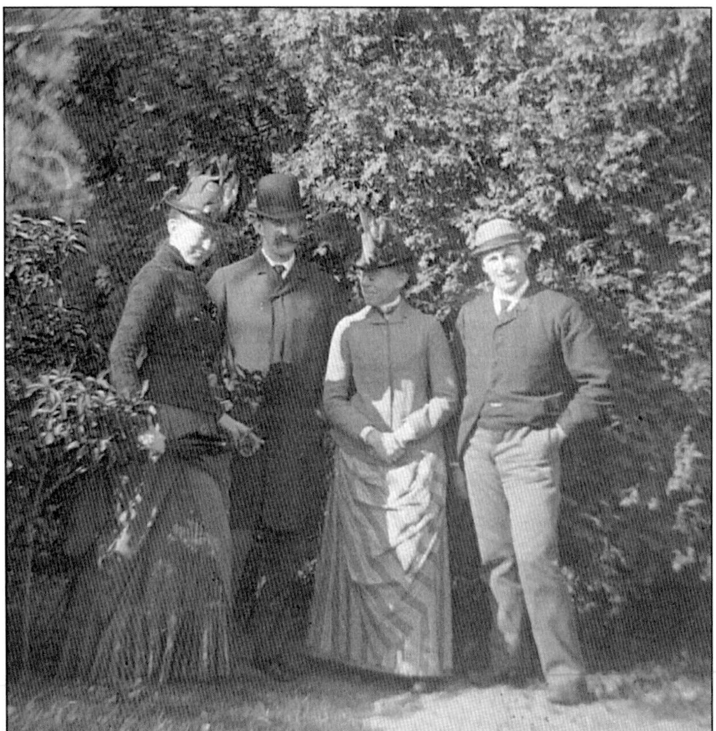

Caleb William Loring and Elizabeth Smith (Peabody) Loring were among the first Bostonians to become summer residents of Prides Crossing. Shown are their children in 1888. From left to right are Katharine Peabody, William Caleb, Louisa Putnam, and Augustus Peabody. Both sons were attorneys. William later became a justice of the Massachusetts Supreme Judicial Court, and Augustus wrote the *Trustees Handbook*, which is still used by trustees and law students today.

Lucy Larcom was a woman of letters in both poetry and prose and was known as an editor and a teacher. She was born in Beverly in 1824 on Wallis Street, now the location of the Larcom Theatre. Her memories of her early childhood in Beverly, her youth in the Lowell textile mills, and her experiences in Illinois as a schoolteacher are enshrined in her book, *A New England Girlhood.* A page from her original manuscript is pictured here. In her later years, Larcom joined with other women of the time who struggled against the restrictions of their society and for the right of women to realize their full potential. Her writings about young women working in New England mills attracted significant attention. She died in 1893 and is buried in Central Cemetery.

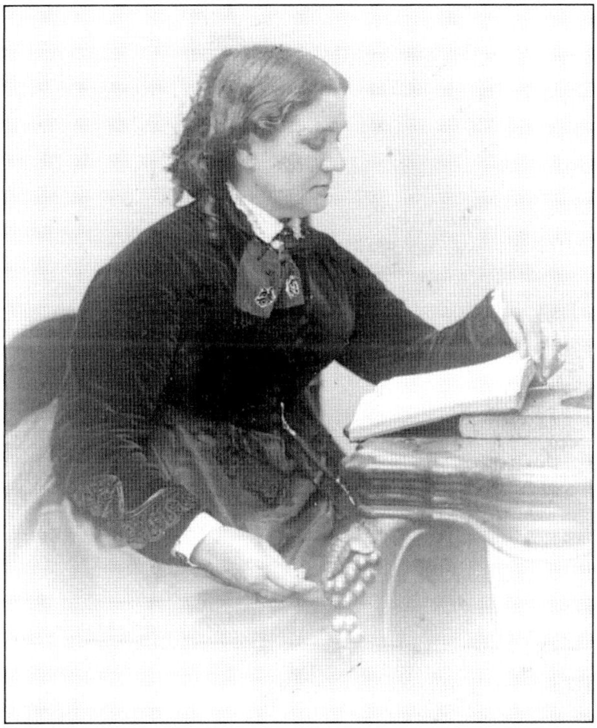

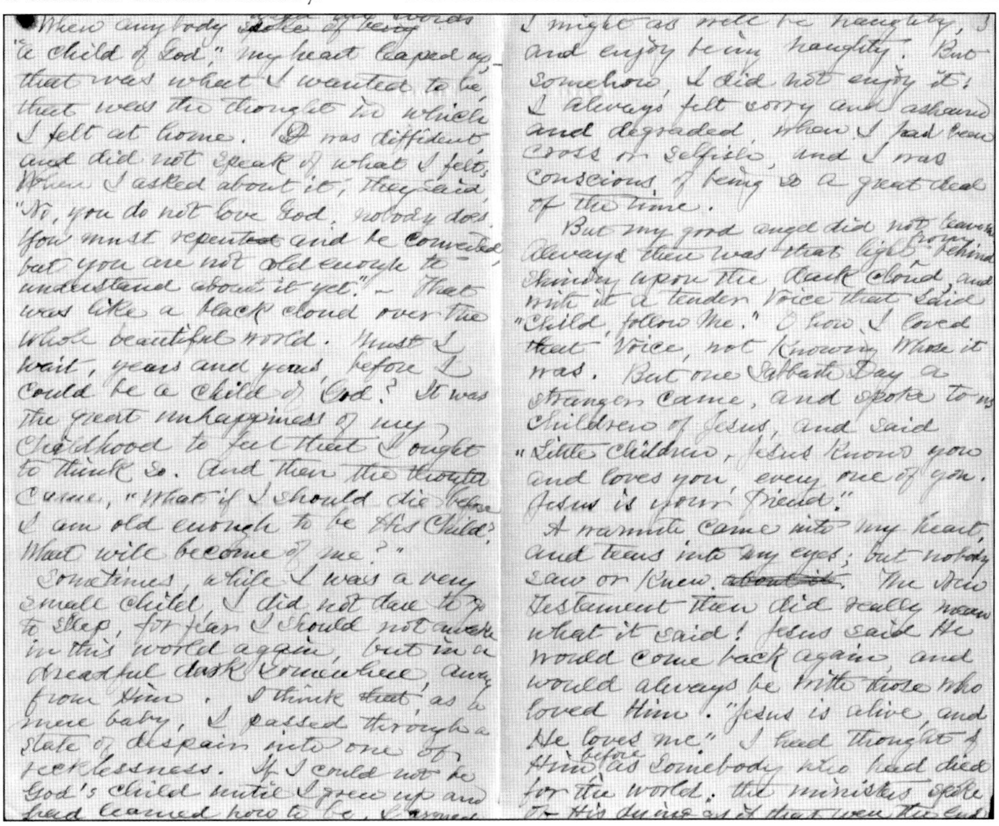

When anybody spoke of being [illegible]
"a child of God," my heart leaped up—
that was what I wanted to be,
that was the thought in which
I felt at home. I was diffident
and did not speak of what I felt.
When I asked about it, they said
"No, you do not love God, nobody does.
You must repent and be converted
but you are not old enough to
understand about it yet." — That
was like a black cloud over the
whole beautiful world. Must I
wait, years and years, before I
could be a child of God? It was
the great unhappiness of my
childhood to feel that I ought
to think so. And then the thought
came, "What if I should die before
I am old enough to be His Child?
What will become of me?"
Sometimes, while I was a very
small child, I did not dare to go
to sleep, for fear I should not wake
in this world again, but in a
dreadful dark somewhere, away
from Him. I think that, as a
mere baby, I passed through a
state of despair into one of
recklessness. If I could not be
God's child until I grew up and
had learned how to be, I …

I might as well be naughty, and
and enjoy being naughty. But
somehow, I did not enjoy it:
I always felt sorry and ashamed
and degraded, when I had been
cross or selfish, and I was
conscious of being so a great deal
of the time.
But my good angel did not leave me.
Always there was that light, shining behind
shining upon the dark cloud, and
with it a tender Voice that said
"Child, follow Me." O how I loved
that Voice, not knowing Whose it
was. But one Sabbath Day a
stranger came, and spoke to us
children of Jesus, and said
"Little Children, Jesus knows you
and loves you, every one of you.
Jesus is your friend."
A warmth came into my heart,
and tears into my eyes; but nobody
saw or knew. The New
Testament then did really mean
what it said! Jesus said He
would come back again, and
would always be with those who
loved Him. "Jesus is alive, and
He loves me." I had thought of
Him before as somebody who had died
for the world; the ministers spoke
of His dying as if that were the end

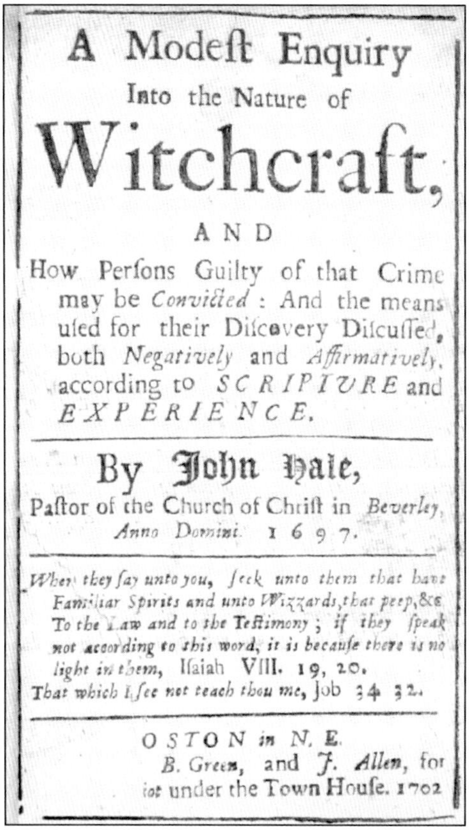

A Modeſt Enquiry
Into the Nature of
Witchcraft,
AND
How Perſons Guilty of that Crime may be *Convicted* : And the means uſed for their Diſcovery Diſcuſſed, both *Negatively* and *Affirmatively*, according to *SCRIPTURE* and *EXPERIENCE*.

By John Hale,
Paſtor of the Church of Chriſt in *Beverley*, *Anno Domini* 1697.

When they ſay unto you, ſeek unto them that have Familiar Spirits and unto Wizzards, that peep, &c. To the Law and to the Teſtimony; if they ſpeak not according to this word, it is becauſe there is no light in them, Iſaiah VIII. 19, 20.
That which I ſee not teach thou me, Job 34. 32.

OSTON in N. E.
B. Green, and *J. Allen*, for
[illegible] under the Town Houſe. 1702

John Hale came to Beverly to preach when it was still known as the Bass River Side of Salem and served as the minister in Beverly until his death in 1700. Hale played a role in the 1692 Salem witchcraft trials and wrote a book, *A Modest Inquiry Into the Nature of Witchcraft*, that was written at Hale Farm. Hale's first wife was Rebecca, with whom he had two children—Rebecca and Robert. Both children were threatened with witchcraft by Margaret Lord, the Hales' cook, who was stealing from the house and who claimed that her accomplice, Dorcas Hoar, was a witch who would harm them or burn their house if they told their parents. After Rebecca died, John married Sarah Noyes, with whom he had four children—James, Joanna, John, and Samuel, the grandfather of Nathan Hale. Hale Farm has a generally accepted construction date of 1694 for its oldest section, but it may be older. Additions were built in the 18th and 19th centuries. At one time Hale Farm included both sides of present Bancroft Avenue and extended to the ocean.

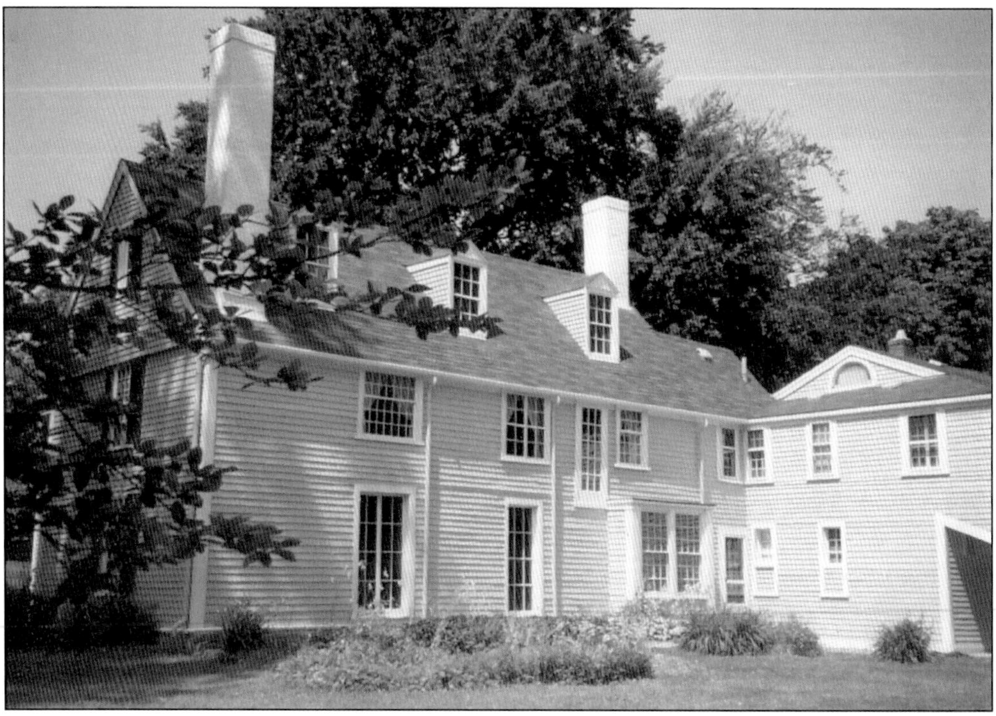

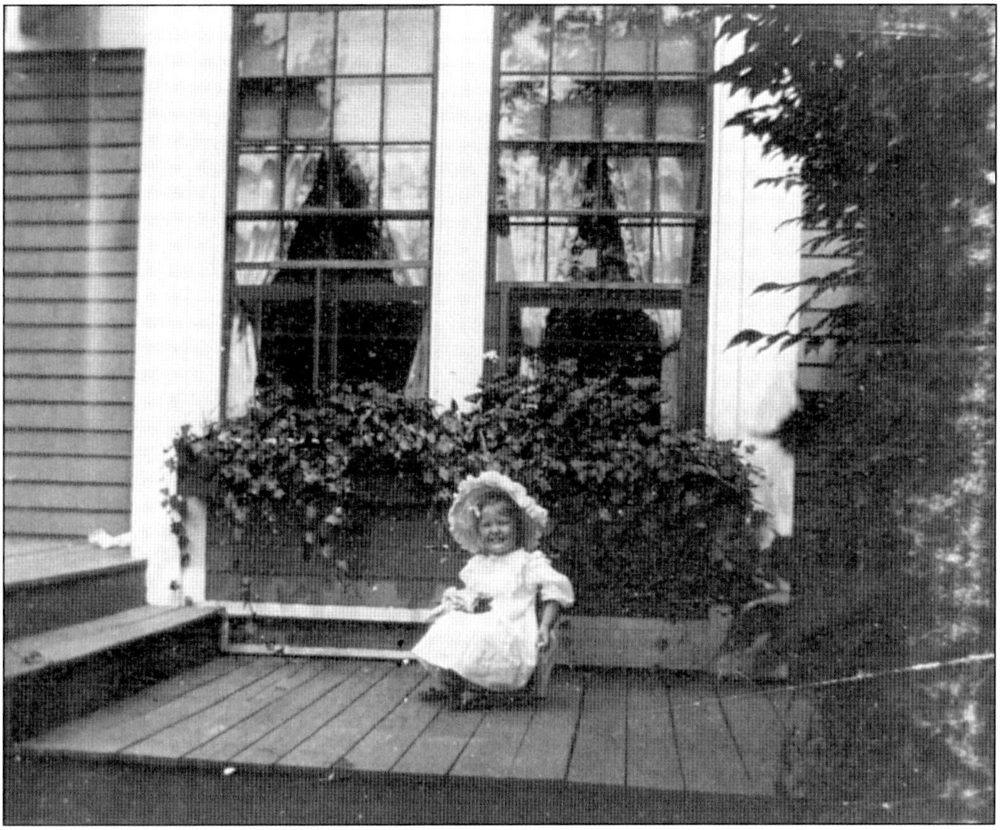

After John Hale's death, his son Robert inherited the property. In 1745, grandson Col. Robert Hale Jr. added the front section of the house, left of the present front door, and the present staircases. The addition consists of two rooms down and two up, along with the gambrel roof that created rooms on the third floor. In the mid-1840s, descendant Thomas Poynton Bancroft of Boston converted the house into a summer estate. Robert Hale Bancroft added the wing, where the apartment is now located, for a new kitchen, laundry, and servant quarters. Eleanor and Hope Bancroft, third-generation summer residents who eventually sold the property to the Beverly Historical Society after the death of their mother Elise in 1936, are shown as little girls playing on the Hale Farm patio and grounds.

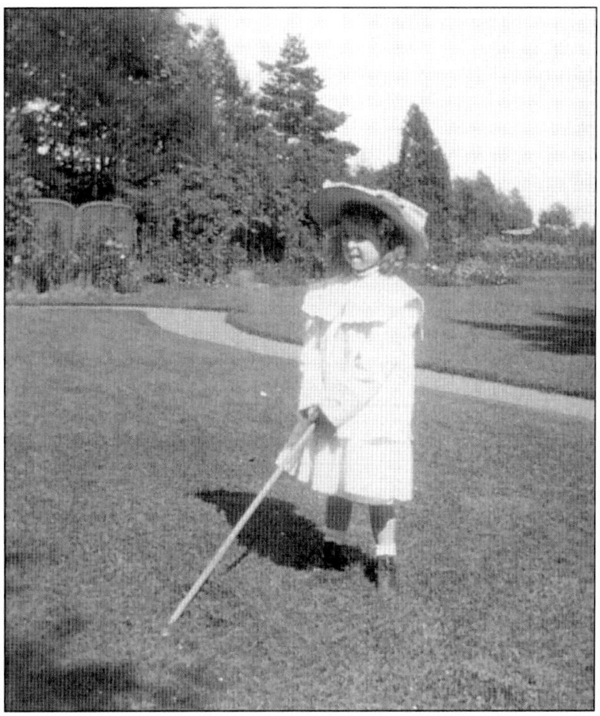

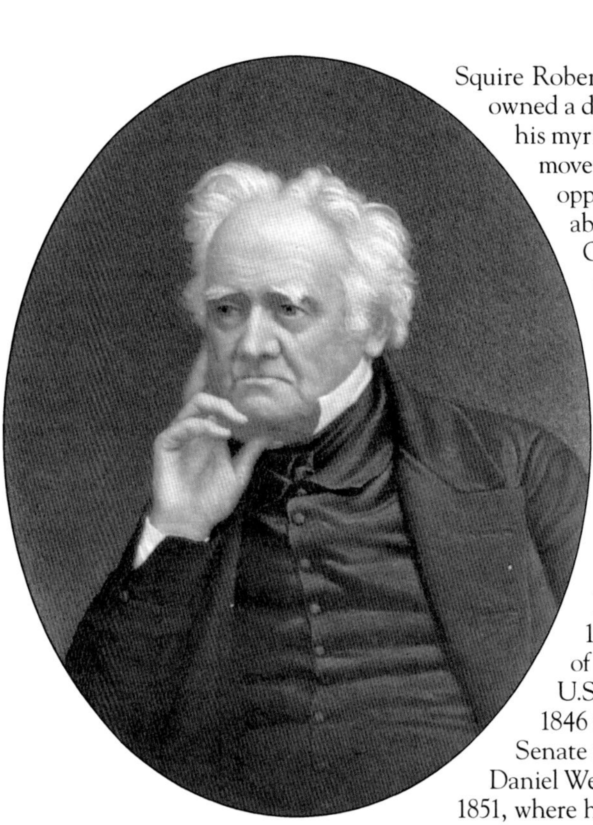

Squire Robert Rantoul was born in 1778. Rantoul owned a drugstore, but it was only a small part of his myriad activities. He was a leader in reform movements, including temperance, education, opposition to capital punishment, and the abolition of slavery. Rantoul served as an Overseer of the Poor in Beverly for more than half a century. He was a delegate to two Massachusetts Constitutional Conventions and served as both a state representative and senator. During General Lafayette's visit to Beverly in 1824, Rantoul delivered the welcome speech on the steps of the John Cabot House. A copy of Rantoul's handwritten speech is pictured below. Rantoul's son, Robert Rantoul Jr., also had a notable career serving as a Massachusetts state representative from 1835 to 1839, on the Massachusetts Board of Education from 1837 to 1842, and as the U.S. district attorney for Massachusetts from 1846 to 1849. Rantoul was elected to the U.S. Senate in 1851 to complete the final month of Daniel Webster's term and was reelected in March 1851, where he served until his death in 1852.

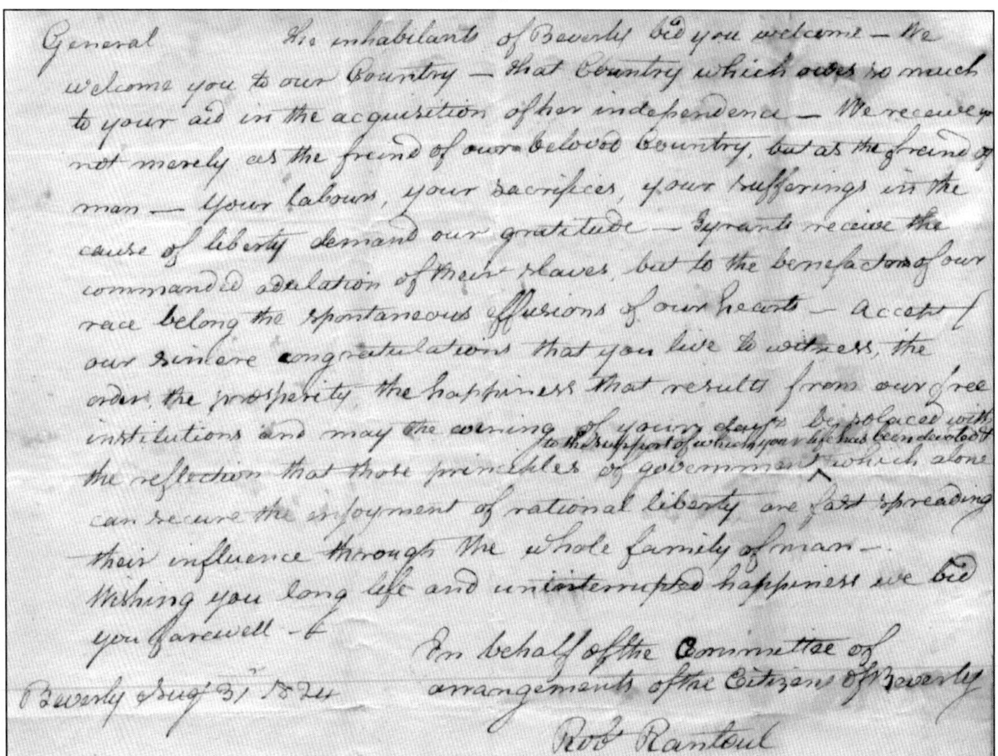

General The inhabitants of Beverly bid you welcome — We welcome you to our Country — that Country which owes so much to your aid in the acquisition of her independence — We receive you not merely as the friend of our beloved Country, but as the friend of man — Your labours, your sacrifices, your sufferings in the cause of liberty demand our gratitude — Tyrants receive the commanded adulation of their slaves, but to the benefactors of our race belong the spontaneous effusions of our hearts — accept of our sincere congratulations that you live to witness, the order, the prosperity, the happiness that results from our free institutions to the support of which your life has been devoted and may the evening of your days be solaced with the reflection that those principles of government which alone can secure the enjoyment of rational liberty are fast spreading their influence through the whole family of man — Wishing you long life and uninterrupted happiness we bid you farewell —

In behalf of the Committee of arrangements of the Citizens of Beverly

Beverly Aug 31 1824

Robt Rantoul

Born in 1821, the daughter of Robert and Joanna Rantoul, Hannah Rantoul was part of a family that believed in community involvement and helping those in need. She found her cause during the American Civil War. The U.S. Sanitary Commission, created by legislation signed by Pres. Abraham Lincoln in June 1861, was formed to coordinate the efforts of women who wanted to volunteer to the Union war effort. Both as associate manager of the New England Auxiliary Sanitary Commission and president of the Beverly Ladies Society in Aid of Massachusetts Soldiers, Rantoul wrote thousands of letters and helped to raise millions of dollars to mitigate the sufferings of soldiers serving their country. Making many lifelong friends through her correspondence with the fighting men, Rantoul was honored by the Beverly post of the Grand Army of the Republic, for her work. She lived all of her life at the family home on Washington Street near the harbor, as seen in the image below; the house still stands. Rantoul died in 1898.

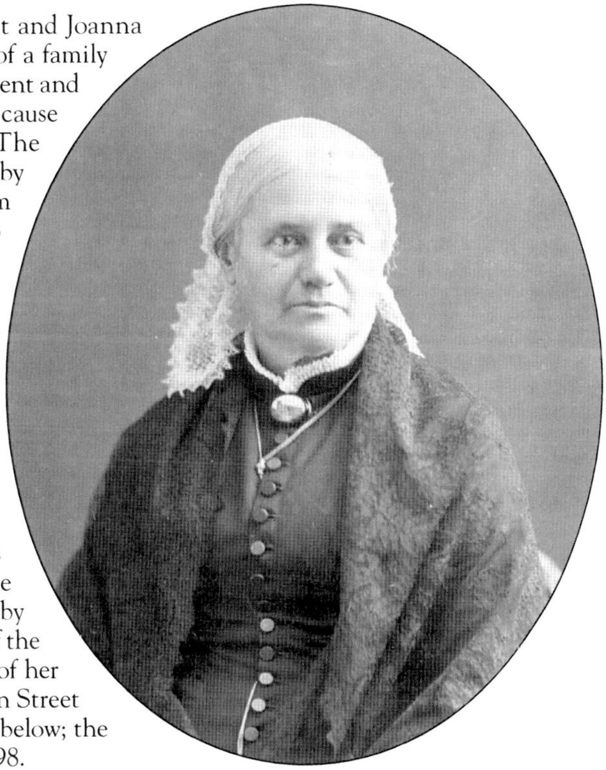

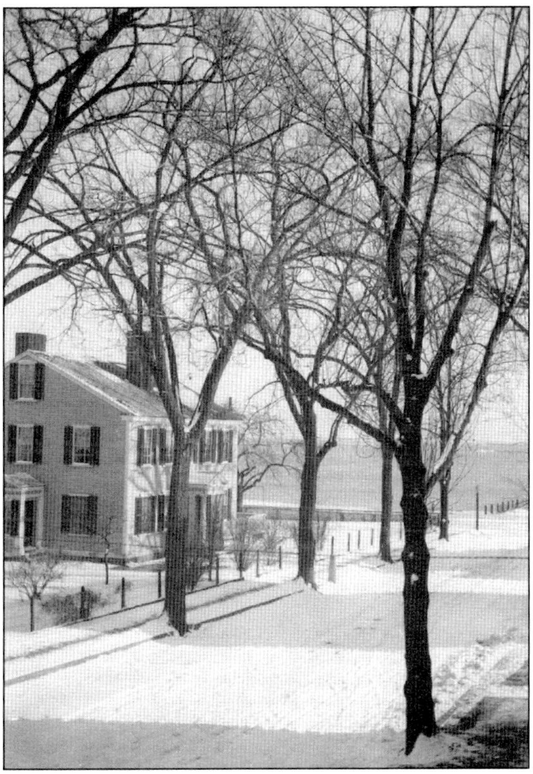

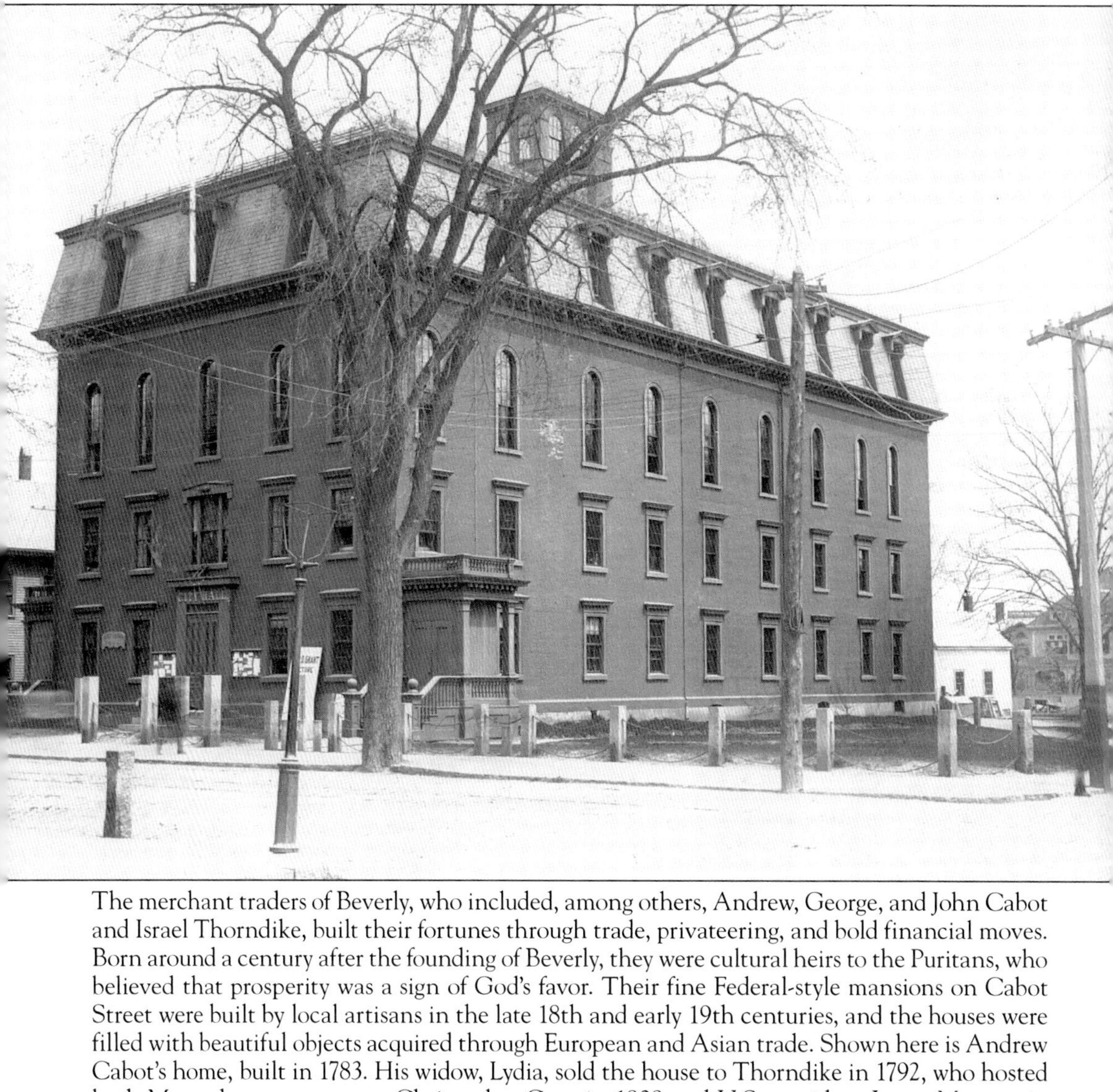

The merchant traders of Beverly, who included, among others, Andrew, George, and John Cabot and Israel Thorndike, built their fortunes through trade, privateering, and bold financial moves. Born around a century after the founding of Beverly, they were cultural heirs to the Puritans, who believed that prosperity was a sign of God's favor. Their fine Federal-style mansions on Cabot Street were built by local artisans in the late 18th and early 19th centuries, and the houses were filled with beautiful objects acquired through European and Asian trade. Shown here is Andrew Cabot's home, built in 1783. His widow, Lydia, sold the house to Thorndike in 1792, who hosted both Massachusetts governor Christopher Gore in 1809 and U.S. president James Monroe in 1817. Thorndike heirs sold the structure to the Town of Beverly in 1841. The building has been altered multiple times since then, but seen from Cabot Street, Beverly's City Hall still retains its 18th-century flavor.

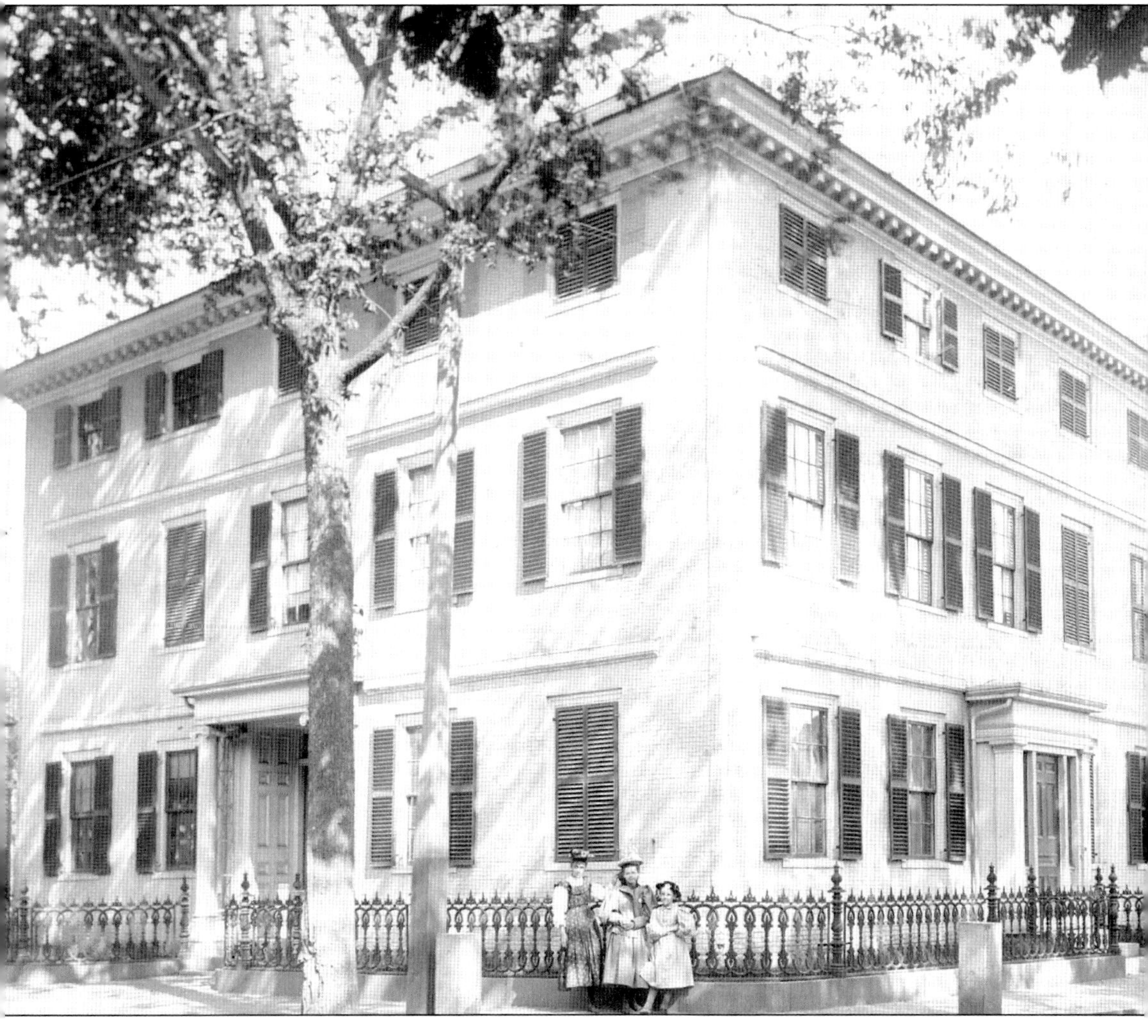

John Cabot's 1781 home, located at 117 Cabot Street, is just around the corner from the Cabot-Lee-Kilham house, which was originally the home of Elizabeth Cabot, mother to the merchant Cabot brothers. Her house still stands, although it was moved from Cabot Street to Central Street in the 1920s, shortly after the George Cabot House was demolished. The John Cabot House was the first location of the Beverly Bank, and it has been the headquarters of the Beverly Historical Society since 1892. Much of the interior layout remains as it was in the Cabots' day, including decorative moldings and Delft tiles around the parlor fireplace. A rear addition was built in the 19th century, which served as living quarters for a caretaker. The John Cabot House serves as an illustration of the life of affluent 18th-century Beverly residents and a contrast to Beverly's smaller and simpler 17th-century structures.

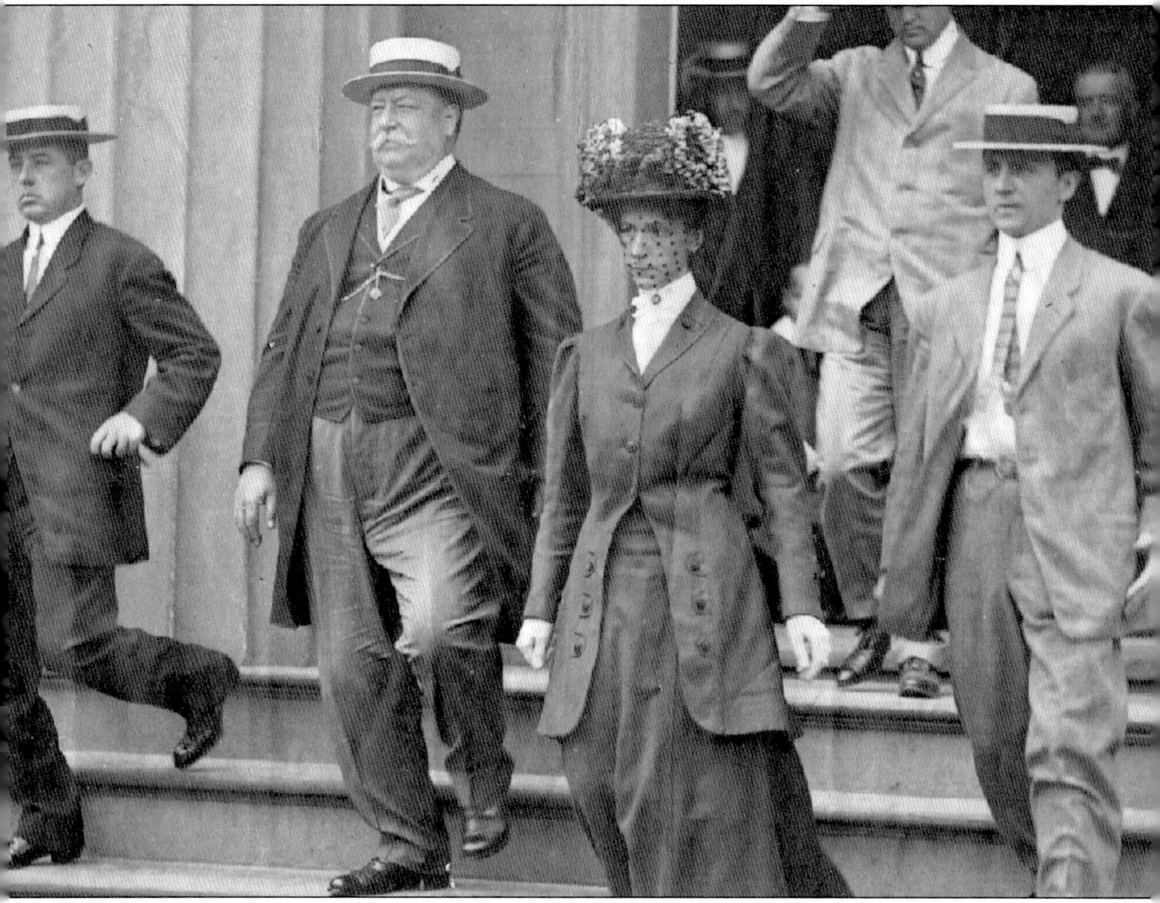

U.S. president William Howard Taft and his wife, Nellie, enjoyed their summer community, and the residents embraced them. Following their eviction from the Stetson Cottage, they were able to secure another residence for the following two summers on Corning Street, in the Montserrat neighborhood of Beverly. It was called Parramatta and was the estate of the late merchant Henry W. Peabody, whose widow, Lucy, painted the house a patriotic white to display her pleasure that the first family had chosen her home. (They even had the option to extend the lease should Taft be reelected for a second term.) The Taft family would attend Sunday services at the First Parish Church, as seen here on the front steps flanked by members of the U.S. Secret Service, and follow it with an automobile excursion throughout the area. Taft had a passion for golf and became a member at both the Myopia Hunt Club and Essex County Club.

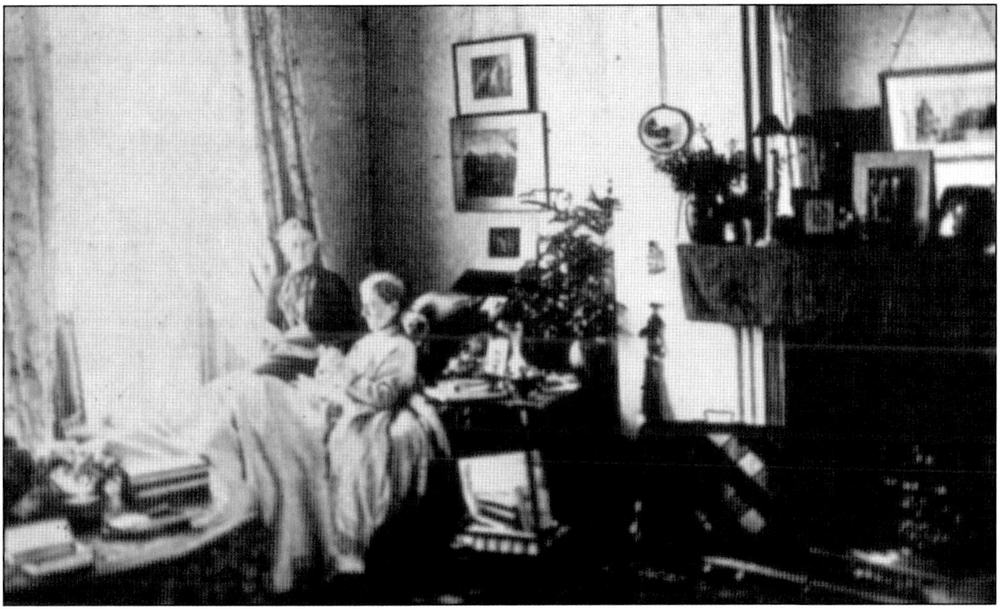

It is difficult to imagine individuals more civic minded or with more community spirit than that evinced by Katharine Peabody Loring and her sister Louisa Putnam Loring. Katharine was a founder and teacher of the Society to Encourage Studies at Home, an organization that taught women by correspondence courses. She is pictured at left above with Alice James, a cofounder and well-known diarist, who was the sister of William and Henry James and a close friend of Katharine. Louisa was an important figure in the local chapter of the American Red Cross. Other society women followed suit, and the photograph below shows a Red Cross lifesaving drill. The terrible Salem fire of 1914 saw both Loring sisters providing much needed aid. They were also active in fighting tuberculosis. Katharine was a trustee of the Beverly Library, a member of the Beverly Improvement Society, and an influential president of the Beverly Historical Society, during a time when the society acquired the Balch and Hale properties.

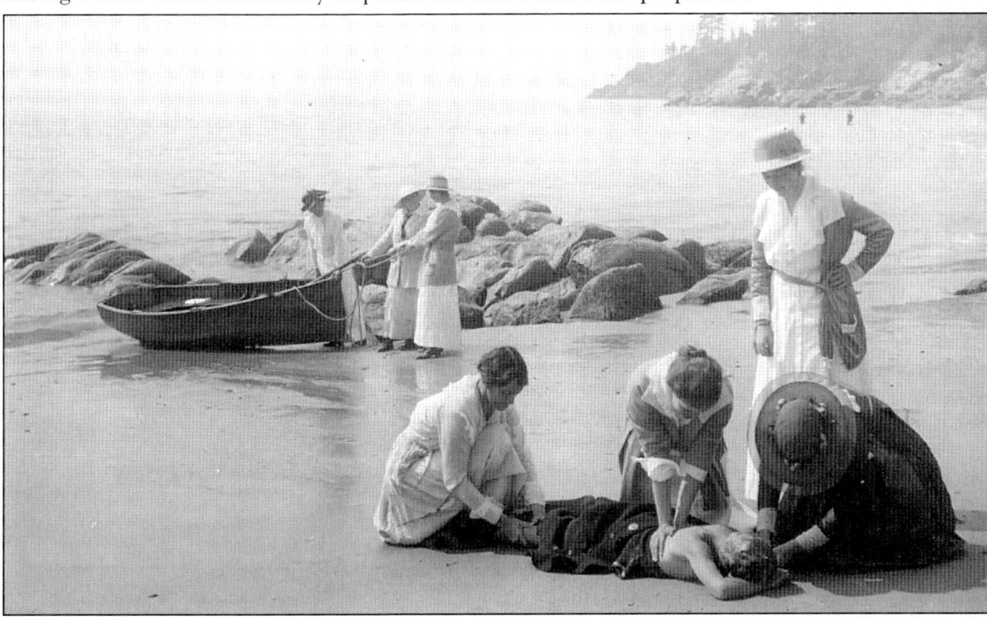

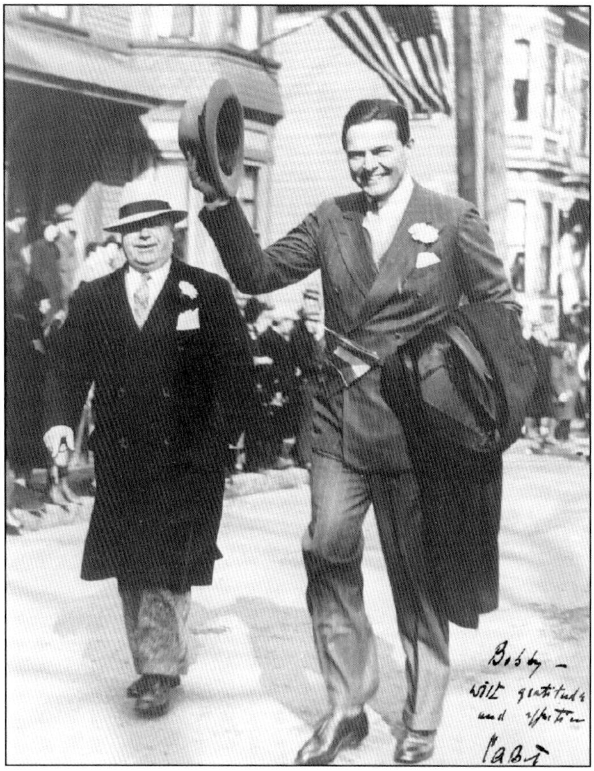

Son of the prominent Lodge family and a descendant of Sen. George Cabot, Henry Cabot Lodge served in the U.S. Senate and as an ambassador to the United Nations, South Vietnam, and West Germany. Lodge ran for vice president with Richard Nixon in 1960, with the ticket narrowly losing to his rival, John F. Kennedy. For many years, Lodge and his wife, Emily, owned a house in Beverly at 275 Hale Street. He died in 1985.

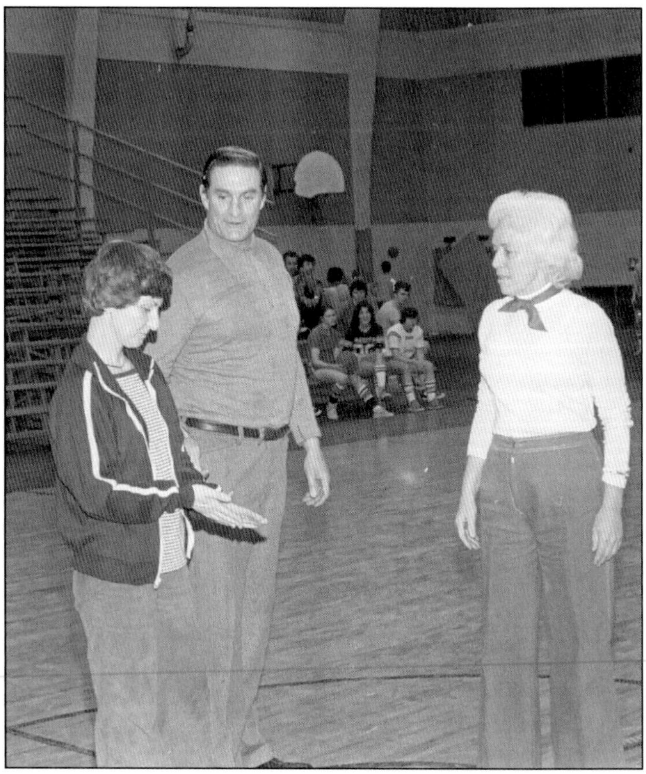

Born in Danvers, Frances Alexander (right) settled in Beverly in 1950 with her family. She started a school called Mrs. Alexander's at her Corning Street home. Alexander was elected to the Beverly School committee in 1970 and, in that capacity, helped establish the Patten Trade School and a public kindergarten. She also served on the Board of Aldermen and in the state legislature from 1983 to 1990. (Courtesy of the *Salem News*.)

Four

TRANSPORTATION

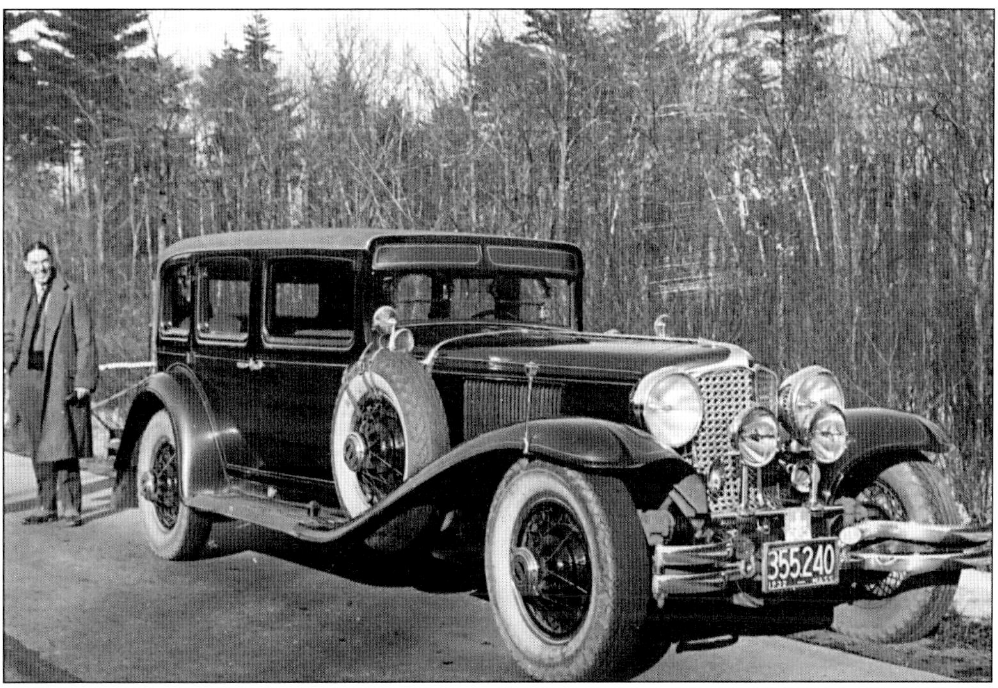

Laurence Breed Walker, who donated the Walker Transportation Collection to the Beverly Historical Society, started his interest in transportation as a youth, sharing photographs and information with other enthusiasts throughout his life. He was a renowned minister and radio talk show host who suffered with polio at midlife. Walker owned several fine automobiles, including this 1932 Cord. He never had a driver's license; his secretary drove for him.

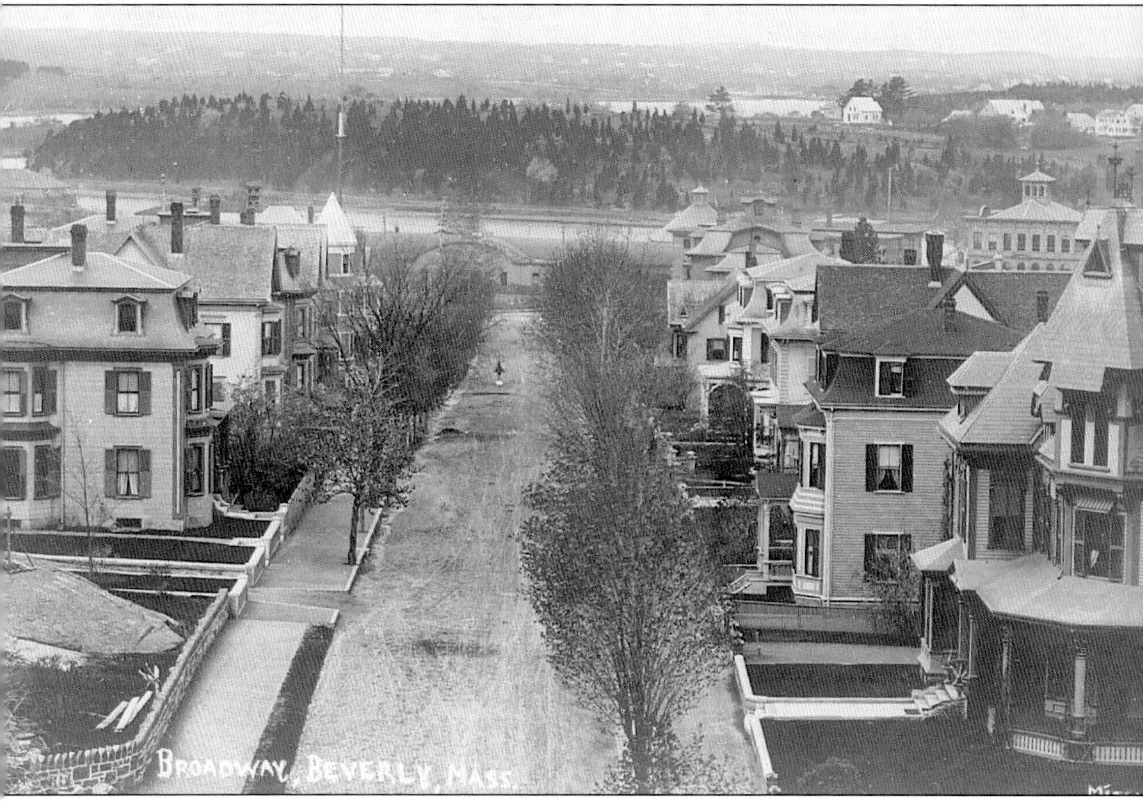

Broadway was constructed as a gateway to the community for travelers coming by train to the "Garden City by the Sea." The first thing visitors would see after leaving the depot would be the handsome structures on the roadway leading to Cabot Street and downtown. The homes on Broadway contain some of the finest examples of architecture on any street in the city of Beverly. Many of the prominent figures in the community began building homes on Broadway as early as 1859, with the construction of William Endicott's home on the corner of Rantoul Street. The development culminated with the groundbreaking for his grandson Robert Rantoul Endicott's stone mansion in 1892. This image looking toward the second depot and the Bass River was taken from the cupola of the Odd Fellows building by Lizzie Mitchell in 1892, with the staging for the Endicott mansion visible in the left foreground.

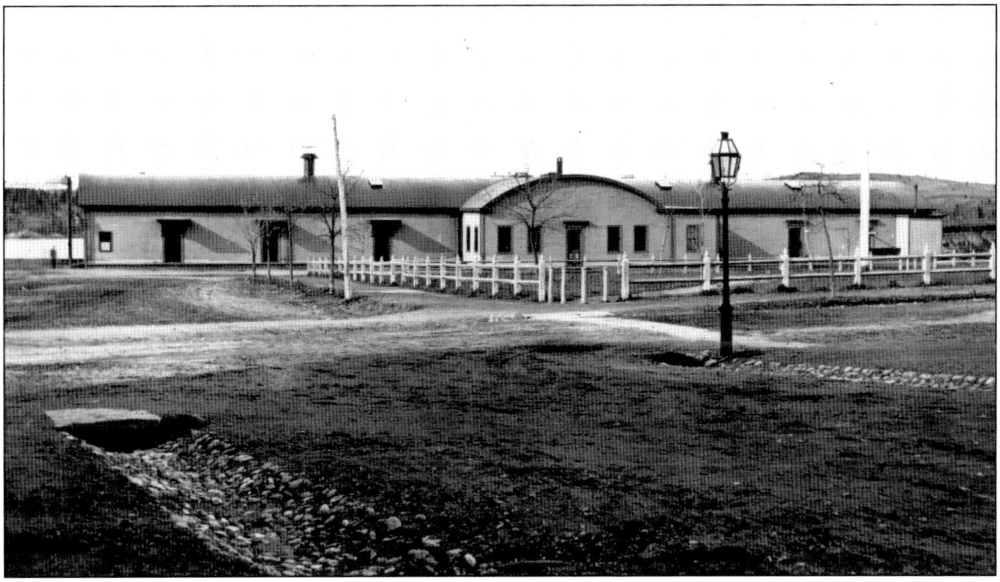

The second Beverly Depot on Park Street is seen from Railroad Avenue across Rantoul Street around 1860. Built by the Eastern Railroad, an early competitor and predecessor of the Boston and Maine Railroad, this station covered the tracks, allowing passengers to avoid inclement weather. It was torn down in 1896 and replaced by the current Beverly Depot in 1897. Note the dirt streets and rudimentary drainage system.

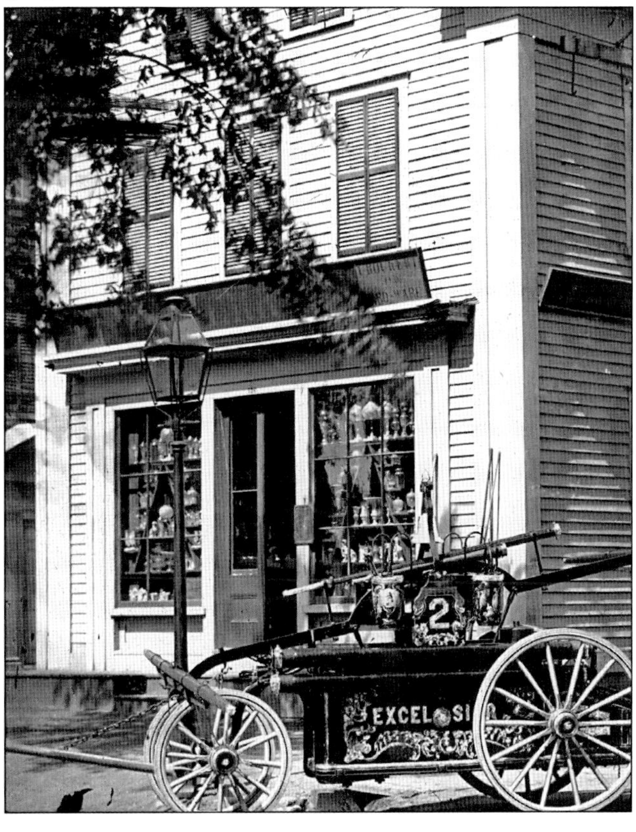

The Beverly Fire Department's Excelsior No. 2 was considered a state-of-the-art firefighting apparatus in its day. Manufactured by Hunneman and Company of Boston, Massachusetts, it was delivered to the city on July 7, 1847. It was one of Beverly's more powerful pumpers and had a crew of 12 to 18 men. The pumper is seen at Cabot Street and Railroad Avenue in the 1850s.

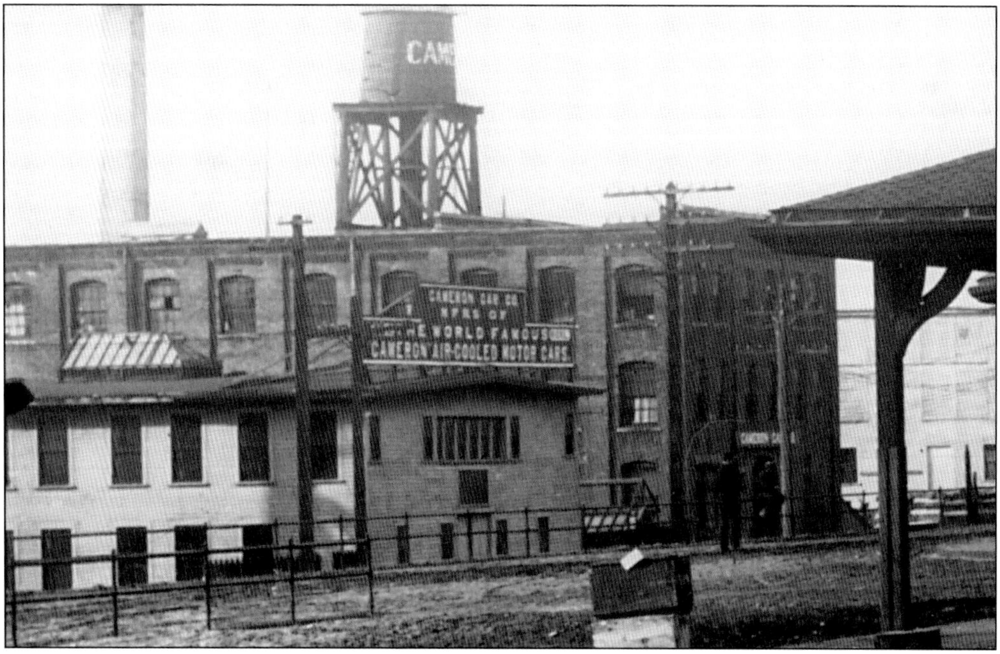

Beverly had six automobile manufacturers at various times, including the Cameron, which was built from 1903 to 1920. Camerons were known for their reliable air-cooled engines and racing exploits around the world. The Cameron plant, seen here on River Street, took over the facility formerly used to build the Upton. Camerons were built in Beverly from 1908 to 1913, when operations were moved to West Haven, Connecticut.

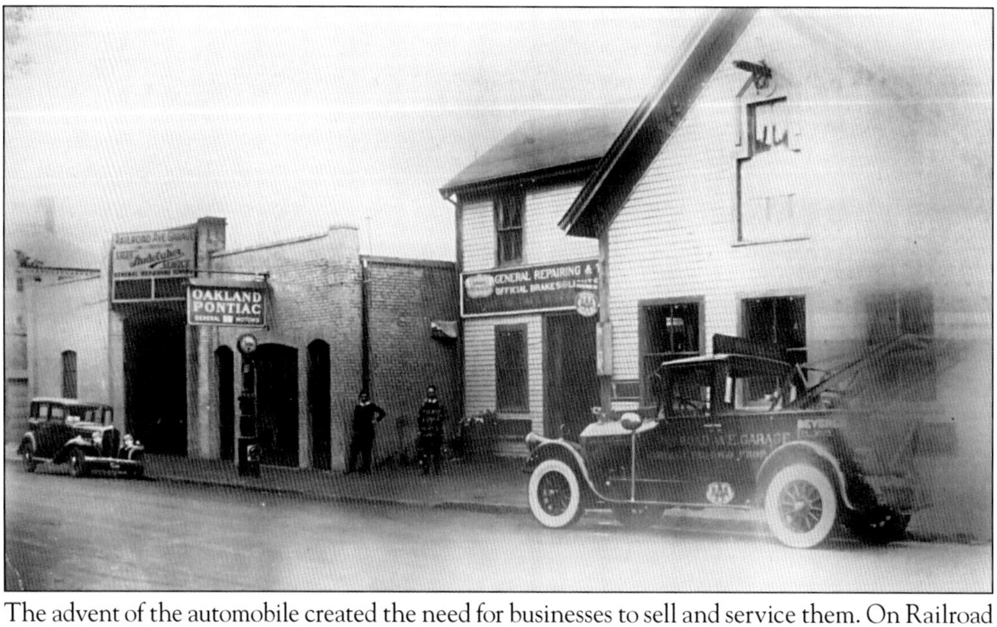

The advent of the automobile created the need for businesses to sell and service them. On Railroad Avenue one could purchase a new Studebaker, Oakland, or its lower-priced companion, the Pontiac. Note the gas pump on the sidewalk and the signs advertising repairs and brake service. The brick building continues to service automobiles today. The tow truck is a Pierce Arrow, a company primarily known for its luxury cars.

Beverly serves as the junction point of the Eastern Division main line to Newburyport and once to Portland, Maine, and the Gloucester Branch to Rockport. At one time, there was a spur track to the United Shoe Machinery Corporation plant on Elliot Street. This signal tower, located north of the Beverly Depot, controlled the movement of trains on these three sections of track. The signal crew poses for this 1914 photograph.

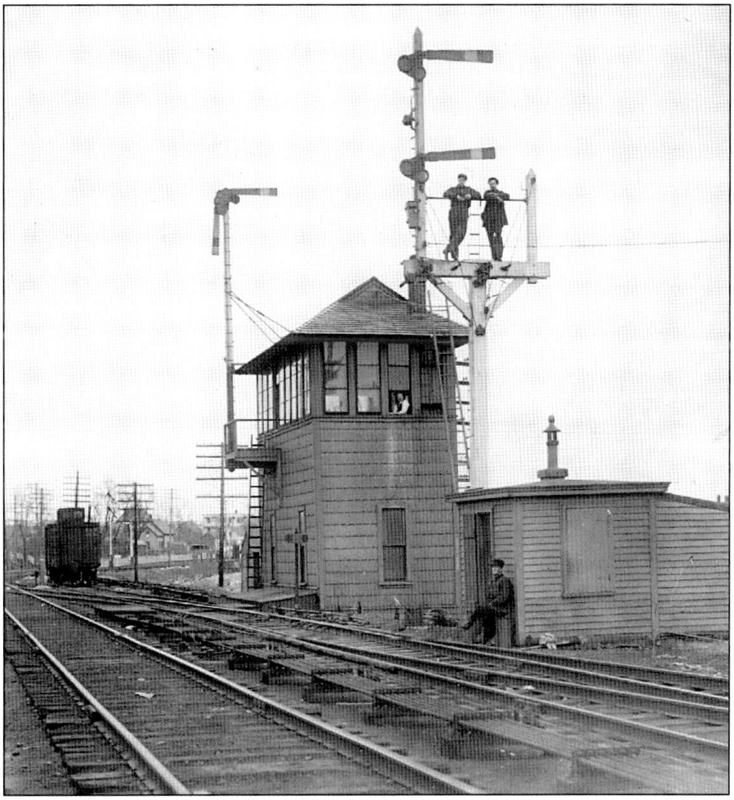

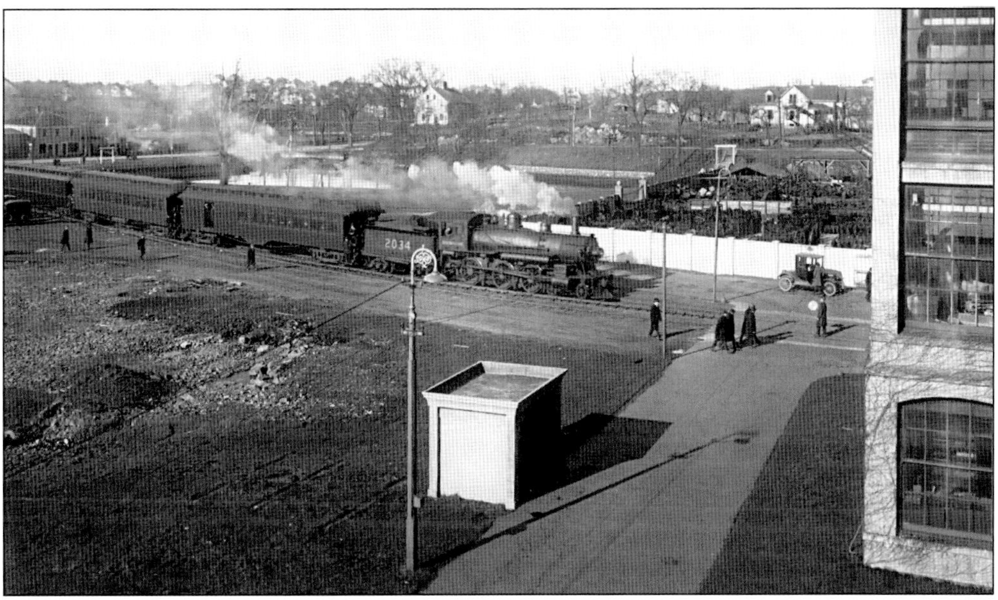

A commuter rail in Beverly has long been in service. The United Shoe Machinery Corporation had its own track and station to better facilitate moving its employees to and from work. Boston and Maine Railroad locomotive No. 2034 had just crossed Elliot Street with a full morning commuter train on April 2, 1921. These tracks were also used to ship raw materials in and finished products out.

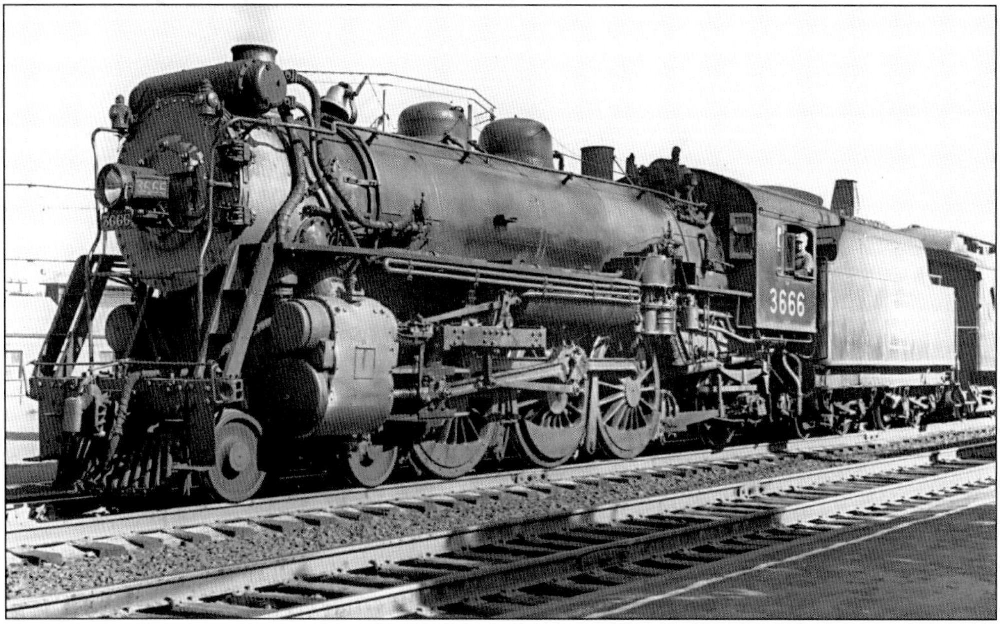

There was once direct train service from Beverly to Portland, Maine. Boston and Maine Railroad No. 3666 is seen at the Beverly Depot on July 3, 1939, before leaving for Portland. Several months later, on a southbound trip, the crew drowned as the locomotive, tender, and baggage coach fell into the Piscataqua River at Portsmouth, New Hampshire. The passenger cars stopped safely. The locomotive still sits at the bottom of the river.

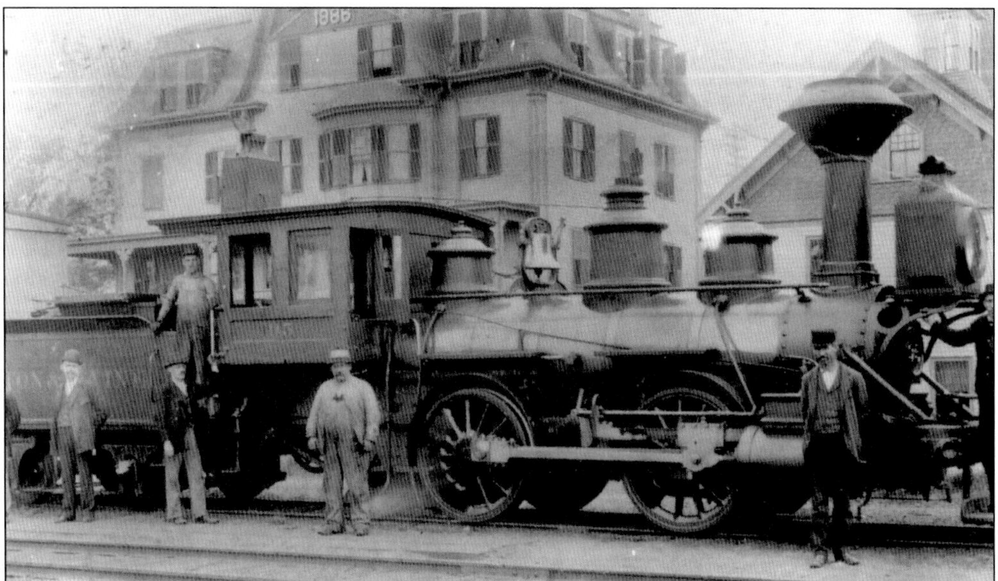

Railroad depots attracted a variety of businesses to serve the traveling public, and a number of railroad motels were located along Railroad Avenue near the Beverly Depot. The Hotel Trafton, built in 1883, was located across the street from the depot and is seen here behind the crew of Boston and Maine Railroad No. 95. The hotel became a rooming house in 1908 and was still in operation in 2010.

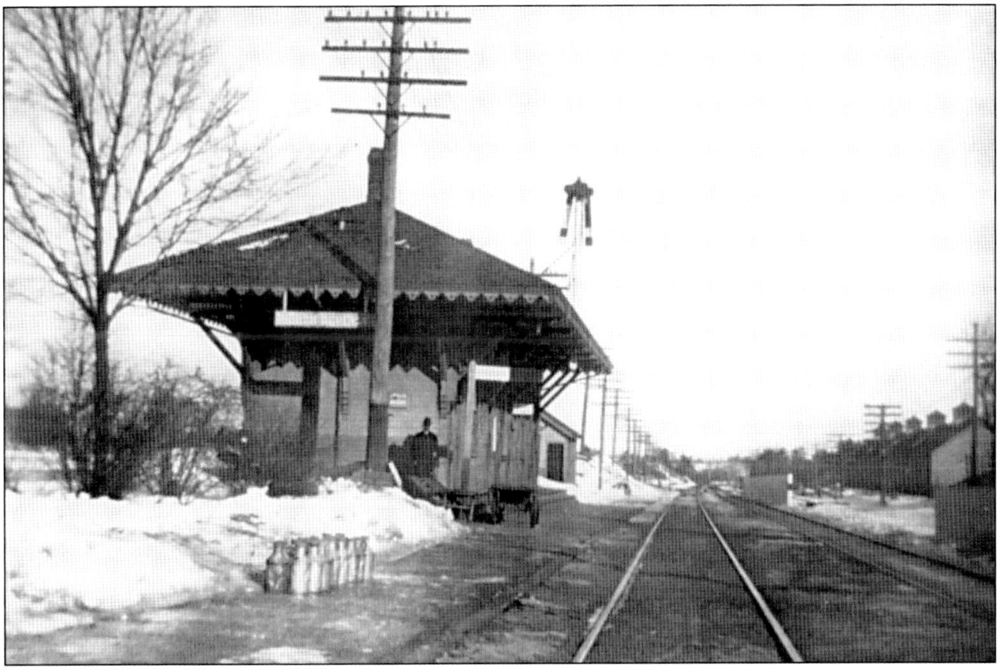

Beverly has had five depots, but only three of the original buildings exist today. This is one of the lost depots, located in North Beverly, where the commuter rail stop is today. This view is looking toward the towns of Wenham and Hamilton. Beyond the depot to the right is a car shed used to store Pullman cars, which were owned by many of the families who lived in the coastal estates of Beverly Farms.

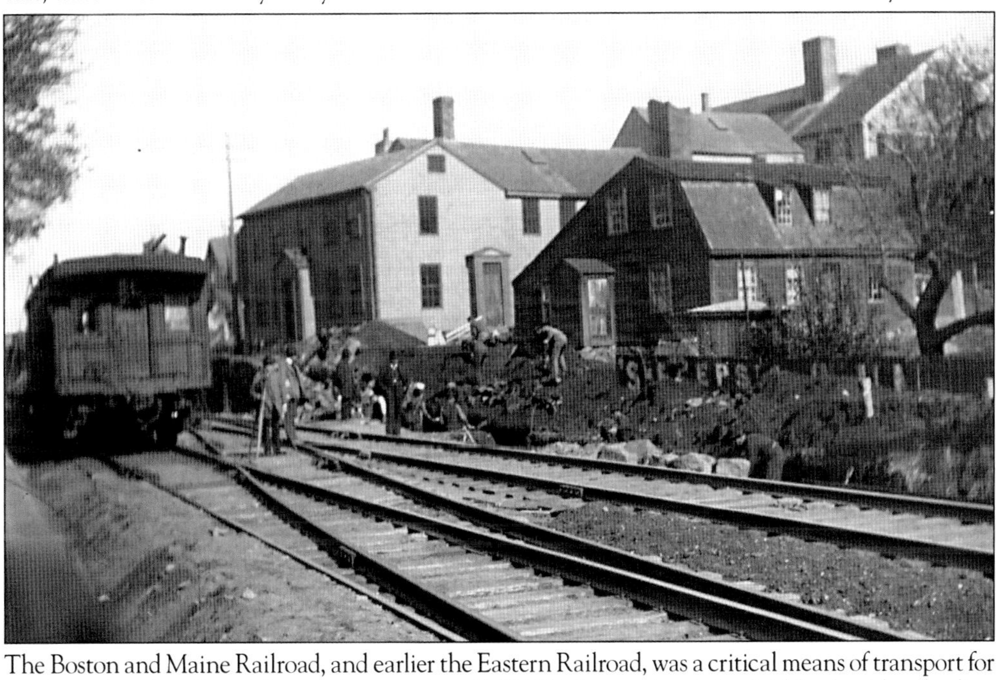

The Boston and Maine Railroad, and earlier the Eastern Railroad, was a critical means of transport for goods produced on Beverly's waterfront, such as Gulf Oil. Here track is being laid for the siding leading to the waterfront. The School Street Bridge crosses the tracks just beyond the passenger coach on the left. This siding was last used on January 12, 1982, for the construction of condominiums.

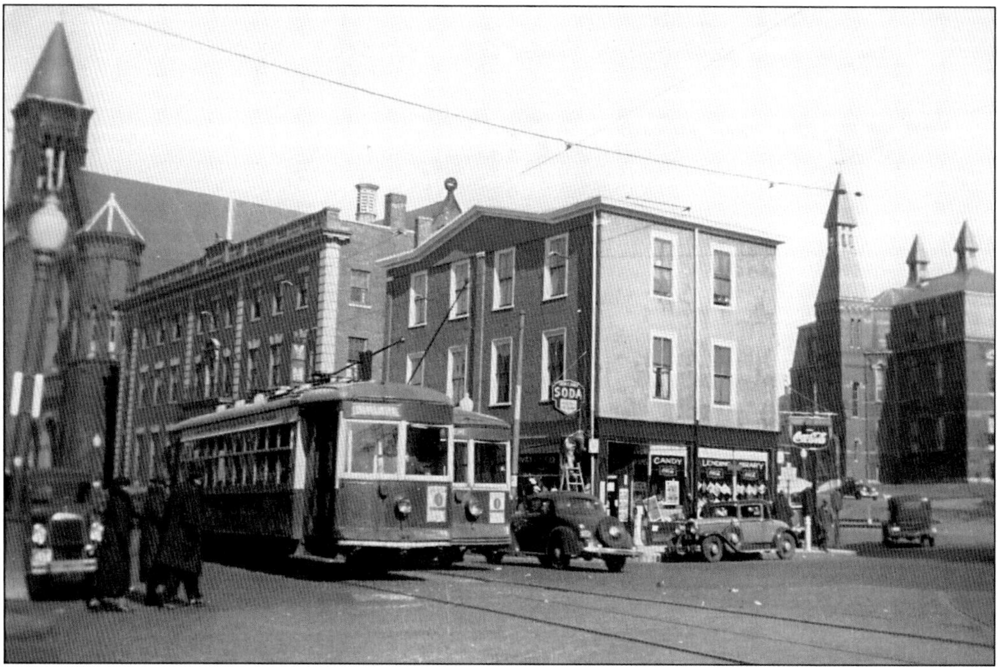

Beverly was served by a number of trolley lines, with the first operated by the Bay State Street Railway Company and later by the Eastern Massachusetts Street Railway. The last run was on February 27, 1937. A capacity crowd ripped up seats and grabbed anything else that was not nailed down as souvenirs of that last ride. These photographs were taken on that last day of service, with the image above showing two Eastern Massachusetts Street Railway trolley cars passing on Cabot Street in Ellis Square. The photograph below, taken at Gloucester Crossing at the intersection of Cabot and Rantoul Streets, shows Eastern Massachusetts Street Railway motormen posing with trolley car No. 7020. The commercial building to the right still exists today.

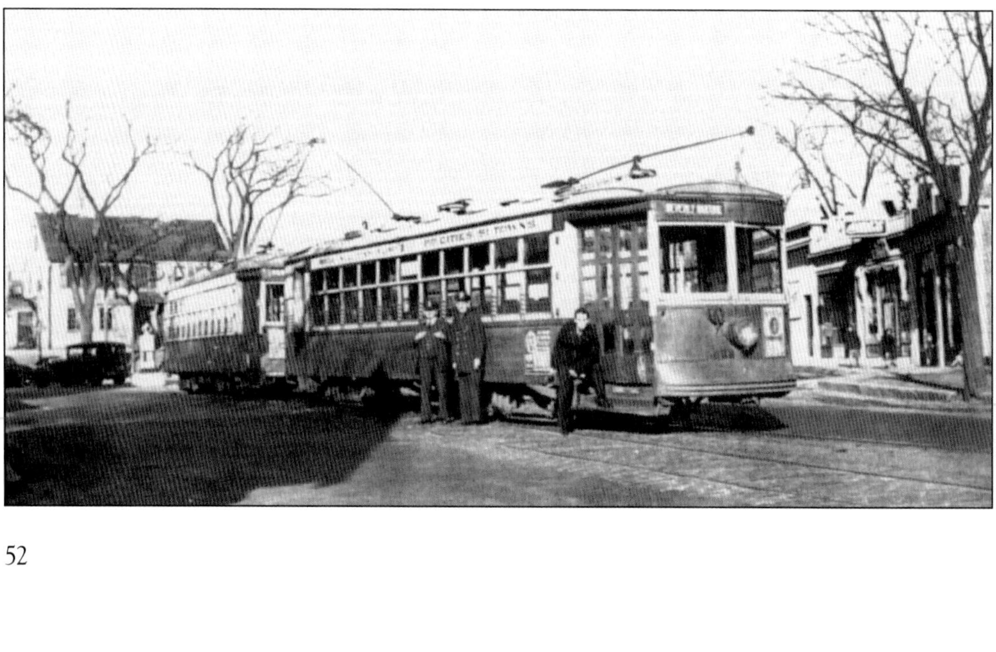

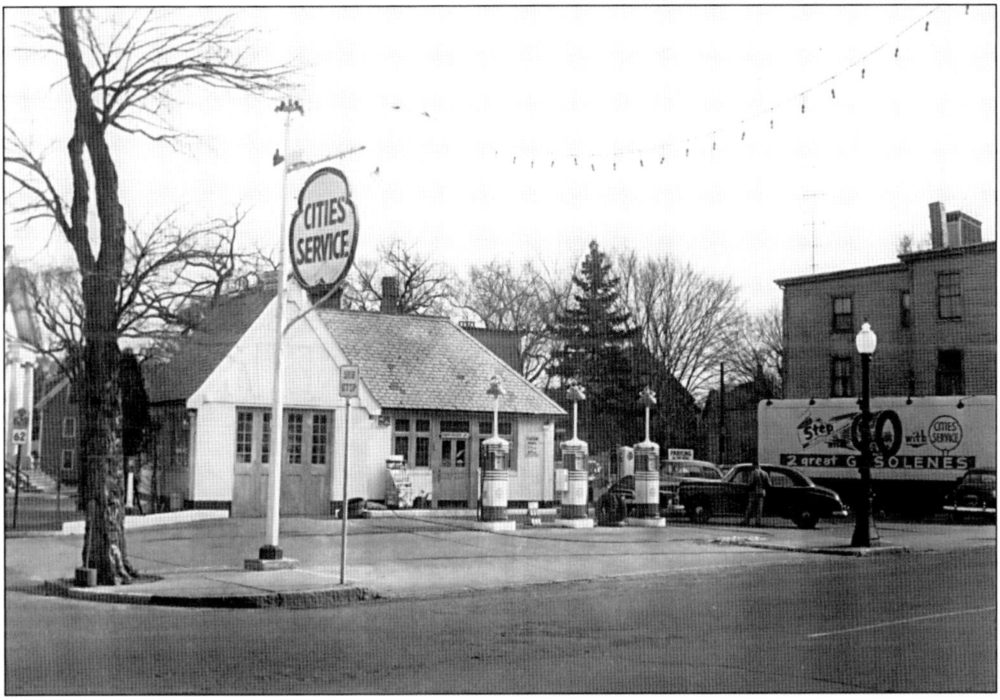

There has been a gas station at the corner of Cabot and Dane Streets since the early 1930s. Cities Service was first operated by the George Pickering Coal Company. It was then owned by Ralph Osgood Jr. from 1952 to 1955. In 1956, it became Dave and Pop's Service Station. When self-service replaced the gas attendant, a modern convenience store and gas station was built in its place.

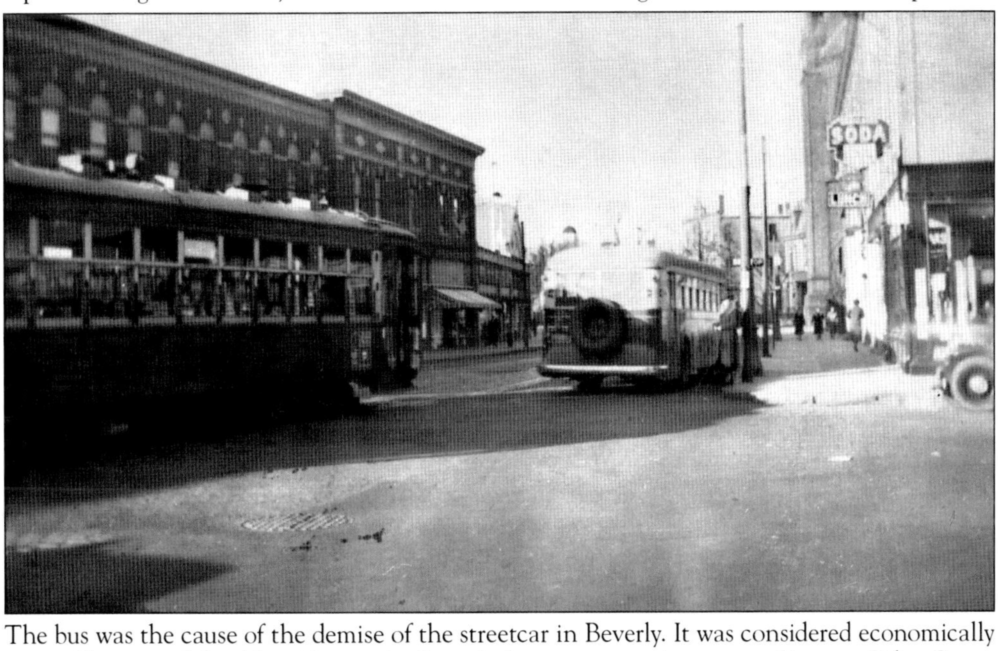

The bus was the cause of the demise of the streetcar in Beverly. It was considered economically more efficient and flexible with practically no infrastructure maintenance. Here on Cabot Street in Ellis Square, an Eastern Massachusetts Street Railway bus is being used to train drivers the route it will take. A streetcar rolls by just days away from its last run at the end of February 1937.

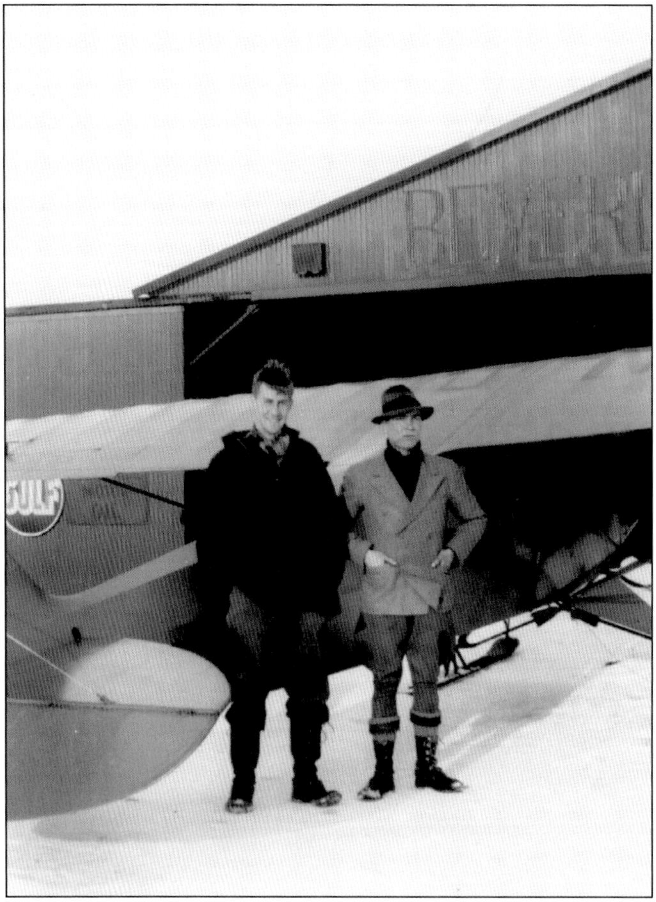

Harold Thompson (left) took over for Larry Thompson (right and no relation) as the acting manager of Beverly Airport when Larry left to fly for the 8th Air Force during World War II. Harold soon left to be a fighter pilot and was shot down overseas after 10 missions. The airport was still a converted cornfield when this photograph was taken in 1939 at the Beverly Aero Club hangar.

The Beverly Aero Club, one of the founding organizations of the Beverly Airport in 1928, held a number of air shows throughout the years. This meet was in 1940. From left to right on the grass field is a Taylorcraft, Piper J5, Piper J3, Luscombe, Piper J5, and another Luscombe. In back is Beverly Aero Club member Harold Morganstern's Stinson SM-8A and Piper J3.

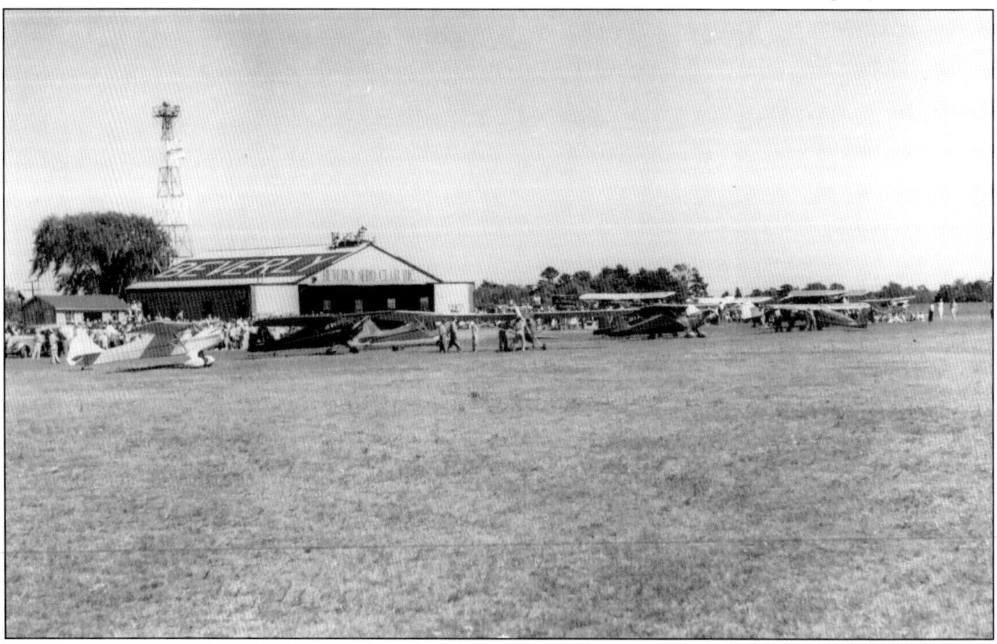

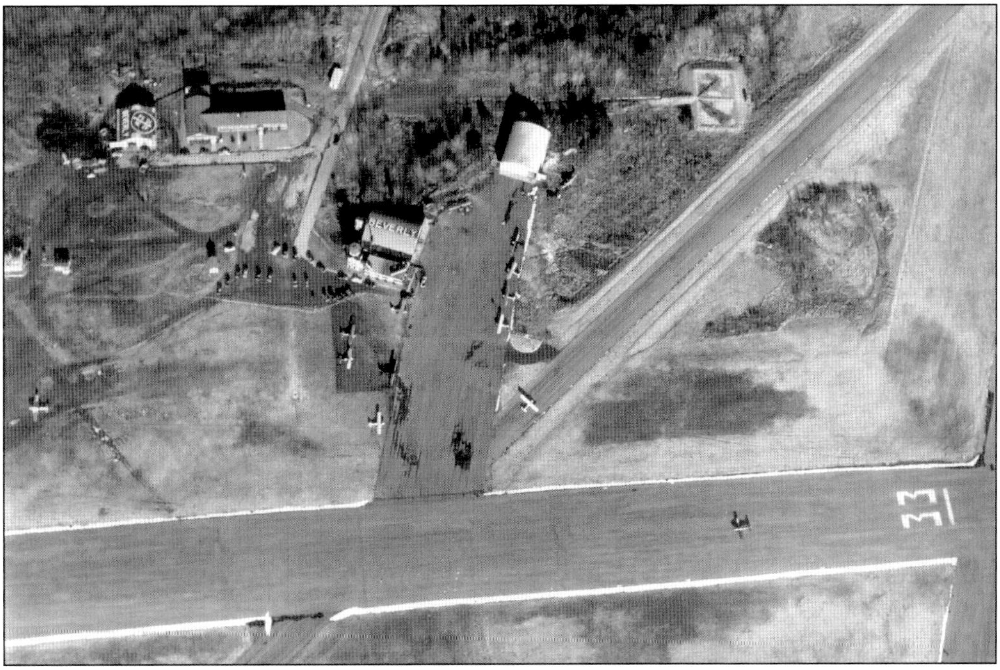

The photograph above is a view of the Beverly Airport taken in 1950, looking west to east. The hangar at the upper left with "Beverly" on the roof was the original location of the Beverly Aero Club hangar, named for the group that pioneered the airport. This hangar was later moved to its current location, at a point about center of runway "33" at the left edge of photograph. Eastern Aviation occupied all of the facilities on the east side of the field. The view below of the Beverly Airport in the early 1940s was taken from northwest to southeast. The circle at the lower right was used to calibrate aircraft compasses and also served as a landmark visible for many miles. The winding dirt entrance road from Route 97 extends from the hangar to the upper left.

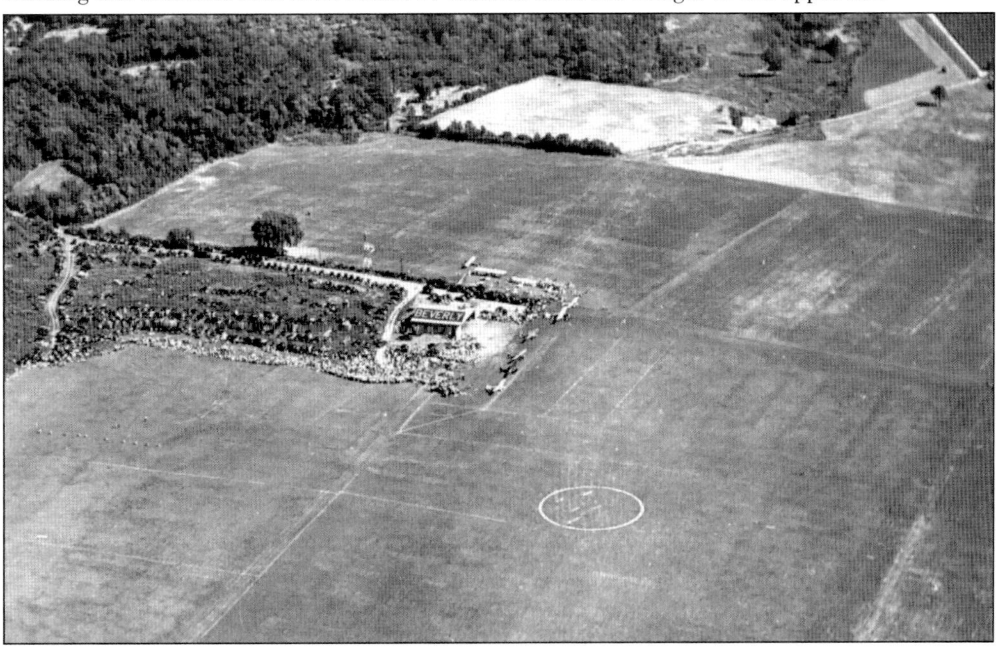

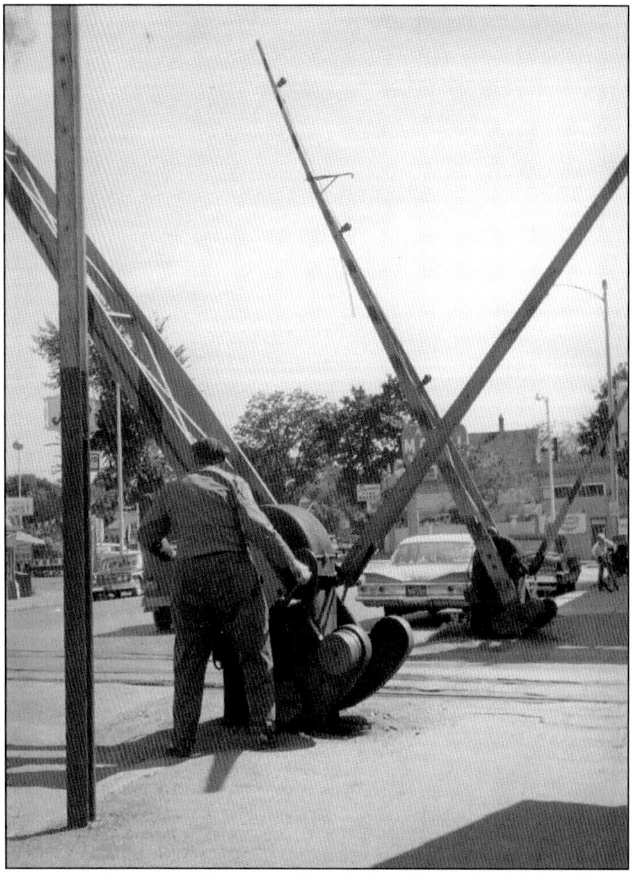

The railroad crossing tender and shanty were once a common sight across New England. This one at Gloucester Crossing shows the crossing tender in June 1963 manually lower the gates before a train rushes across Cabot Street. Even though the gates are now automatic, Gloucester Crossing is one of three remaining manned crossings in the Greater Boston area because of the complex intersection with Rantoul and Colon Streets.

Beginning in 1872 as lunch wagons, diners eventually evolved to the type seen here on Cabot Street in Gloucester Crossing, where the Miss Beverly Diner was moved in December 1950 by Al Hedblom. Through the years it had a number of owners until 1974, when it became a Buffalo Bill's Roast Beef. It still exists today as a national sandwich chain, but with a brick facade.

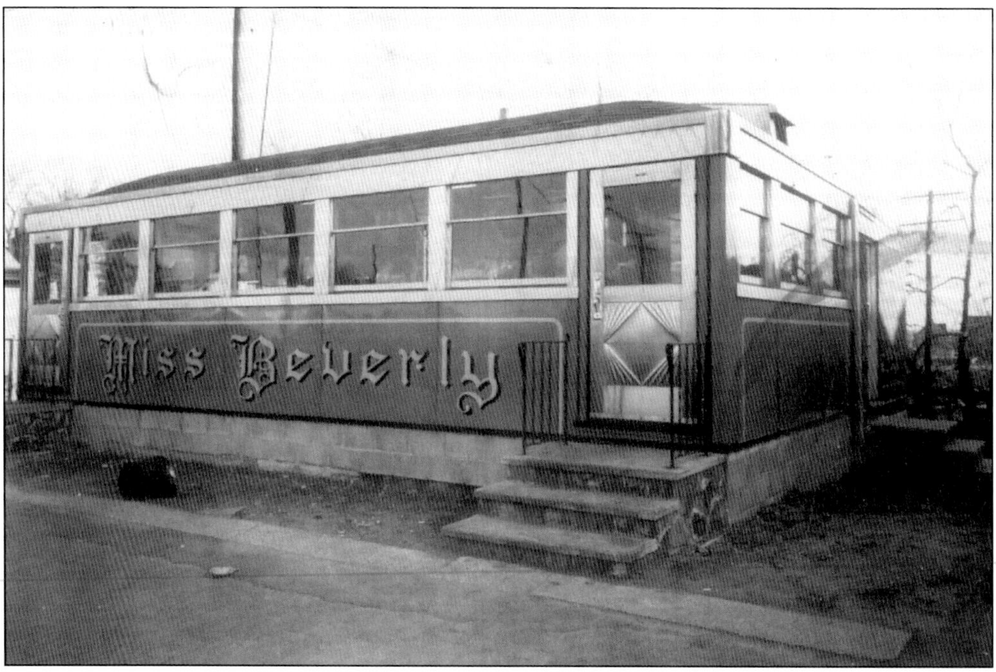

Five

Business and Industry

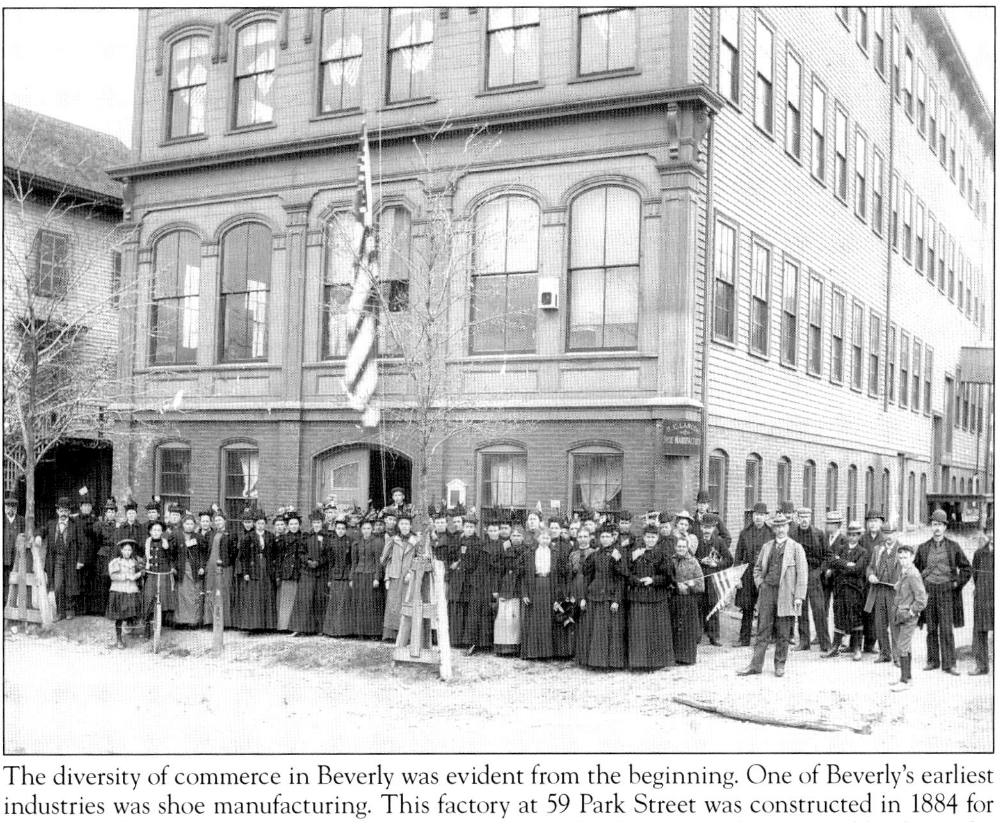

The diversity of commerce in Beverly was evident from the beginning. One of Beverly's earliest industries was shoe manufacturing. This factory at 59 Park Street was constructed in 1884 for shoe manufacturer Charles H. Creesy and Company. The factory was later owned by the Rufus E. Larcom Shoe Manufacturing Company. Here employees are seen on the day in 1898 that the men left Beverly to serve in the Spanish-American War.

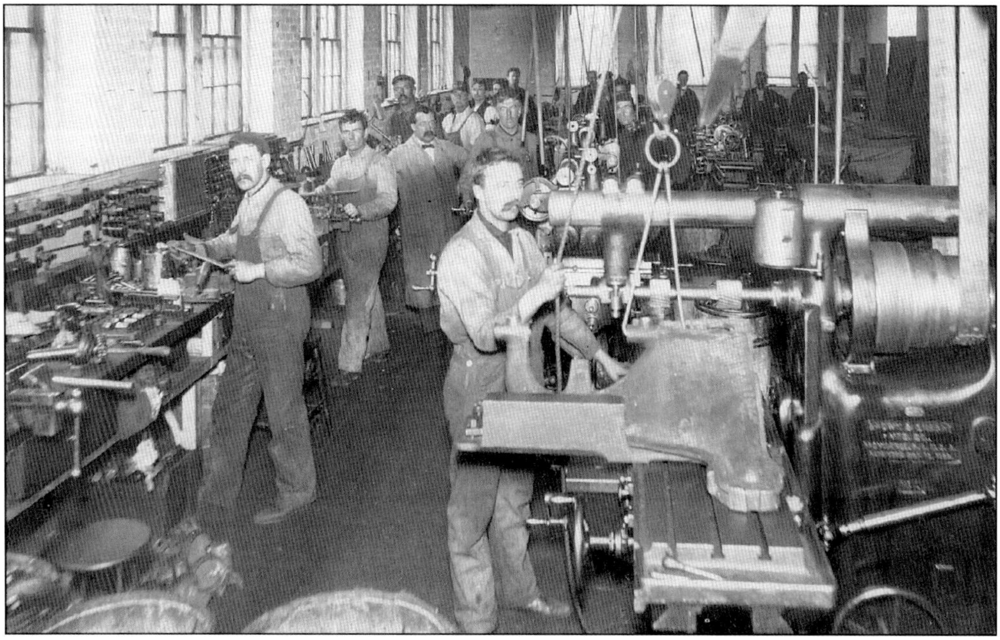

Shoemaking was, at first, a piecework business. So-called "ten footers"—small sheds where one to five men could work—were common. Women were employed to sew leather uppers at home. The first small factories were built in Beverly in the 1820s, but as fishing declined as an industry, the importance of shoemaking increased, employing a third of all working men and women by 1890. Eventually large factories on Rantoul and Park Streets were producing shoes for men, women, and children. The Beverly Building Association, on Rantoul Street, housed many shoe manufacturers. The photograph above was taken in 1899. Many of the shoe factories manufactured articles for the war effort during World War I, including the company below, also located there. By the late 1930s shoemaking had mostly ceased, and the mills are now gone or converted into apartments.

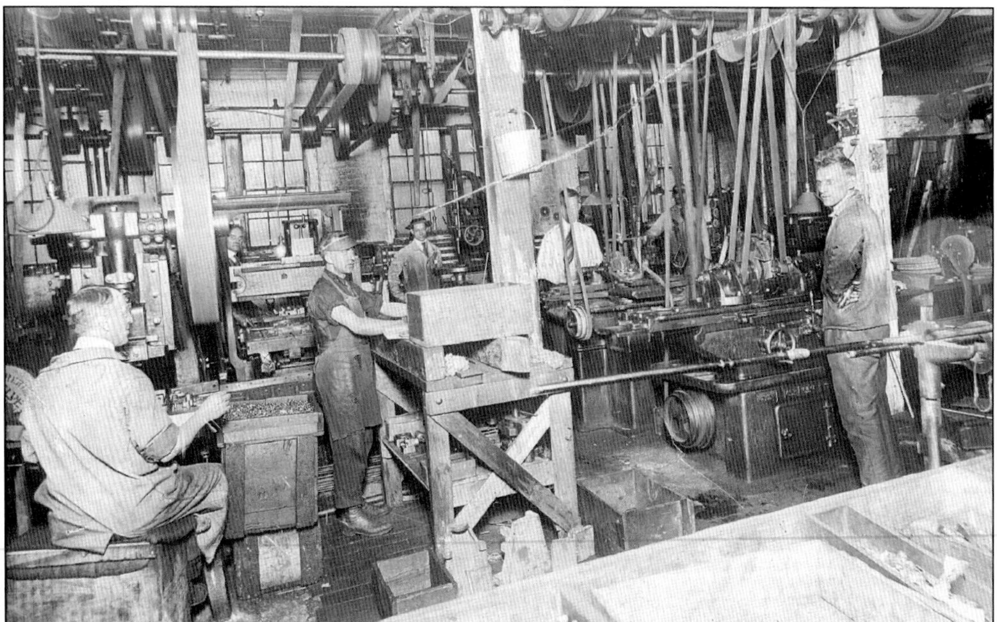

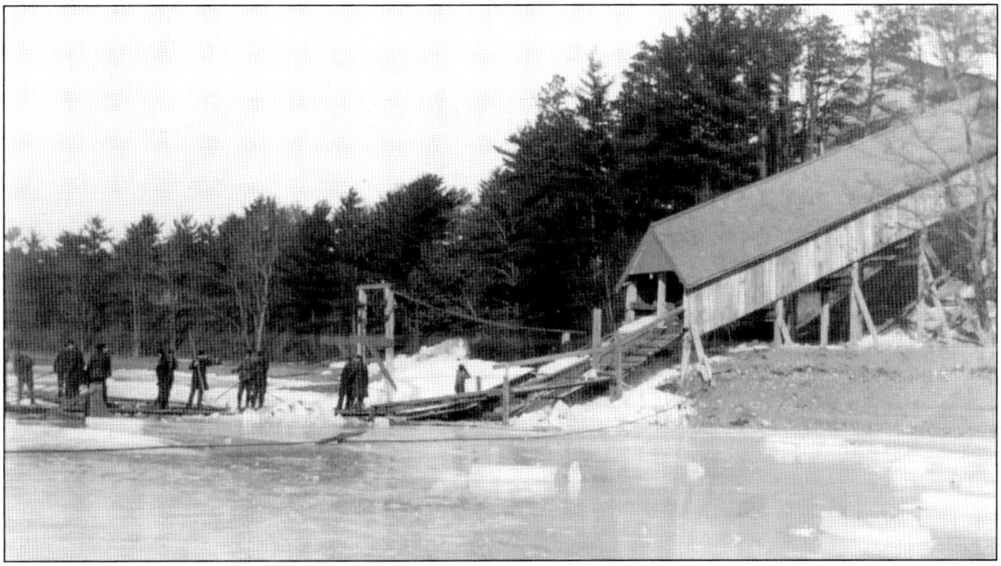

Frederick Tudor, known as the "Ice King," began harvesting ice from Wenham Lake in the early 19th century. This ice was considered the finest available and was the only type that Queen Victoria would use. Ice harvesting continued at Wenham Lake through the early 20th century, when the lake was set aside by the Salem and Beverly Water Supply Board as a reservoir. The Beverly Ice Company, which was founded by John C. Kelleher, harvested ice beginning around 1910. Other ice dealers, including F. B. Davis, Ernest Wright, W. A. Caldwell, and B. N. Dodge, also made a living from Wenham Lake. Residents placed cards in the windows of their homes to notify the dealer of how much ice would be needed for the icebox. Major fires, exacerbated by the sawdust that insulated the ice, hit the icehouses frequently, and that, combined with the development of refrigeration, put an end to the industry.

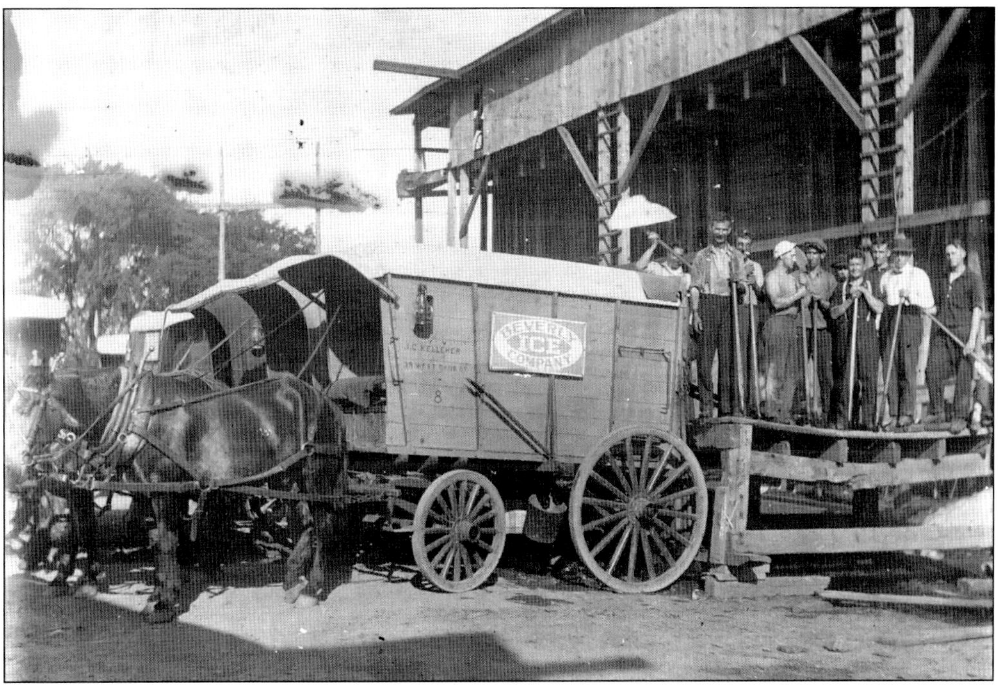

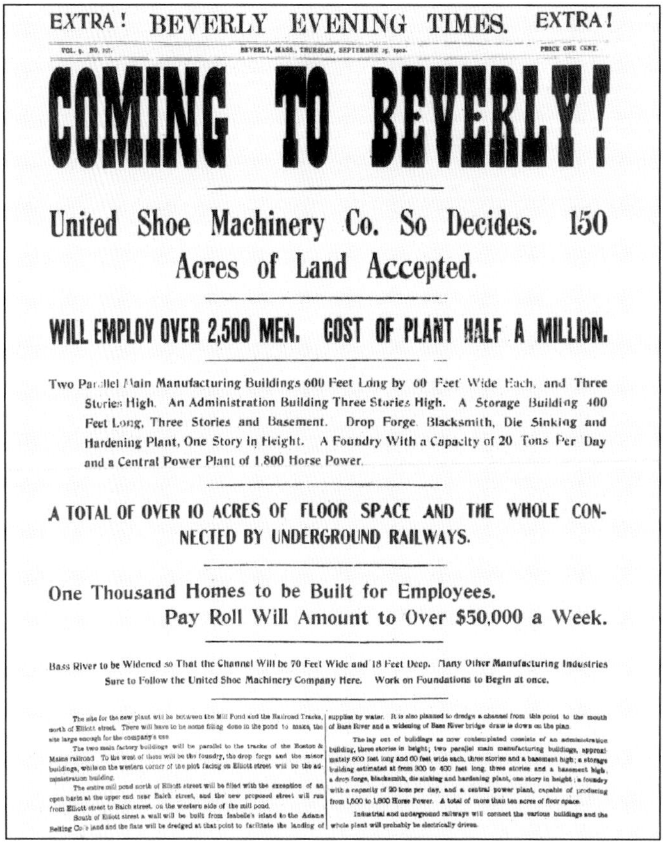

EXTRA! BEVERLY EVENING TIMES. EXTRA!

VOL. 9. NO. 107. BEVERLY, MASS., THURSDAY, SEPTEMBER 25, 1902. PRICE ONE CENT.

COMING TO BEVERLY!

United Shoe Machinery Co. So Decides. 150 Acres of Land Accepted.

WILL EMPLOY OVER 2,500 MEN. COST OF PLANT HALF A MILLION.

Two Parallel Main Manufacturing Buildings 600 Feet Long by 60 Feet Wide Each, and Three Stories High. An Administration Building Three Stories High. A Storage Building 400 Feet Long, Three Stories and Basement. Drop Forge, Blacksmith, Die Sinking and Hardening Plant, One Story in Height. A Foundry With a Capacity of 20 Tons Per Day and a Central Power Plant of 1,800 Horse Power.

A TOTAL OF OVER 10 ACRES OF FLOOR SPACE AND THE WHOLE CONNECTED BY UNDERGROUND RAILWAYS.

One Thousand Homes to be Built for Employees. Pay Roll Will Amount to Over $50,000 a Week.

Bass River to be Widened so That the Channel Will be 70 Feet Wide and 18 Feet Deep. Many Other Manufacturing Industries Sure to Follow the United Shoe Machinery Company Here. Work on Foundations to Begin at once.

The site for the new plant will be between the Mill Pond and the Railroad Tracks, north of Elliott street. There will have to be some filling done in the pond to make the site large enough for the company's use.

The two main factory buildings will be parallel to the tracks of the Boston & Maine railroad. To the west of these will be the foundry, the drop forge and the minor buildings, while on the western corner of the plot facing on Elliott street will be the administration building.

The entire mill pond north of Elliott street will be filled with the exception of an open basin at the upper end near Balch street, and the new proposed street will run from Elliott street to Balch street, on the western side of the mill pond.

South of Elliott street a wall will be built from Isabelle's island to the Adams Belting Co.'s land and the flats will be dredged at that point to facilitate the landing of supplies by water. It is also planned to dredge a channel from this point to the mouth of Bass River and a widening of Bass River bridge draw is down on the plan.

The lay out of buildings as now contemplated consists of an administration building, three stories in height; two parallel main manufacturing buildings, approximately 600 feet long and 60 feet wide each, three stories and a basement high; a storage building estimated at from 300 to 400 feet long, three stories and a basement high; a drop forge, blacksmith, die sinking and hardening plant, one story in height; a foundry with a capacity of 20 tons per day, and a central power plant, capable of producing from 1,500 to 1,800 Horse Power. A total of more than ten acres of floor space.

Industrial and underground railways will connect the various buildings and the whole plant will probably be electrically driven.

In late September 1902, an extra edition of the *Beverly Evening Times* trumpeted the news that the United Shoe Machinery Corporation had picked a 150-acre site off Elliott Street in Beverly for its massive complex, which would be like an industrial city. Construction began the next year on the more than 10 acres of floor space in three buildings, along with a foundry and drop forge. Many Italian immigrants came to work on the construction, and some stayed there. "The Shoe," as it came to be known, was for many years Beverly's largest employer. It even had its own stop for passenger rail.

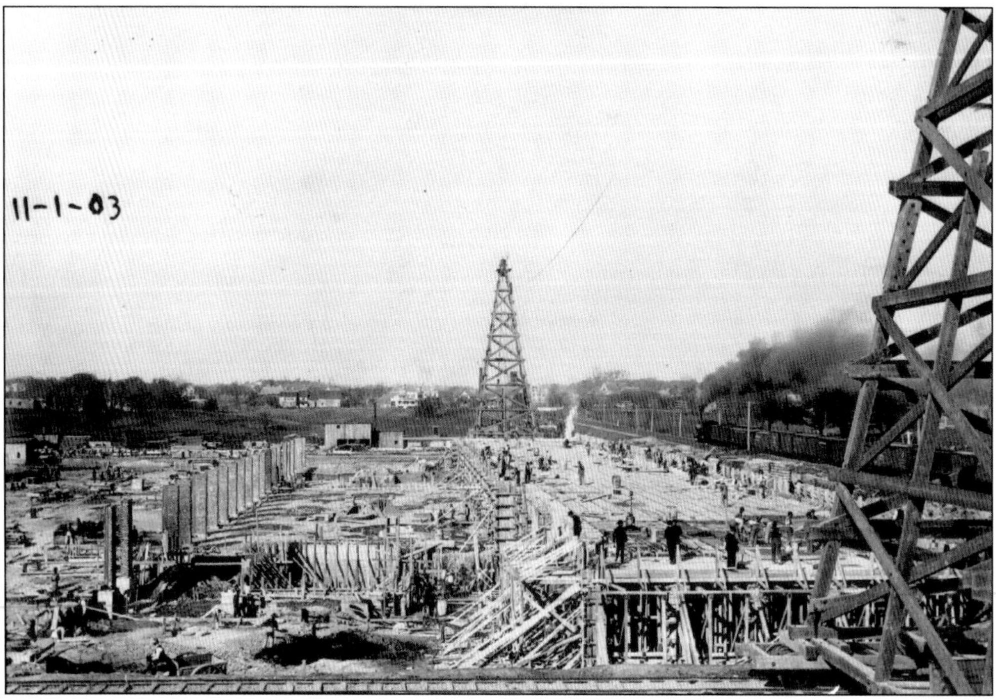

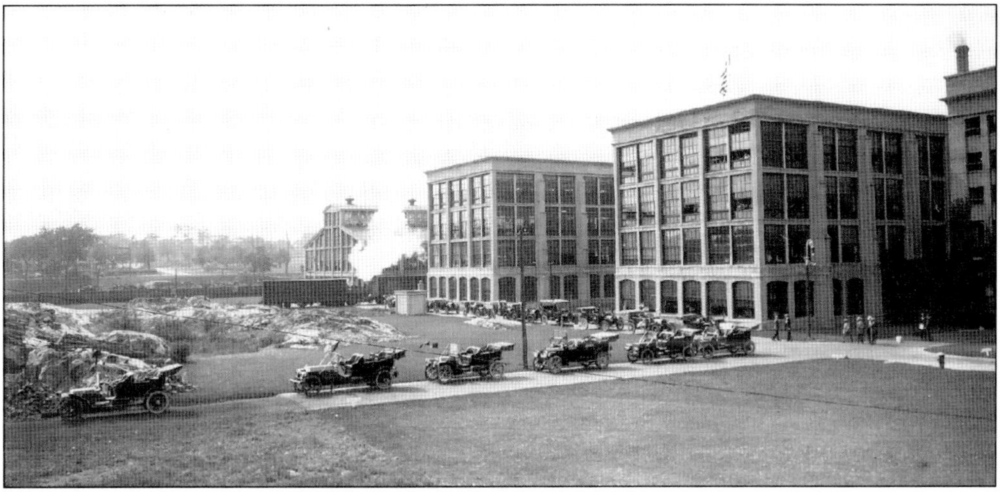

The Shoe complex was so massive that messengers carried documents around the buildings on roller skates. The company even employed a staff of inventors on site as it developed and built machinery for assembling footwear. The company's name was changed in 1968 to USM Corporation, and it dominated the industry worldwide. By then antitrust rulings against the company were cutting severely into its business, and in the early 1980s, the Beverly operation was phased out. The complex was neglected for several years—its size a liability. Now known as the Cummings Center, it is home to a variety of businesses. The buildings contain wonderful photographs and objects from the days of the Shoe.

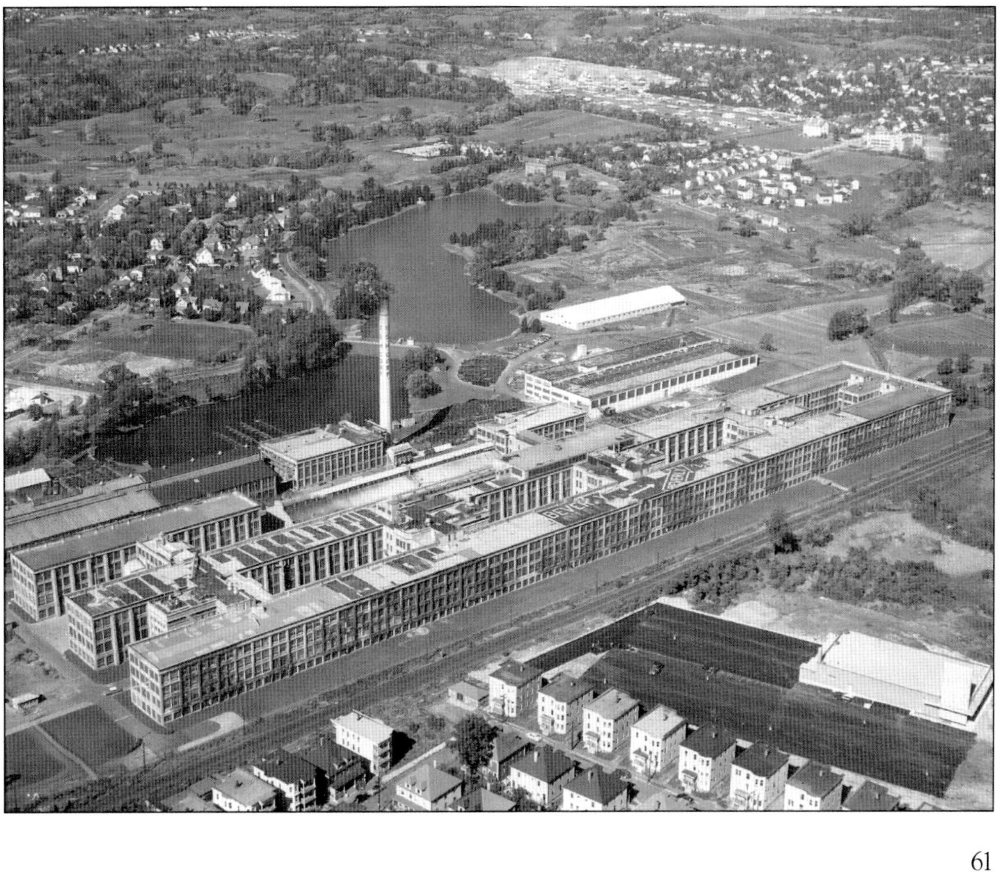

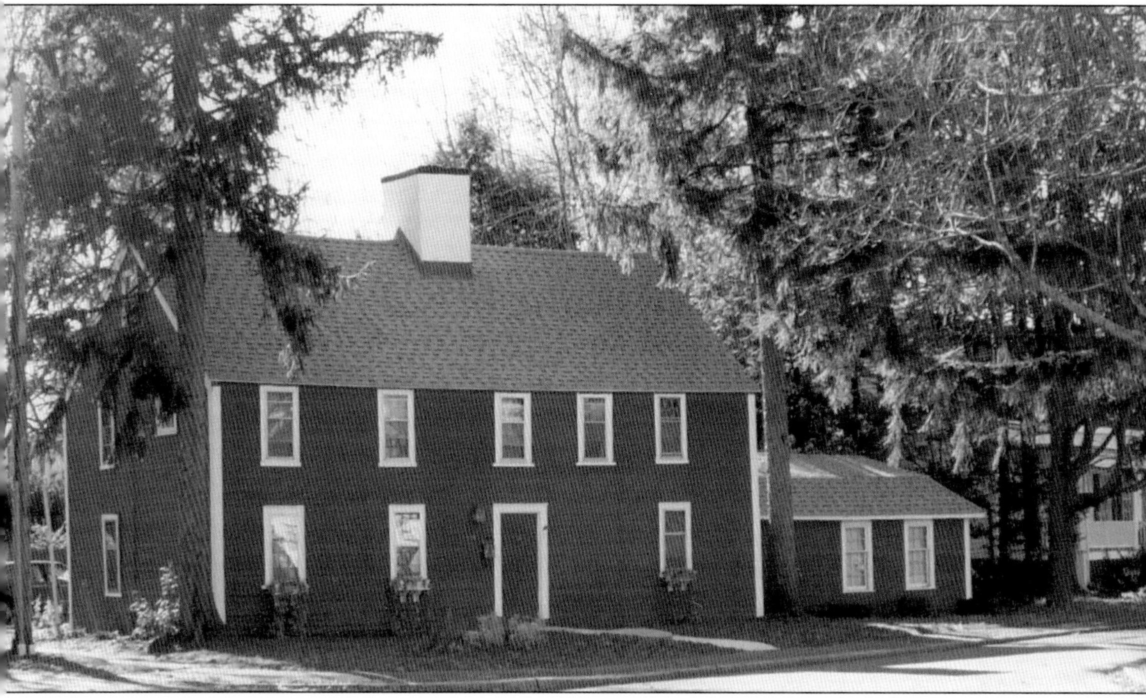

John Woodbury was one of the first English settlers in the area, settling first on Cape Ann, then Naumkeag, the original name for Salem. He finally moved to the Bass River Side (later Beverly) in 1635 as one of the Old Planters, who received land grants of 200 acres. The many members of this prominent family built homes all over town. This house was built before 1690 on the corner of Woodbury and Hale Streets. Five generations of the Woodbury family lived in this historic house. It became a tavern and stagecoach stop between Salem and Gloucester where passengers could enjoy good food and a comfortable place to sleep. It opened as a restaurant in the 1930s, serving lobster, steak, chicken, and lamb. Today the Woodbury Tavern is a private home. Woodbury (also spelled Woodberry) descendants still live in the area.

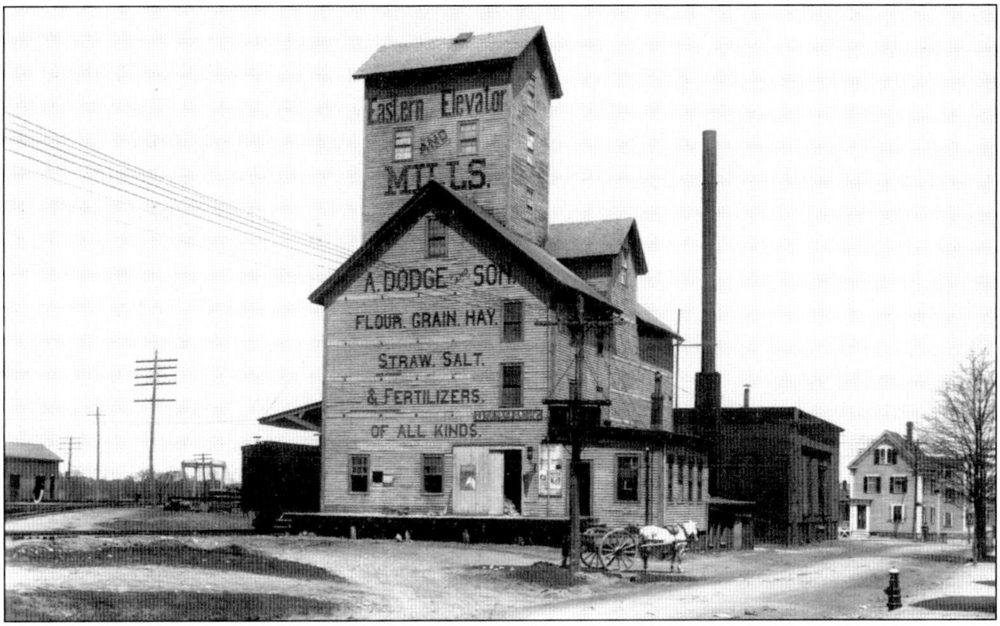

Albert Dodge was president of both Eastern Elevator and Mills and A. Dodge and Son, located at 70 Park Street, in the early 20th century. This firm was just down the road from the Beverly Depot. According to the 1910 Beverly City Directory, Dodge dealt in meal, corn, oats, fine feed, hay, and straw, while Eastern Elevator was noted for flour, grain, and feed.

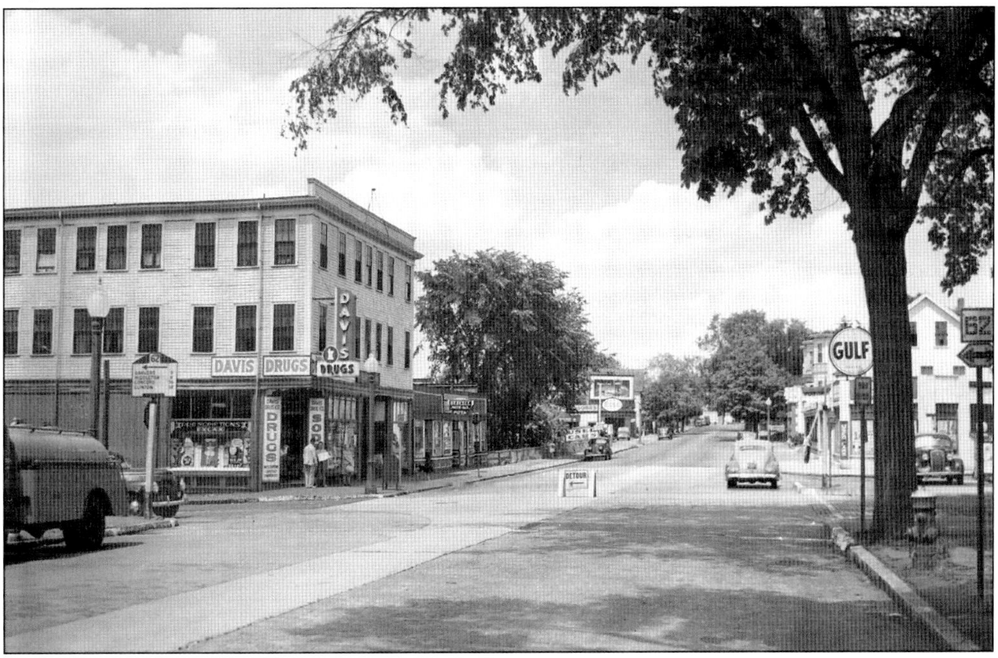

Davis Drug opened on the corner of Rantoul and Elliott Streets in 1941 and continued in business until July 4, 1984, when a terrible fire broke out in the rooming house above the store. Elliott Chambers was known as a tinderbox by the fire department, and this proved to be tragically true. Although fire trucks responded within two minutes, the building was already engulfed; 15 people died in the blaze.

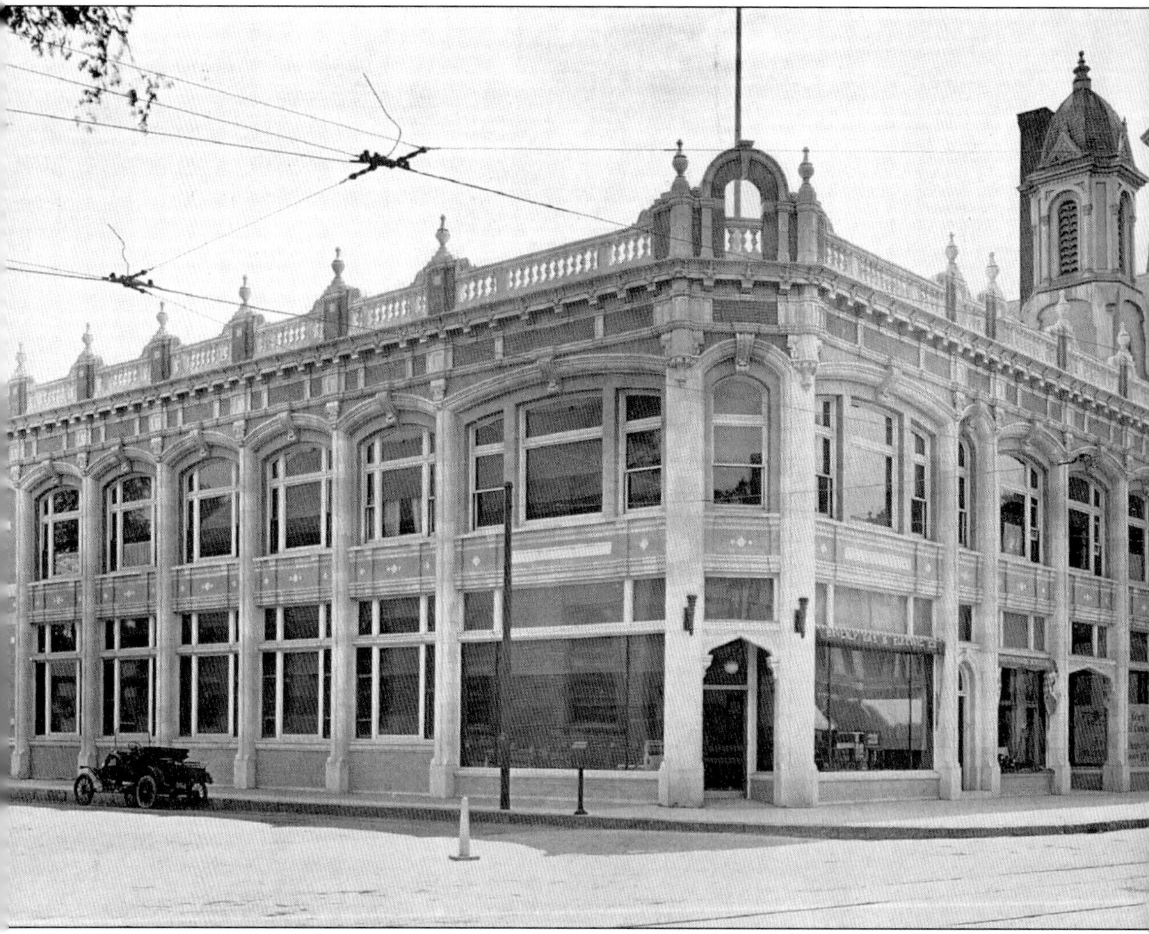

In 1915, the Beverly Gas and Electric Company built this lovely Renaissance Revival–style building at 223 Cabot Street. It is difficult to imagine the difference for the community by providing gaslight, then electricity; the company called gaslights "the perfect servants." In addition to providing gas and electricity, Beverly Gas and Electric sold stoves, radiators, hot-water heaters, and fans. Andrew W. Rogers was secretary and treasurer of the company and was also president of Beverly National Bank. He owned a home at 36 Hale Street, across from Hale Farm. The house was demolished after his death, and three homes were built on the lot. The stone wall still survives. In 1976, the building became the headquarters of the bicentennial committee; everything from information, to souvenirs, to walking tour tapes were available there. The company decided to sell the building shortly after the First Baptist Church burned, and the church purchased it for $90,000 in 1976. The building was torn down to make way for the new church.

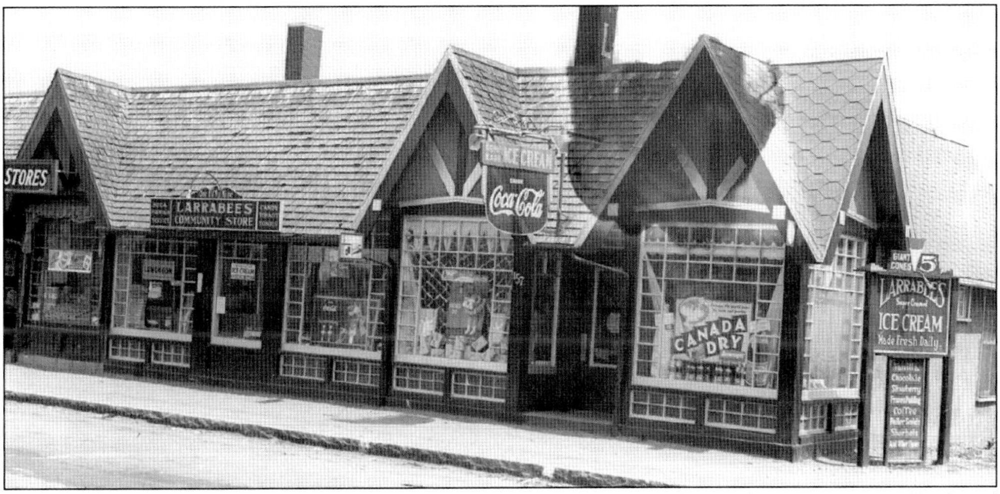

Neighborhood stores played an important role in the life of Beverly residents. Anyone who lived in Montserrat in the second half of the 20th century remembers Larrabee's. It opened in 1947 as an ice cream shop and convenience store; it was the place for children to buy treats as they walked to school and for their parents to purchase milk and bread. "Meet Your Friends at Ralph's" was more than just a slogan for the popular grocery store in Ryal Side. For decades it truly was a gathering place for local residents. Businessman Ralph Parisella opened a small grocery store on Bridge Street in the mid-1950s that grew to be an important fixture in the neighborhood. Parisella went to the state's highest court with a case challenging the Sunday blue laws, setting a precedent for all businesses in Massachusetts.

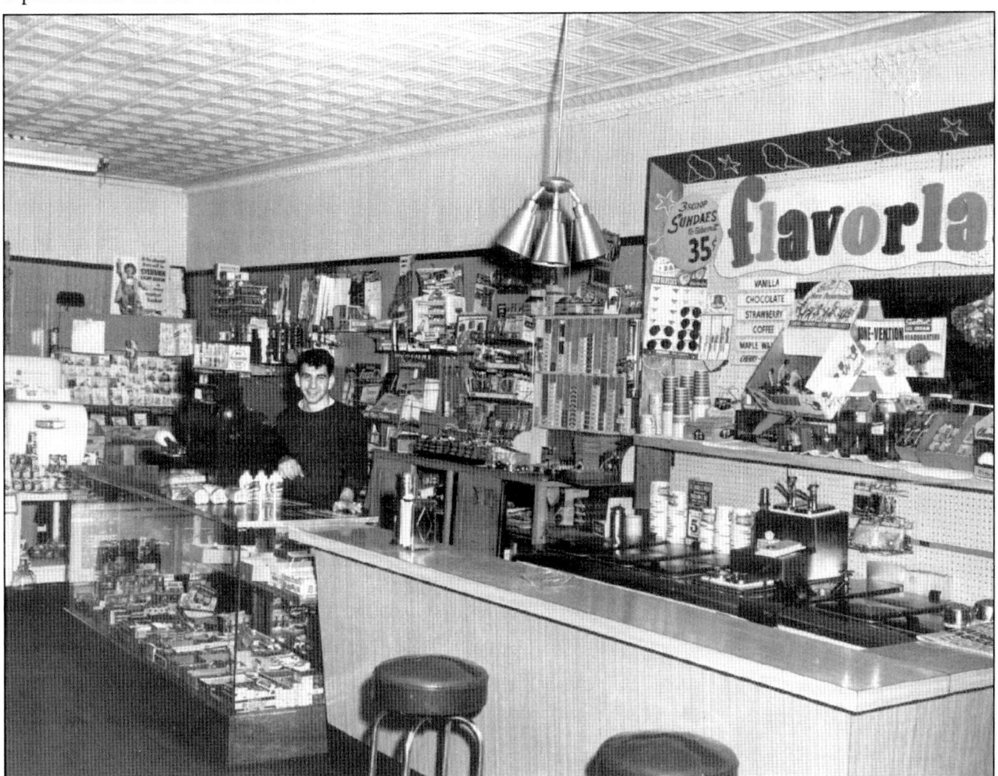

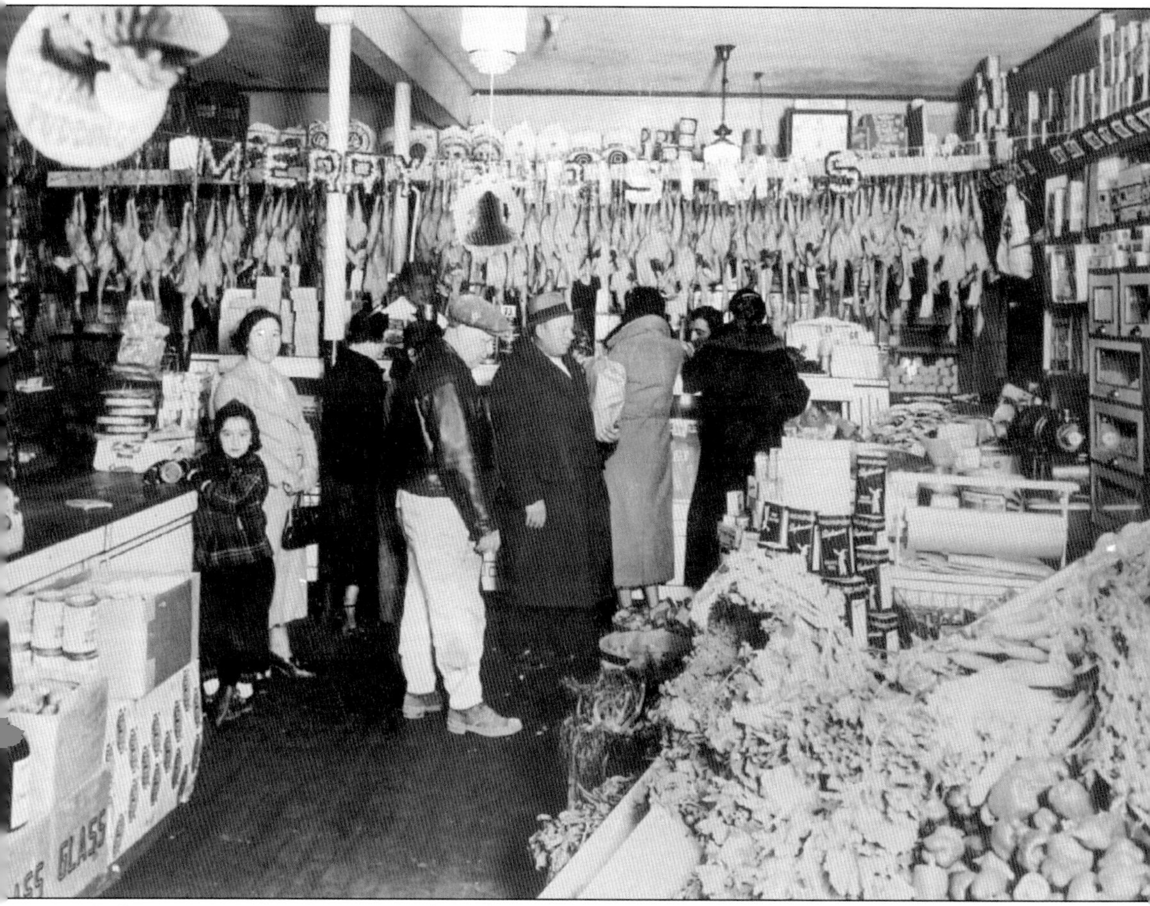

Italian immigrants came to Beverly at the beginning of the 20th century with the hope of starting a new and prosperous life. Many came seeking work as stonemasons and gardeners on the large estates that were being built on the coast or to work on the construction of the United Shoe Machinery Corporation plant. Charlie Bucci immigrated to the United States from Italy in 1906, and after a few decades in Pennsylvania, he moved to Beverly in 1928. Bucci was the longtime proprietor of Bucci's Market, where he was known for his generosity and thoughtfulness, providing customers with food on credit when they did not have the money to buy groceries. He served as city assessor and was also a member of the school committee. Bucci was the founder of the 13 Black Cats and Charlie Bucci's Lousy Band and was known for his portrayal of Santa Claus for more than 30 years, including in Beverly's longtime Santa parade.

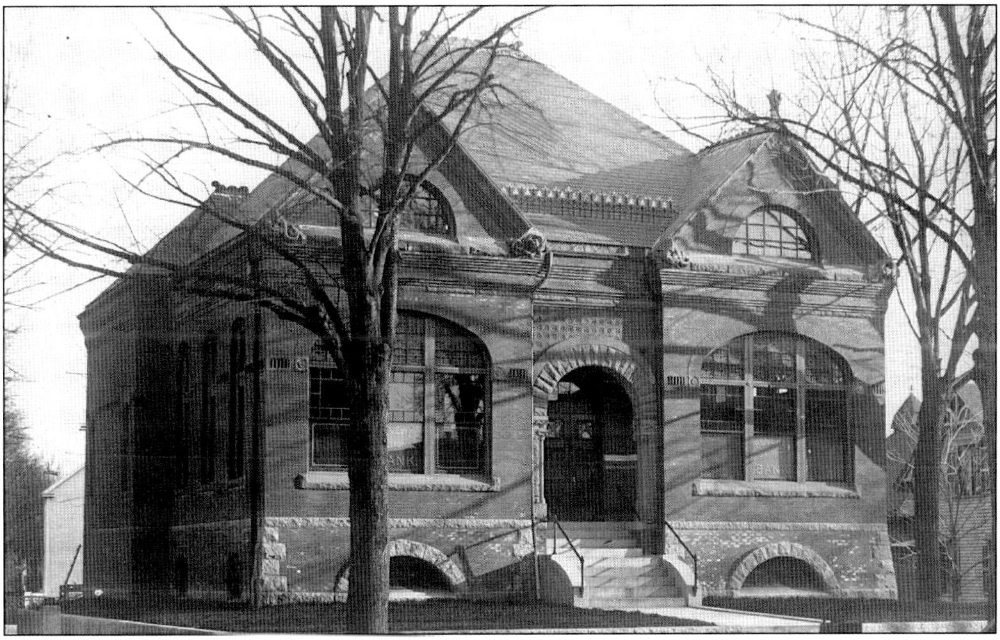

The Beverly Bank, one of the oldest in the country, was founded in 1802 by some of the community's leading citizens. It was moved from its original home on the first floor of the John Cabot House in 1868, and after a short tenure at another location, was moved again to the building in the above image in 1885. Beverly saw tremendous growth in the following years with the rise of the shoe industry and the influx of summer visitors. The bank was their financial anchor. In 1925, Beverly National moved to its final location at 240 Cabot Street, once the location of President Taft's summer office. This structure (seen below) was destroyed in a 1954 fire. The bank was rebuilt and later expanded into the adjoining space in 1984, where it continued to be a vital financial and philanthropic part of the Beverly community.

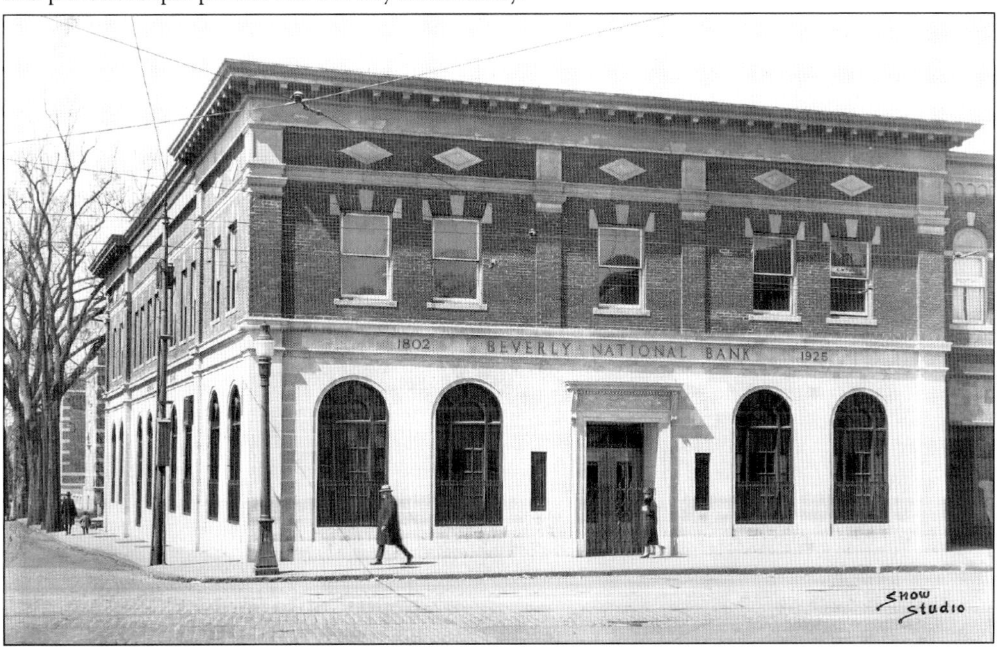

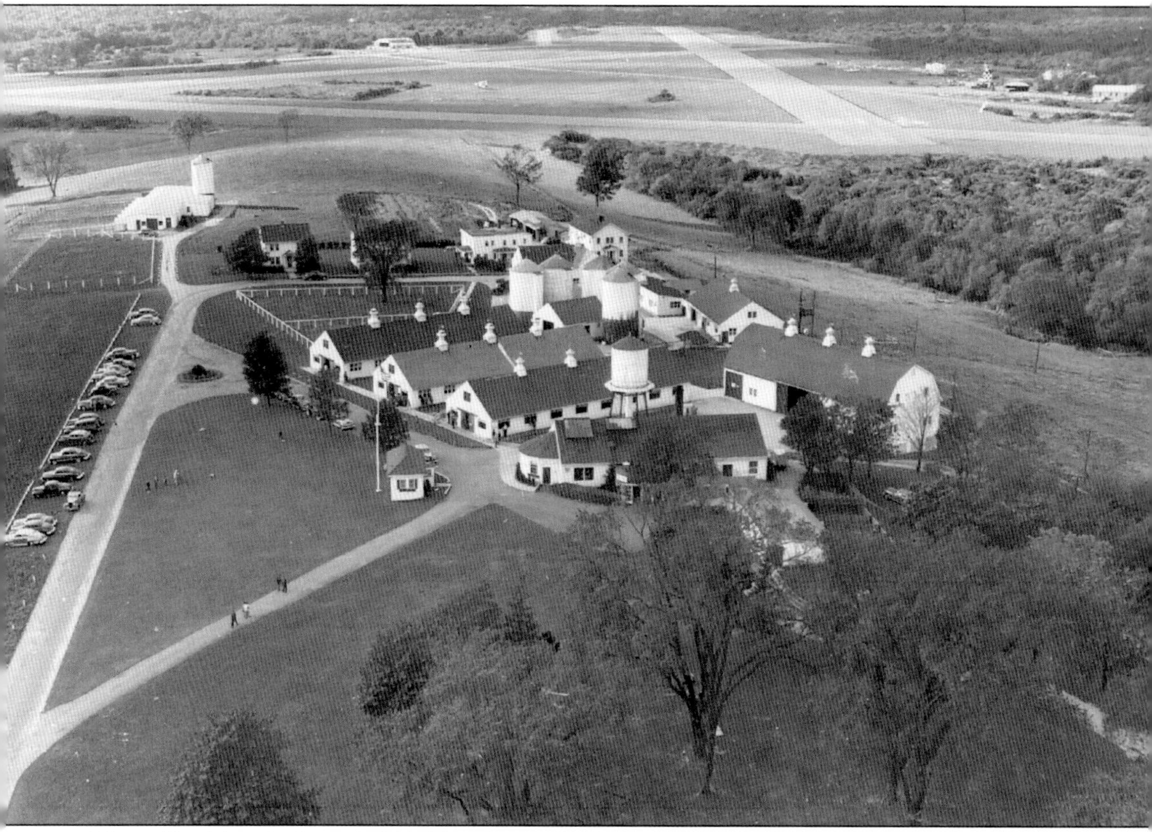

The Alford family farmed the property now known as Cherry Hill beginning in 1650. Cherry Hill was purchased by the H. P. Hood Company in 1912. During its years as a dairy farm, an estimated 3 million visitors enjoyed the beautiful view and the recreational facilities, which included volleyball, badminton, horseshoes, and softball. Families and school groups toured the barns, learning about the prize-winning Holsteins and the history of the farm and enjoying ice cream treats as a part of their day in the country. Charles Reynolds followed his father, Ralph, into the dairy business at Cherry Hill, first working on the farm and then driving a milk truck all over the area from the 1950s to mid-1990s. In an interview in 2002, Reynolds described the importance the farm put on providing safe, consistent quality for all its milk products. In 1965, Cherry Hill was developed into an industrial park.

Six

The Gold Coast

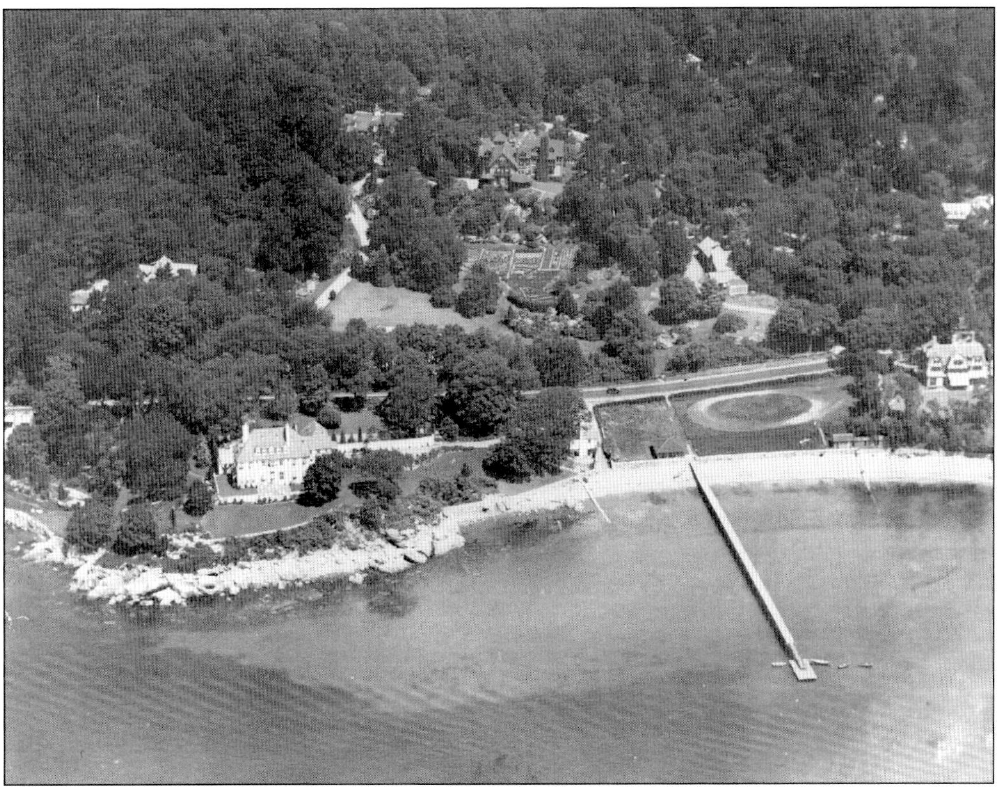

This aerial view of Prides Crossing illustrates the evolution of this neighborhood in Beverly. Many of the estates in this area were built by wealthy industrialists who came here in numbers after rail service began in 1847, looking for a summer escape. Herbert Sears owned Woodrock, seen in the center of the picture, as well as the pier. These properties are now owned by Endicott College.

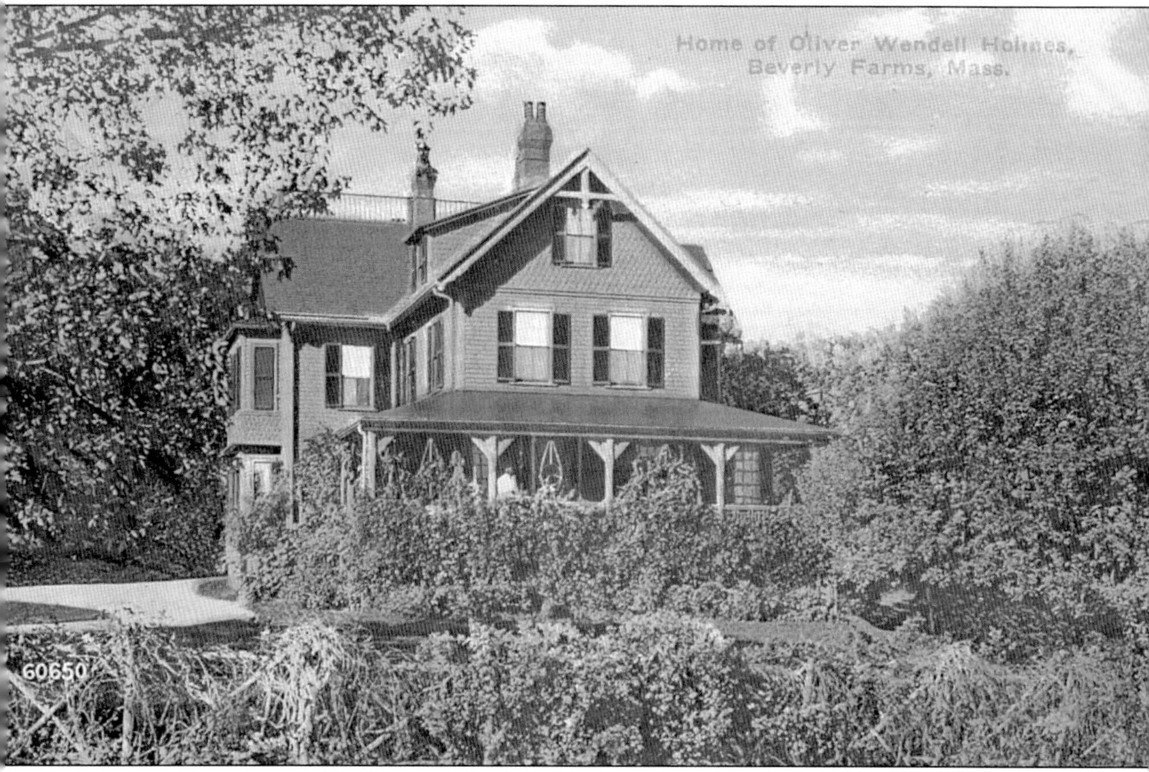

U.S. Supreme Court Justice Oliver Wendell Holmes Jr. (1841–1935) spent his summers at this Victorian house on Hale Street in Beverly Farms, which was built in the 1870s by Asa Obear Marshall. It still stands today. Holmes served for three years during the Civil War with the 20th Massachusetts Volunteers and was wounded three times. He graduated from Harvard Law School and then practiced law in Boston for several years until he was appointed a justice of the Supreme Judicial Court of Massachusetts in 1882. He became chief justice of that court seven years later. Holmes was appointed to the U.S. Supreme Court by U.S. president Theodore Roosevelt in 1902. He was known for his prolific writing and for often being in the minority. Holmes served for 30 years until his retirement, due to ill health, and died three years later.

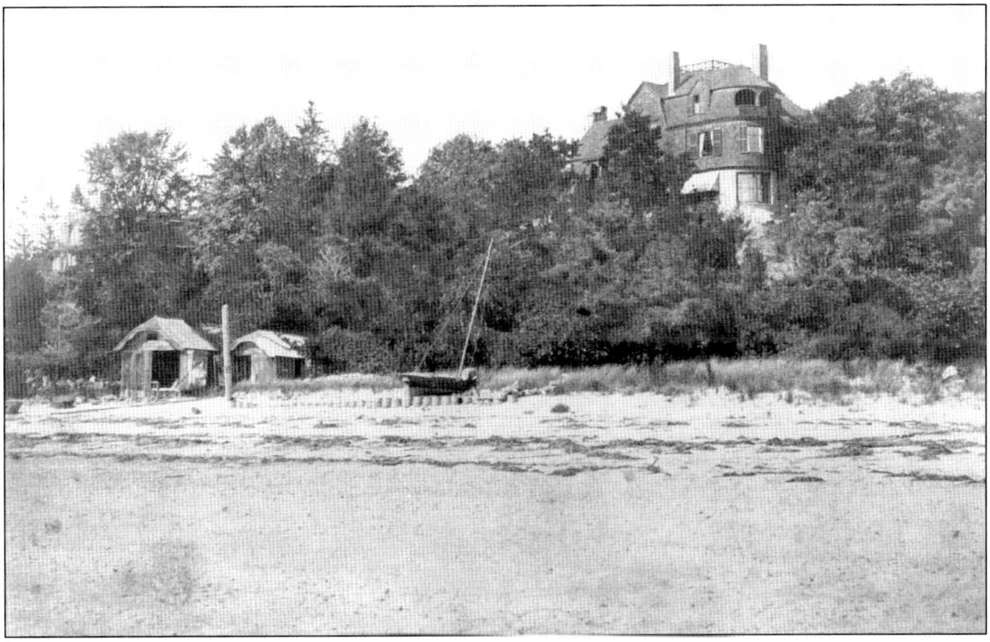

The home of Gen. Charles Greeley Loring Jr., this 1881 shingle-style house overlooking Plum Cove, was known as Pompey's Garden. It was designed by William Ralph Emerson, a founding member of the Boston Society of Architects. Loring, a Civil War veteran, developed an interest in Egyptian art and served as the director of the Museum of Fine Arts in Boston from 1881 to 1902.

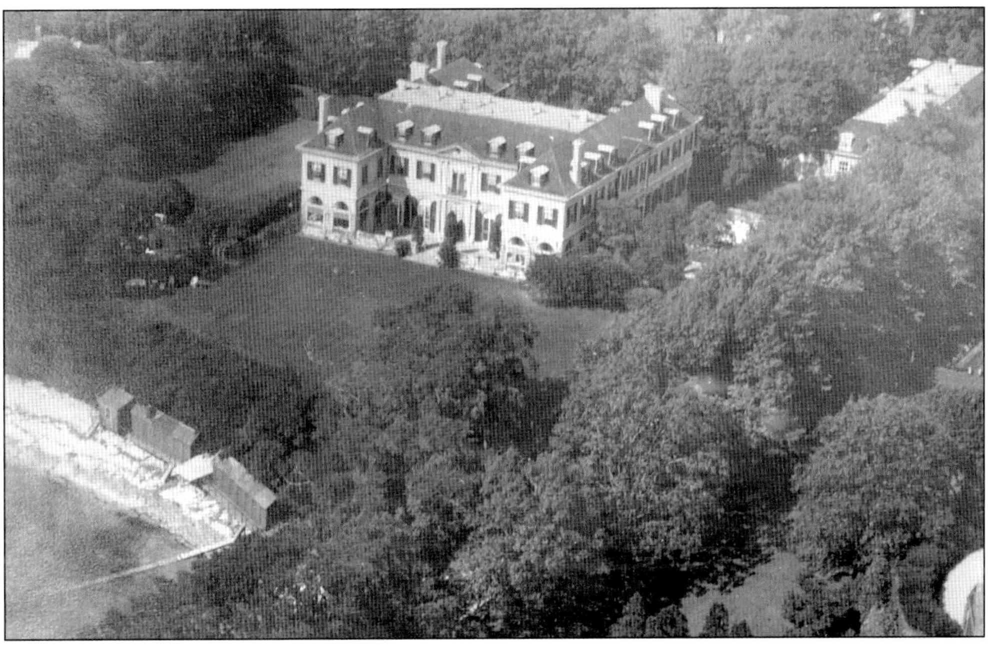

High Wall was the summer residence of Oliver Ames, president of the shovel manufacturing business Ames Shovel Company. This dwelling, which was constructed in 1904, was designed by renowned Boston architect Ogden Codman Jr. Its nickname was probably given due to the high wall that enclosed the property. High Wall was demolished in 1950, but the stable still stands and has been converted into a private residence.

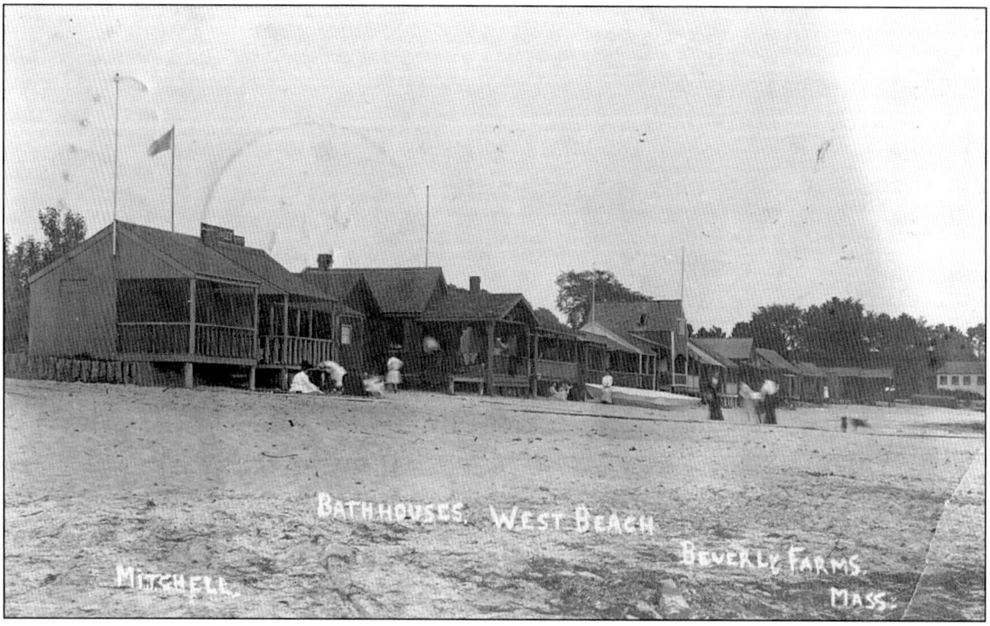

The private West Beach Corporation of Beverly Farms was formed in 1852 to end disputes over harvesting seaweed. By the 1890s, privately owned bathhouses had been erected. The corporation ordered them removed in 1911 to build a grand pavilion, which burned in 1948 and was replaced by the current bathhouse.

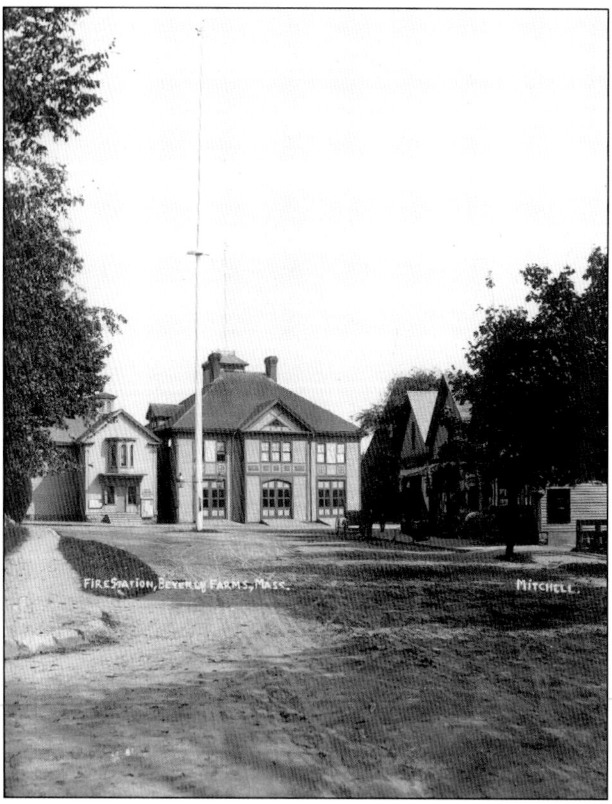

The Beverly Farms fire station on West Street was authorized by a Beverly town meeting in an attempt to placate divisionists who wanted the Beverly Farms neighborhood to secede from the town. Before this structure was built in 1887, the area had nothing more than a shed with a hand tub. In front are a steam pumper, hose reel, and hook and ladder. The building was torn down in 1958.

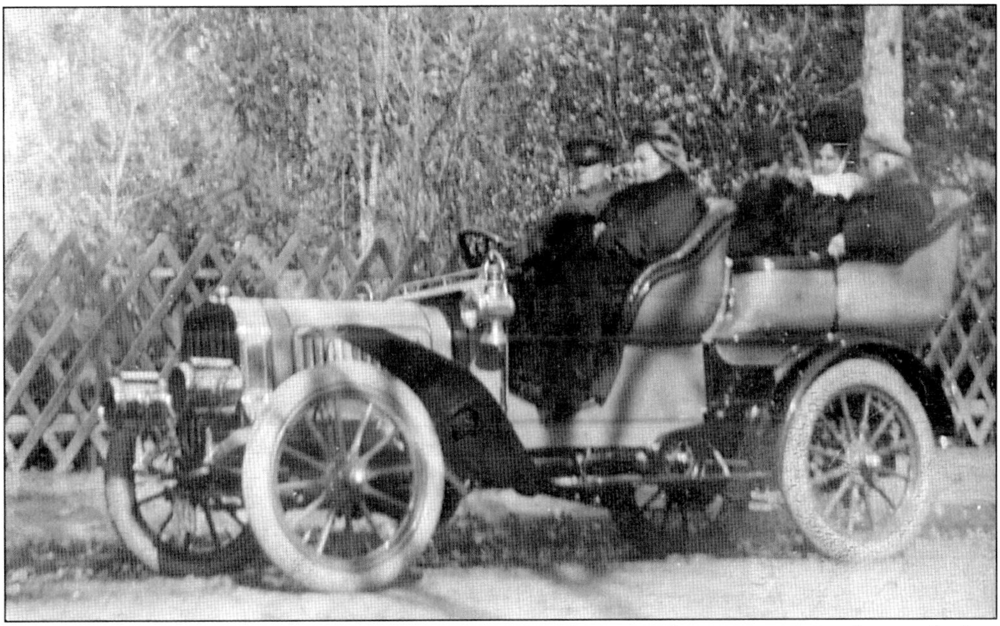

Daniel Linehan was born in Ireland and emigrated to the United States at 25. He first worked in a furniture factory but soon formed a construction company. His firm helped build many of the summer homes along the Gold Coast. His success enabled him to purchase a large tract in the Beverly Farms section of town, as well as one of the first automobiles seen on the North Shore. The above photograph shows chauffeur Dreuean Smith and Mary Linehan in front, with John and Sarah Linehan in the backseat. The image below shows the construction of a retaining wall at Paine's Beach. Among those pictured are Daniel Linehan (in the white overalls) and John Linehan (in jacket and derby); the others are unidentified.

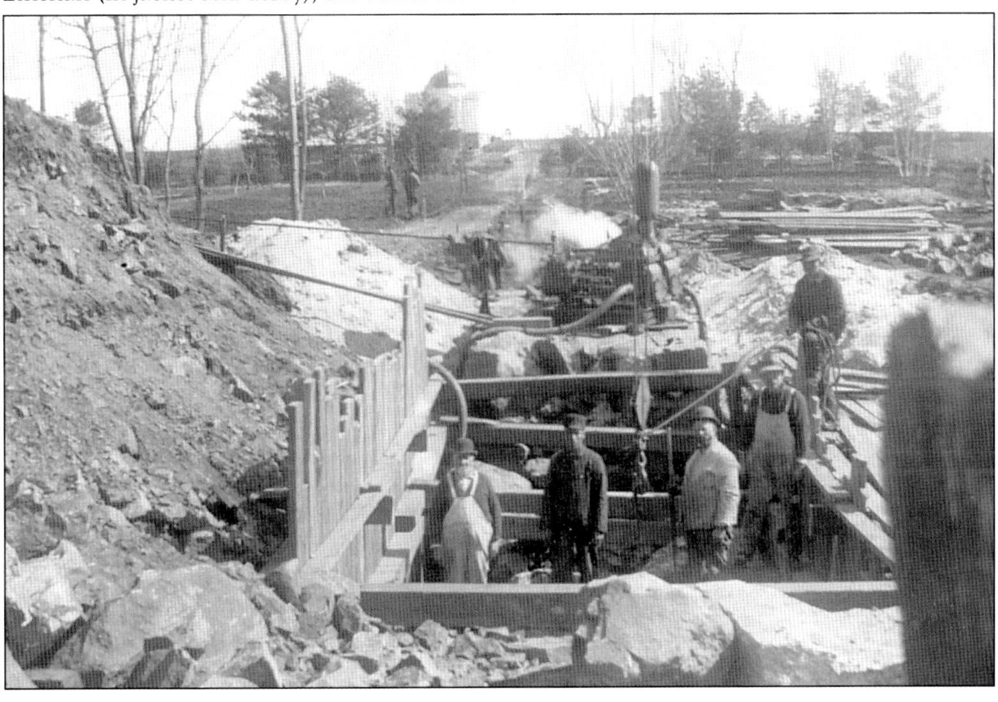

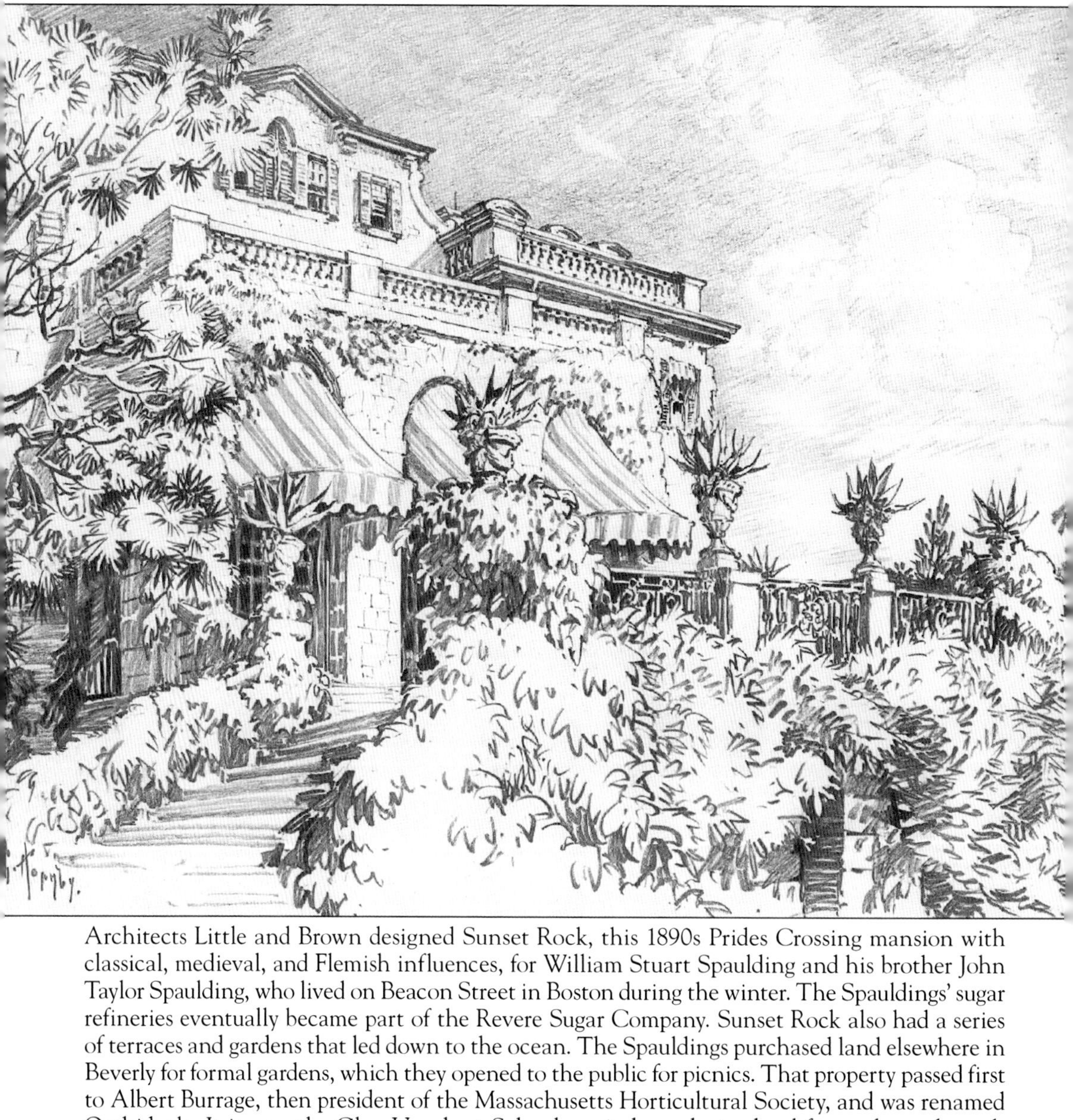

Architects Little and Brown designed Sunset Rock, this 1890s Prides Crossing mansion with classical, medieval, and Flemish influences, for William Stuart Spaulding and his brother John Taylor Spaulding, who lived on Beacon Street in Boston during the winter. The Spauldings' sugar refineries eventually became part of the Revere Sugar Company. Sunset Rock also had a series of terraces and gardens that led down to the ocean. The Spauldings purchased land elsewhere in Beverly for formal gardens, which they opened to the public for picnics. That property passed first to Albert Burrage, then president of the Massachusetts Horticultural Society, and was renamed Orchidvale. It is now the Glen Urquhart School, an independent school for students through eighth grade. Much of Sunset Rock was demolished in 1951. This pencil sketch was one of a group of drawings of Sunset Rock done by Lester Hornsby that were privately published for the Spaulding family in 1924.

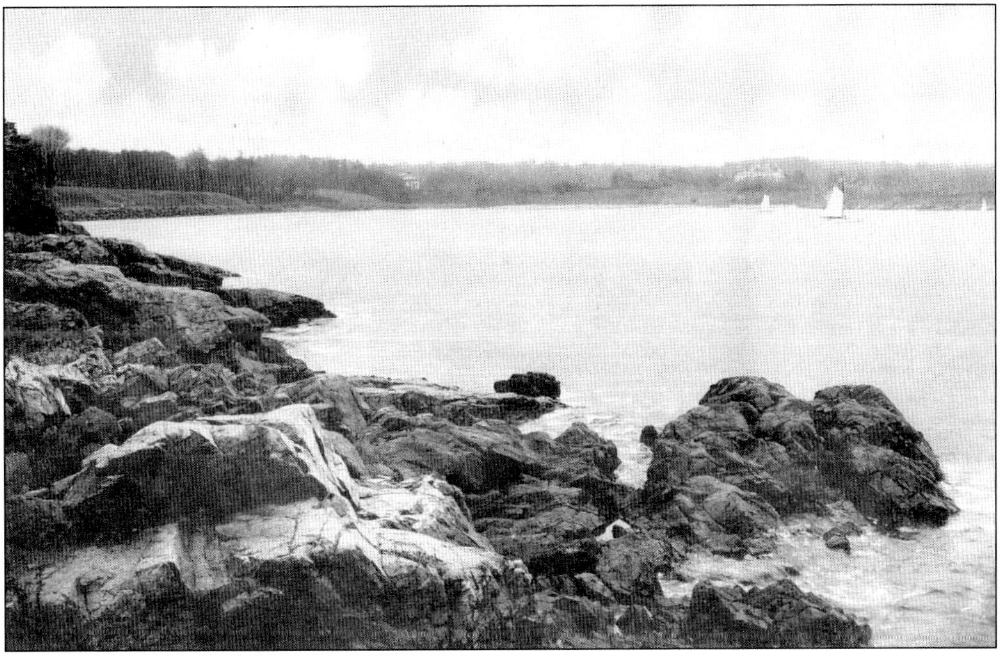

The coastal view above is an early photograph of Brackenbury Cove. Richard Brackenbury was one of Beverly's earliest settlers, receiving a land grant in 1636. His daughter Elizabeth was the first female child born in the Massachusetts Bay Colony. This area was known for a time as Patch's Beach for a Brackenbury descendant, but it is now a public beach named for Brackenbury. The painting below by artist John Frederick Kensett (1816–1872) is representative of his later work, which was dominated by views of Rhode Island and the North Shore. It is believed that Kensett produced more then 20 works of Beverly sites such as Mingo Beach, Plum Cove, and Smith Point, the subject of this painting titled *Coast Scene*. Kensett first came to the North Shore in the 1850s to explore the natural environment of Nahant. The beauty of the Beverly shoreline was one of the chief attractions for the many affluent New Englanders who came here in the summer.

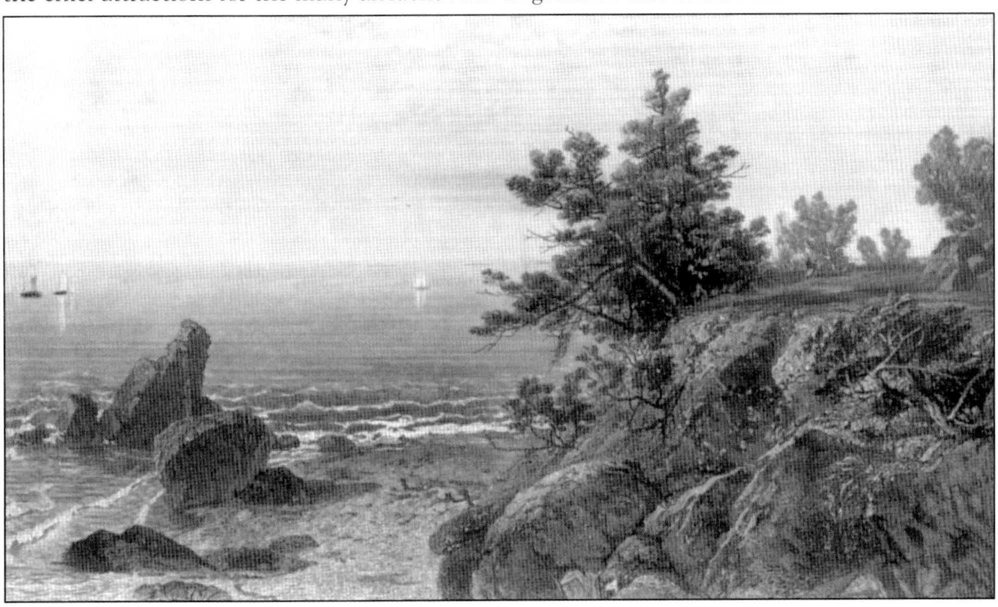

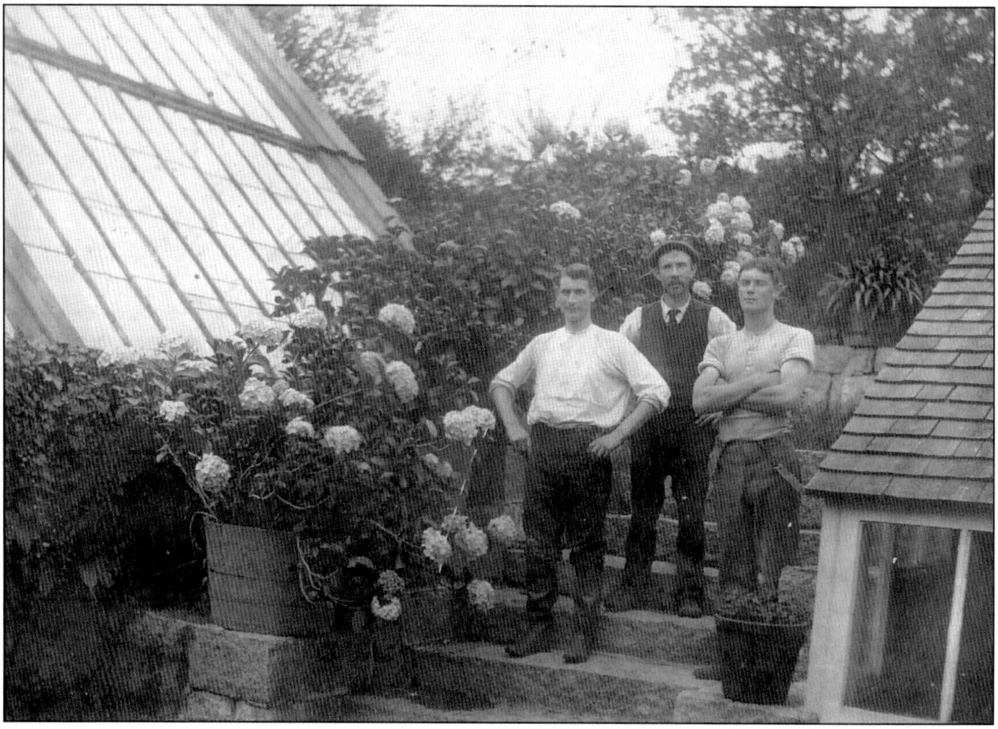

This c. 1912 photograph shows staff at the estate of attorney and gentleman farmer Augustus P. Loring, located on Thissell Street. From left to right are Sam Cinnemond, chauffeur; John O'Sullivan, foreman gardener; and Tom Griffin, stableman. Cinnemond and O'Sullivan lived on the estate, as was common at the time, although Cinnemond may have moved with the family to Boston in the winter.

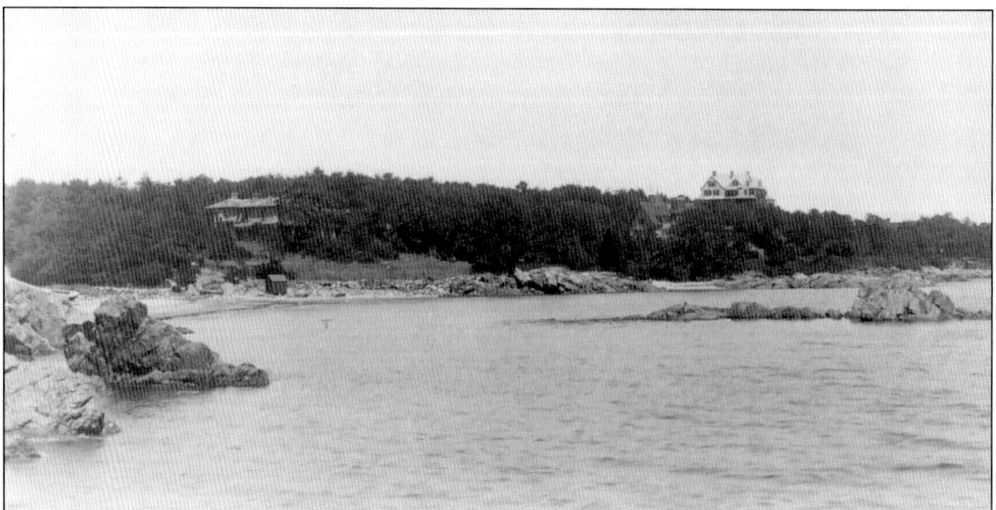

Caleb William Loring, a prominent Boston attorney and president of the Plymouth Cordage Company, built a summer residence known as Burnside in Plum Cove in 1851. His father, Charles Greeley Loring, was one of the first summer residents of Beverly. Burnside became Loring's permanent residence in 1872. Loring's children—William, Augustus, Katherine, and Louisa—became involved in the community, particularly his daughters.

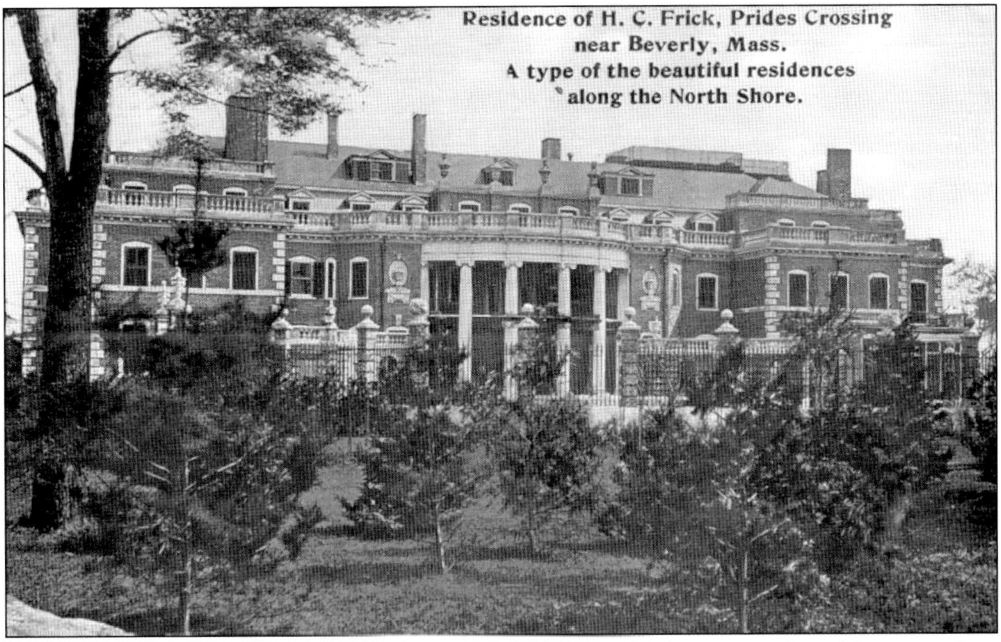

The fence on Hale Street marks the location of Eagle Rock, the estate of steel baron and art collector Henry Clay Frick. The house was a neoclassical summer retreat and was known as one of the grandest mansions north of Newport. Designed by Little and Brown, the main house was demolished in 1969. The brick garage and electric powerhouse, stucco gardener's cottage, and carriage house survive.

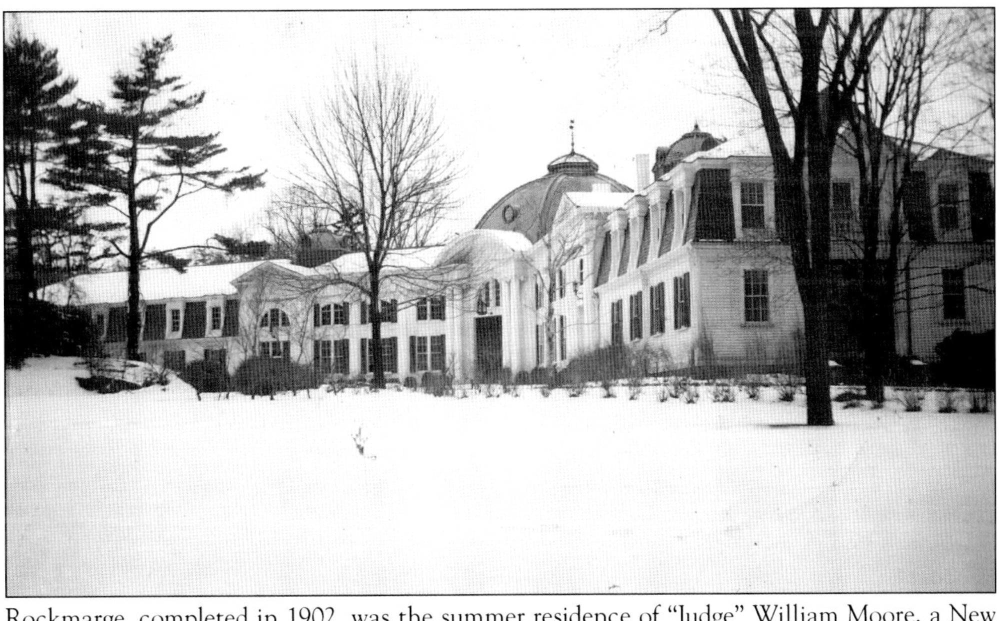

Rockmarge, completed in 1902, was the summer residence of "Judge" William Moore, a New York attorney and financier. His nickname came from his shrewd business deals and keen eye for thoroughbreds. Horses played an integral role in his life in Prides Crossing. Moore spent twice as much money on the stable (shown here) and exercise track as on the house. Rockmarge was demolished in 1957, but the stable and bathhouse remain.

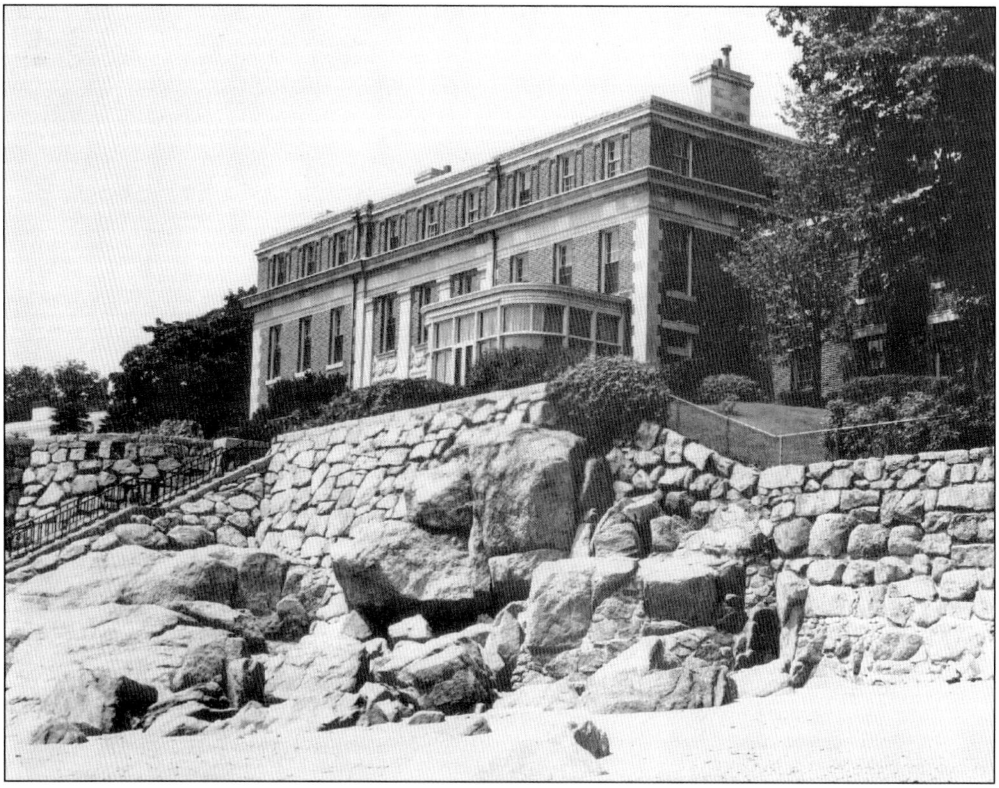

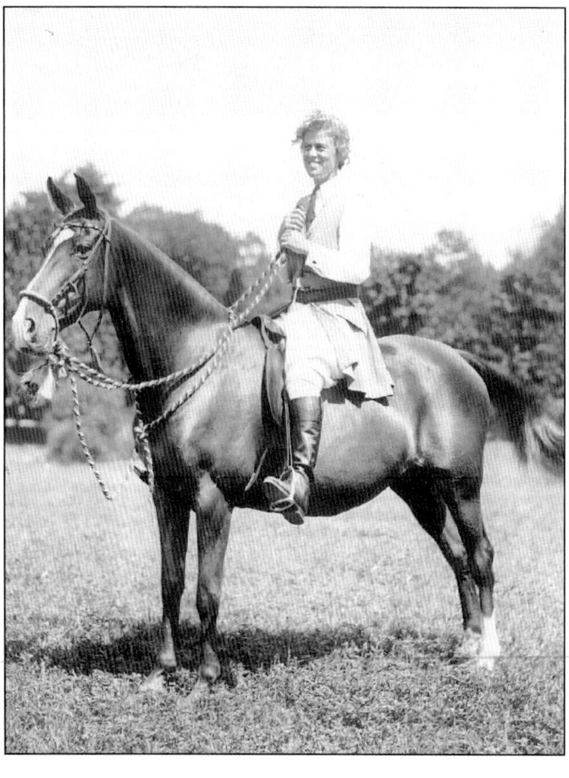

Rock Edge was built for Marian A. Sargent, a widow and the great-great-granddaughter of Thomas Jefferson. Completed in 1911, this Georgian Revival–style estate overlooks Beverly Harbor. After Sargent's death in 1924, the house passed to her niece Eleonora Sears. Born in 1881, Sears was a great beauty among Boston's elite. She is best remembered as a superb athlete known for breaking barriers in women's sports and a strong, eccentric personality. Sears was an accomplished equestrienne, a pioneering squash player, and a nationally ranked tennis player. She won the national doubles championship four times, twice with the legendary Hazel Wightman. Sears was also known for walking long distances, both in California and from Providence to Boston, which she did more than once. One of the earliest women to own an automobile (and to be arrested for speeding), she was also the first Boston woman to pilot an airplane alone.

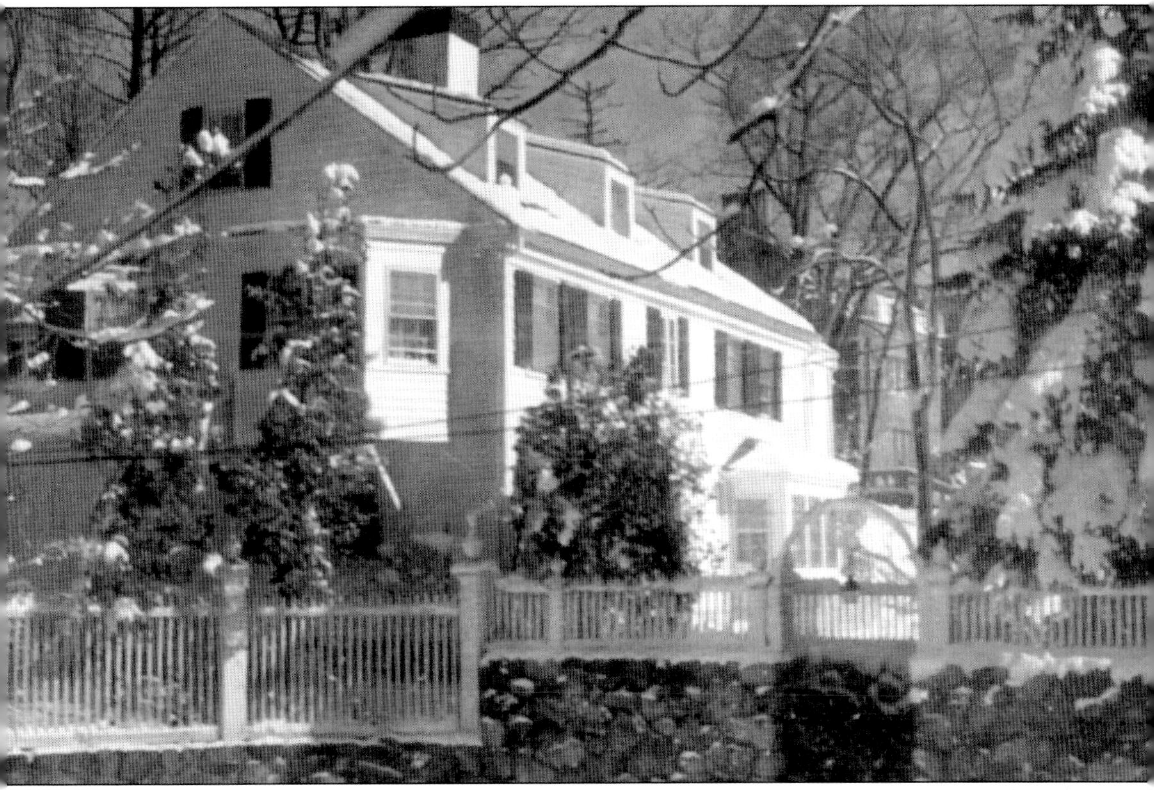

Alhambra was originally built elsewhere on Hale Street as a farmhouse around 1760 by a member of one of Beverly's Old Planter families, the Woodberrys. Alhambra was once a tavern and stagecoach stop on the Salem-Gloucester line. It served as summer housing in the 19th century for some of New England's intellectual elite, including Edward Everett Hale, James Russell Lowell, and Isabella Stewart Gardner, before Bostonians began to purchase coastal land for summer estates. It was moved to its present location near Mingo Beach in the 1920s. It is now the oldest building on the campus of Endicott College, which was founded as a women's college in 1939 by Dr. Eleanor Tupper and her husband, Dr. George O. Bierkoe. It has been used as campus housing since 1940. The first use of the name is uncertain but may date to the Tupper years.

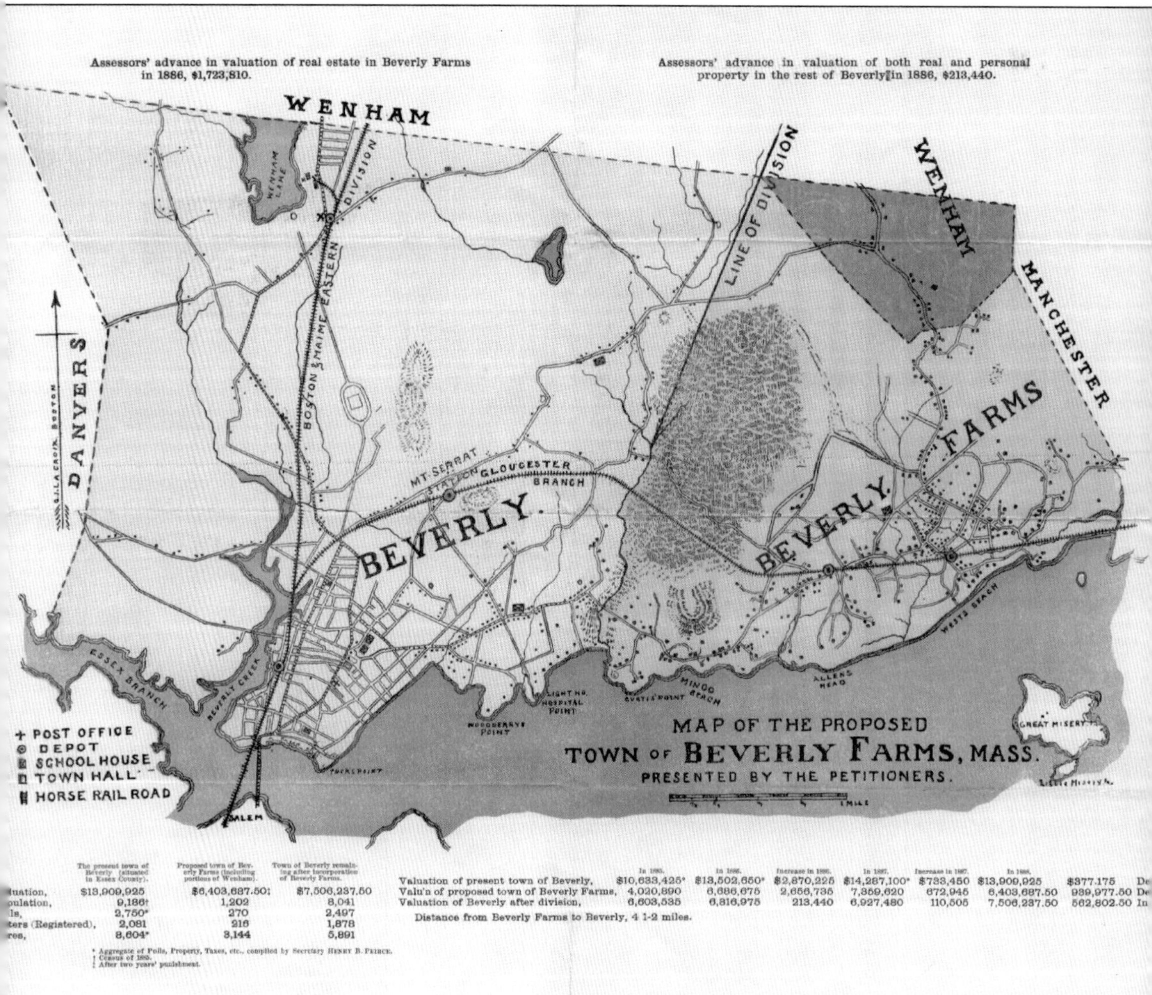

From 1886 to 1888, residents of the neighborhood of Beverly Farms, known as divisionists, launched an all-out attempt to break away from Beverly to form a separate town. The participants were angry about high property valuations, a lack of municipal services like public safety, and a perceived separation from the rest of the town. A few homeowners from Little Comfort, a nearby neighborhood in Wenham, were also interested. They almost succeeded in 1887, when both houses of the Massachusetts Legislature passed the bill, but it was vetoed by Gov. Oliver Ames under pressure from Beverly interests. Lacking enough votes to override the veto, the plan was defeated. A subsequent bill the next year also failed to pass. The proposed town was the shaded area of the map; the division line would have been just west of Curtis Point (Prince Street).

Seven

SPORTS

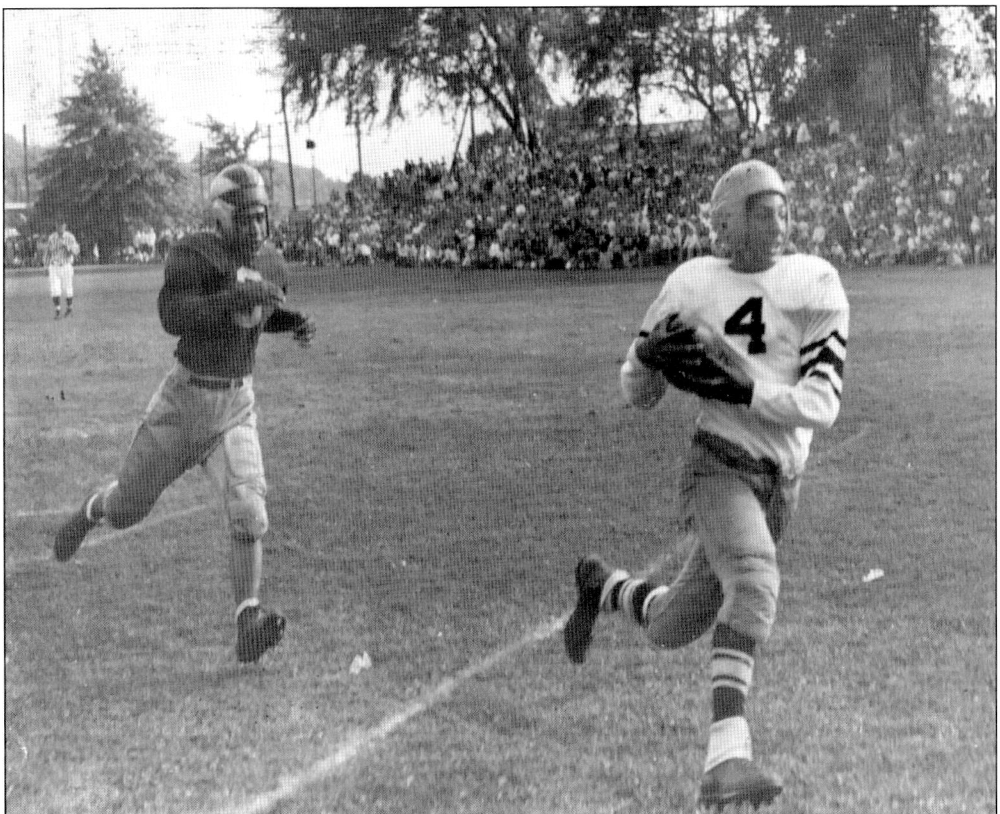

Beverly was and still is a sports town. Charlie Manuel, the first of the Manuel brothers to star on the Beverly High School football team, has both hands on the ball as he breaks away for a touchdown run in 1951. The location looks unfamiliar; it may have been in Revere. Coach Charlie Walsh's 1951 team started with a 6-0 loss to Haverhill, then earned eight consecutive wins while outscoring the opposition 190-47.

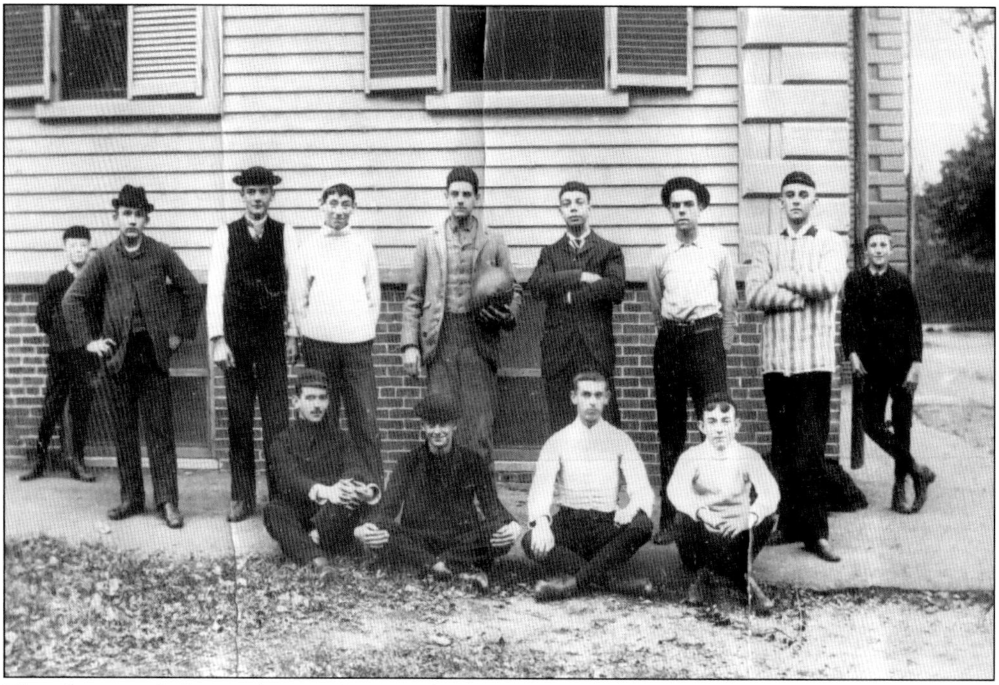

This photograph shows what may be Beverly's first football team in 1890. From left to right are (first row) William Quiner, E. Waldo Dudley, Max Lovell Butler, and Charles Dane Woodberry; (second row) Lawrence Stanton, George Beckford, Charlie Bennett, Harry Fraser, Harold Wormwood (with football), William Foster Jr., Arthur Kent, Charles Farnham, and Ora Currier.

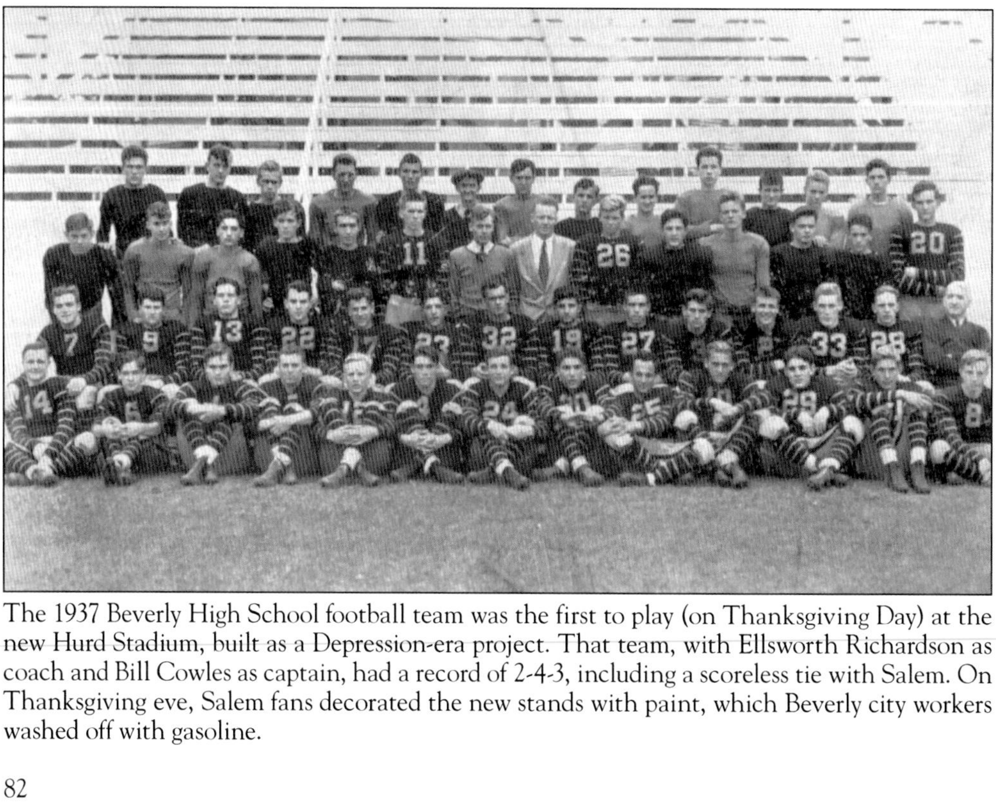

The 1937 Beverly High School football team was the first to play (on Thanksgiving Day) at the new Hurd Stadium, built as a Depression-era project. That team, with Ellsworth Richardson as coach and Bill Cowles as captain, had a record of 2-4-3, including a scoreless tie with Salem. On Thanksgiving eve, Salem fans decorated the new stands with paint, which Beverly city workers washed off with gasoline.

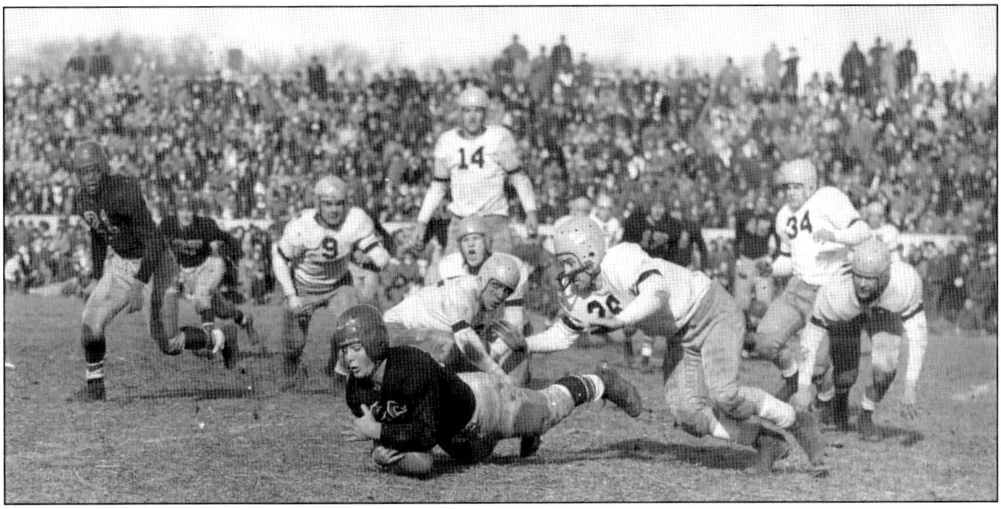

The 1947 Thanksgiving Day football game between Beverly and archrival Salem was played at Hurd Stadium. Beverly lost 7-0 but had a 5-5 season under coach Charlie Walsh. Salem's Eddie Lane fumbled here after being upended by Jimmy Weaver (center, behind Lane), and Sandy Kessaris (at far right) recovered. Other Beverly players are Truck Petrosino (No. 9), Mike Toomey (No. 14), Walter Hayes (center, in front of Toomey), Jack Donovan (No. 26), and Frank Chamberlain (No. 34).

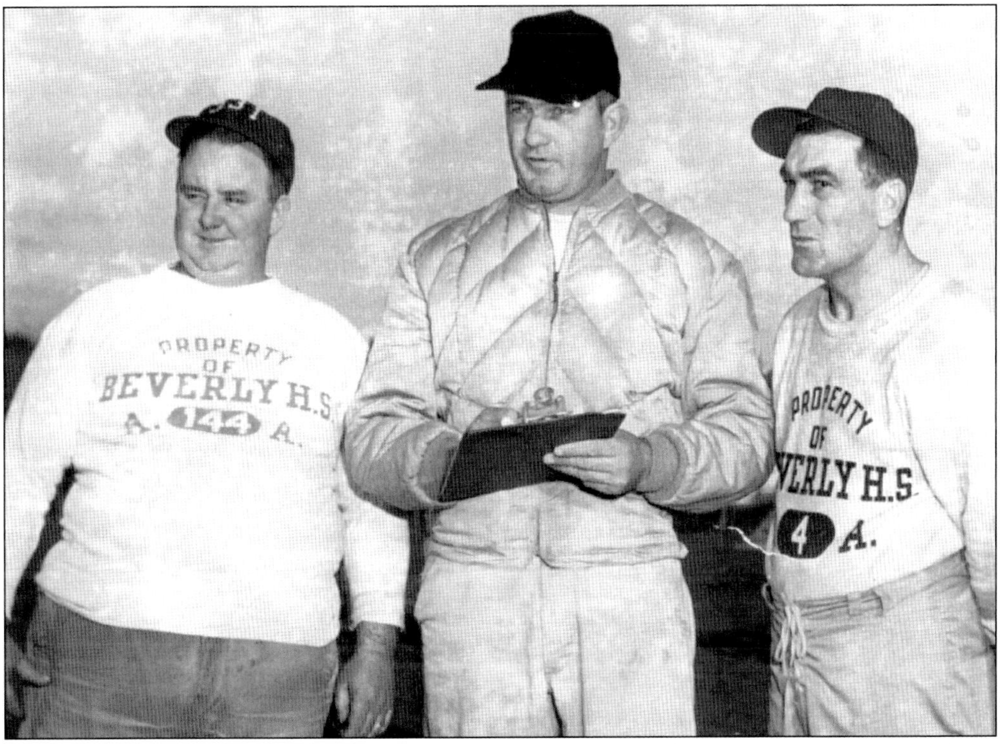

The guiding lights behind a dominant era of Beverly High School football are shown about 1950. From left to right are Clarence "Clammy" Foster, team trainer for over a decade; Charlie Walsh, longtime head coach serving from 1944 to 1958 (including two undefeated seasons) and then athletic director until 1975; and Charlie Pelonzi, a former BHS captain and quarterback, assistant coach under several coaches, and a member of St. Anselm's College Hall of Fame.

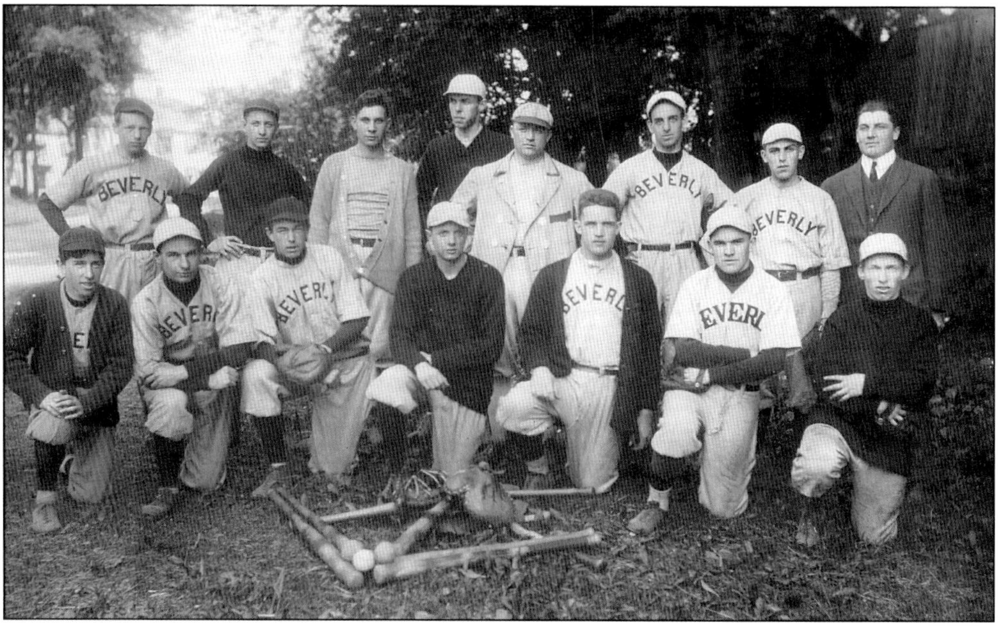

Nothing is known about this photograph of a Beverly men's baseball team from the early 1900s, but the only known city-representative club of that time was Dick Madden's highly regarded semipro team, which played its games at Peabody's Field near the Montserrat depot. If so, it is possible the youthful-looking player standing second from right in the second row might be future Major League star John "Stuffy" McInnis.

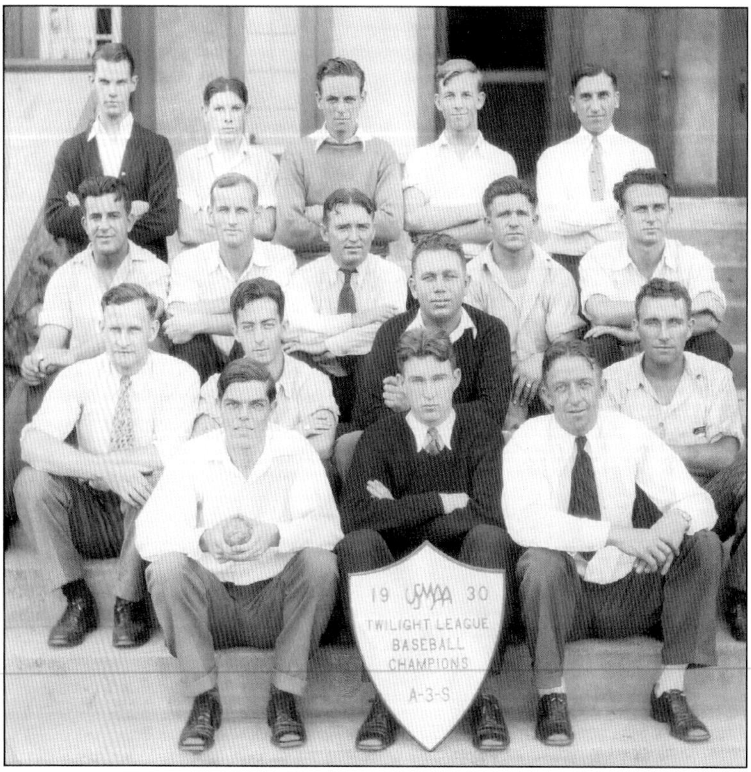

The United Shoe Machinery Corporation's Twilight Baseball League champions for 1930 are shown here. From left to right are (first row) Bunny Chapman, Charlie Markham (captain), and Ty Peterson; (second row) Andy Hurley, Austin Ritchie, Chet Mattern, and Jack Rix; (third row) Joe Gorini, Sam Nash, Joe Sinnott, Bob Gorini, and Scoffy Tibbetts; (fourth row) John Eastwood, Dan Hughes, Jack Powers, Rupe Watts, and Jerry Giancola (coach).

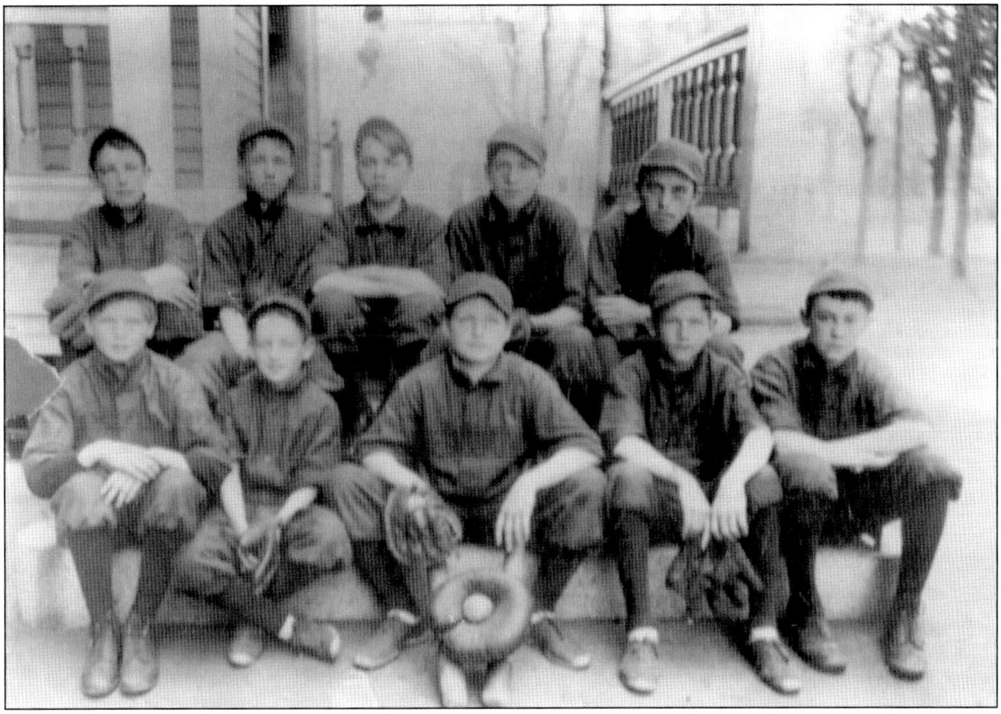

Pictured around 1910 are players on the South School team who played in a grammar school league. From left to right are (first row) Henry M. Beck, Jeremiah Murphy (a future *Boston Globe* journalist), Guy Fossiano, Daniel McLean (mayor of Beverly from 1937 to 1948), and Arthur "Mecca" Brown; (second row) Cornelius Riordan, Murray Greenlaw, William Terry, Harold Marley, and Edward Foley. Both Terry and Marley served on the Beverly Police Department.

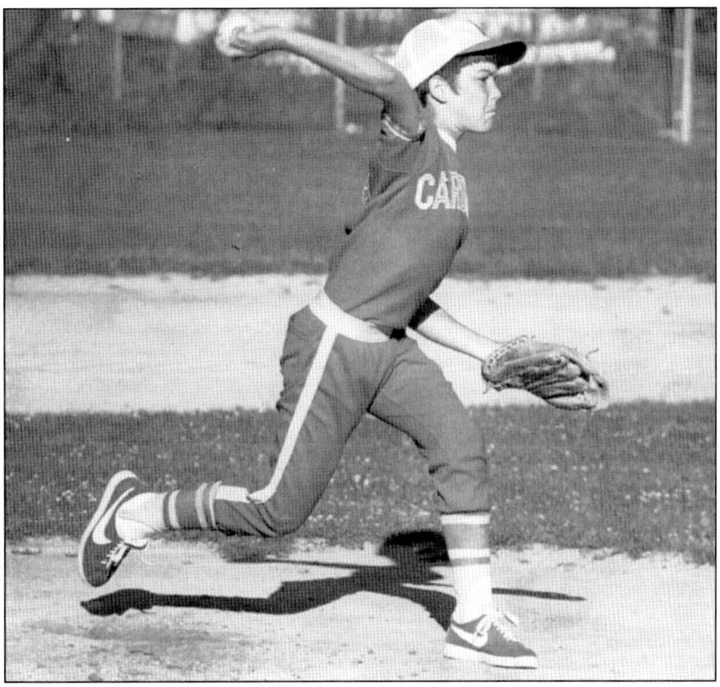

Timmy Hough, now Dr. Timothy J. Hough of Beverly, pitched and played shortstop for the Beverly Little League Cardinals in 1977–1978. Beverly introduced Little League Baseball to Massachusetts in 1950. In the mid-1990s, with the aid of volunteer tradespeople and using its own funds, the Beverly Little League constructed its spectacular home park at Harry Ball Field on Essex Street, with a clubhouse, batting cages, and two lit diamonds.

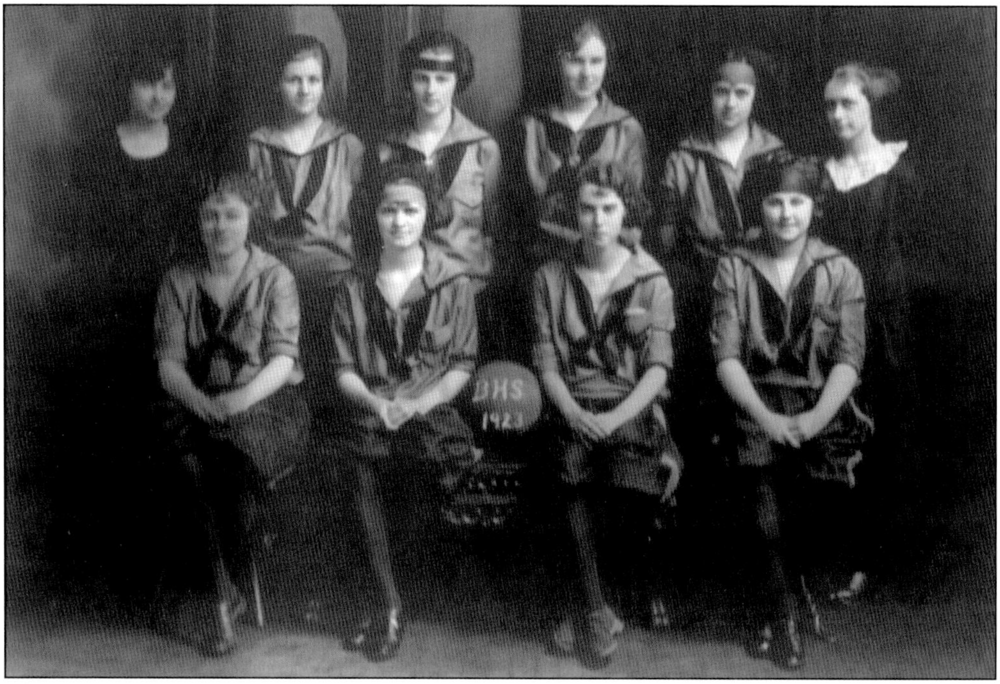

The 1932 Beverly High School girls' basketball team line up for a photograph outside the school, then located at Sohier Road and Colon Street. Girls' rules in those days called for a half-court game with dribbling greatly restricted, and players were not allowed to cross the center line. That year the team was coached by Martha Richards, and the captain was Elizabeth Gorse.

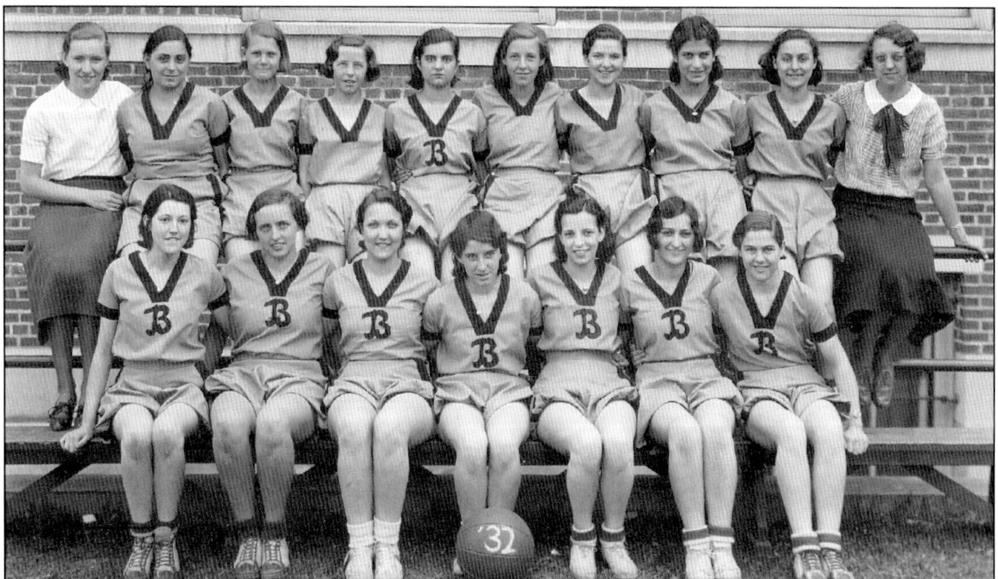

The Beverly High School girls' basketball team of 1923 pose proudly here in uniforms they sewed themselves, as one team member later remembered, "of cotton sateen, orange blouse, and black bloomers." The uniforms were first worn when BHS defeated the YWCA (Young Women's Christian Association) team 52-14, paced by what the school paper called the "clever shooting" of Pearl Macdonald and Marie Brown. The girls also defeated Essex Aggie but lost to Melrose and Gloucester.

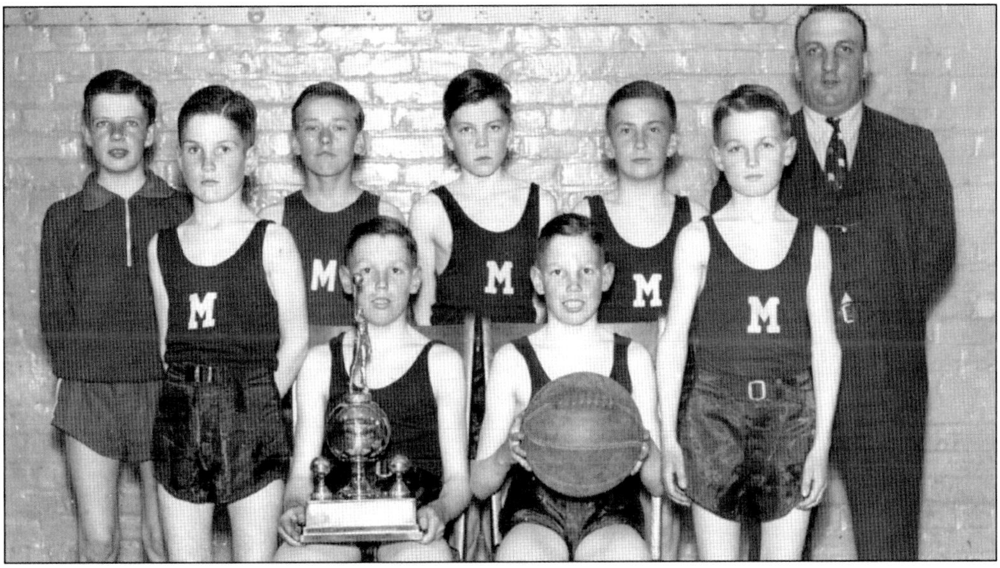

For several decades, a "Pygmy" winter basketball league for boys was organized at the tiny basement gym of the Edwards School by John Carbone. The 1939 champions were the Mustangs. From left to right are (first row) Jerry Murphy, the Bradley twins Jack and Bill ("Bucket") seated with the trophy and game ball, and Jack Murphy; (second row) Bob Bossie, Bibber McMahon, Fred Healey, Don Richards, and Carbone.

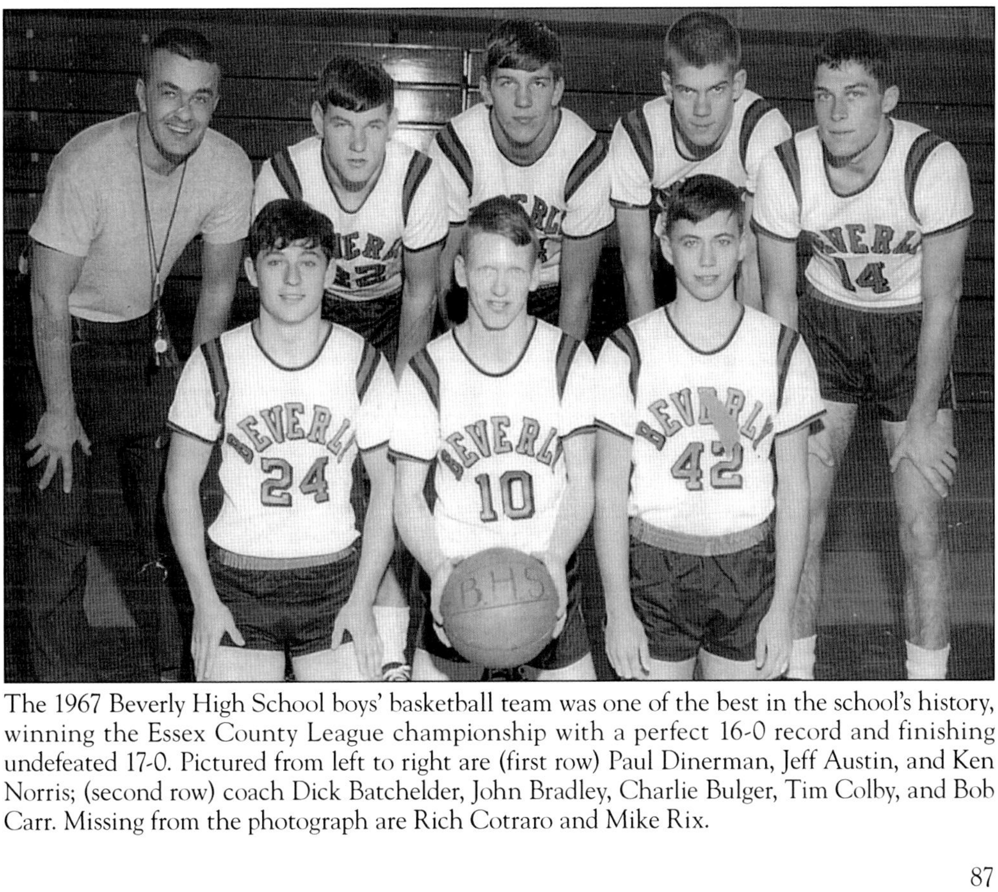

The 1967 Beverly High School boys' basketball team was one of the best in the school's history, winning the Essex County League championship with a perfect 16-0 record and finishing undefeated 17-0. Pictured from left to right are (first row) Paul Dinerman, Jeff Austin, and Ken Norris; (second row) coach Dick Batchelder, John Bradley, Charlie Bulger, Tim Colby, and Bob Carr. Missing from the photograph are Rich Cotraro and Mike Rix.

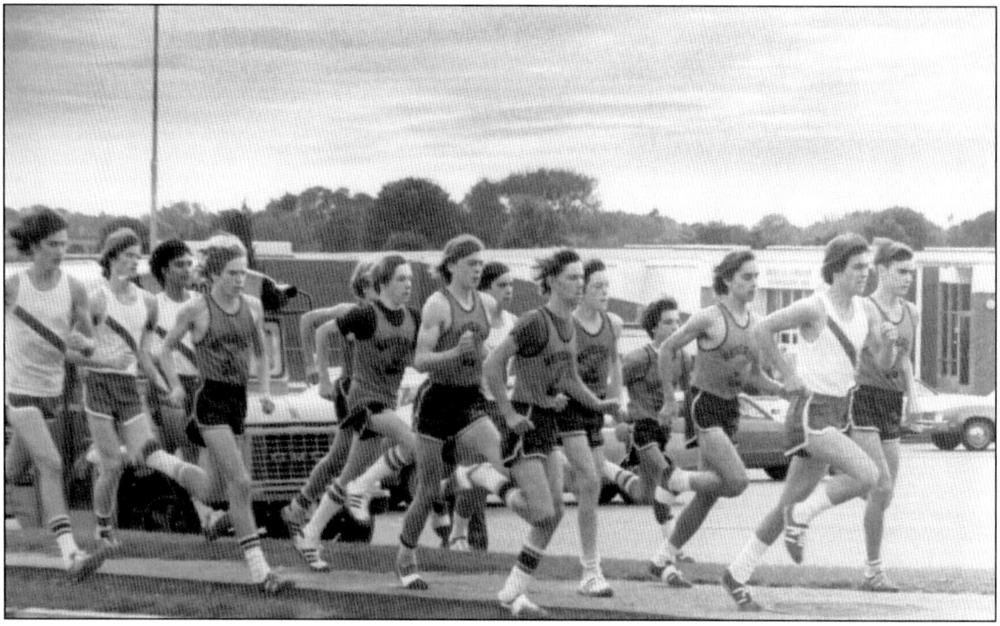

Cross country teams from Beverly and Saugus answered the starter's gun from the parking lot of the high school. Pictured from left to right in the dark-colored uniforms are Ed Burgess, Dave Richard, Barry Reinhold, Richard Frost, Steve Miranda, Dan Ossoff, and Frank Mangan. The photograph was taken by the late Charlie Corse, who captured images of numerous local school and amateur sports events.

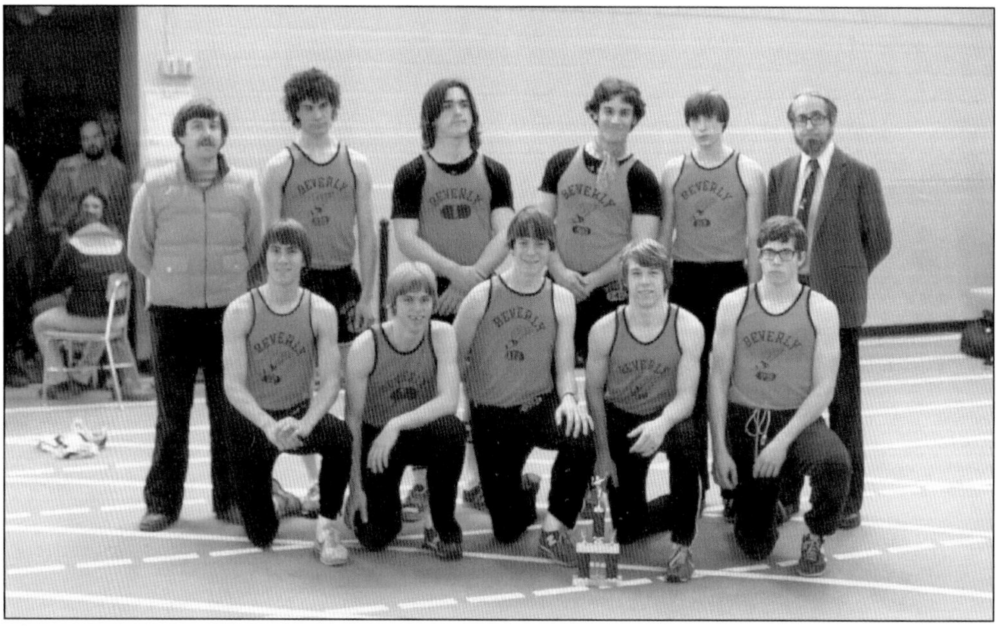

The 1978 Northeastern Conference winter indoor track champions came from Beverly High School, and the team followed up with a third-place finish in the Class A state meet. From left to right are (first row) Paul Revard, Dave Mahan, John Norris, Dave Richard, and Joel Richardson; (second row) assistant coach John Hilton, Scott Cashman, Bill Shea, Bruce Carito, Don Wilson, and coach Fred Hammond.

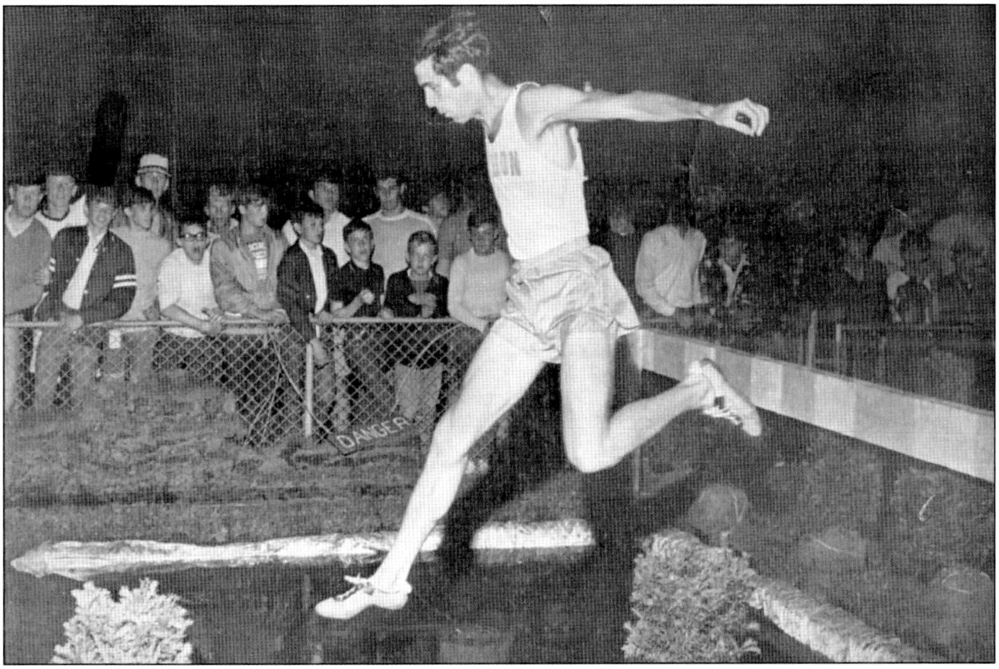

Beverly's Bill Norris, shown here clearing a water hurdle during a steeplechase race in Danvers, was one of Beverly High School's best track athletes of all time. Norris was a seven-time champion in the mile run while at BHS. He went on to a stellar career at Boston College and was selected as an alternate to the 1968 U.S. Summer Olympic Team. The 1962 Beverly High School graduate had the opportunity in April of that year to meet track star John Thomas, who held several world records in the high jump and won the bronze and silver medals in the 1960 and 1964 Olympics, respectively.

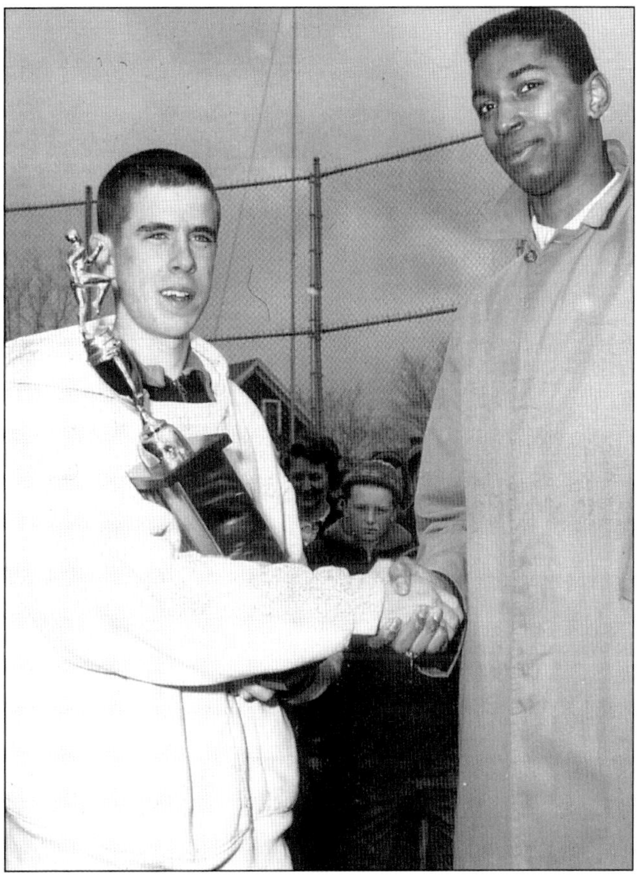

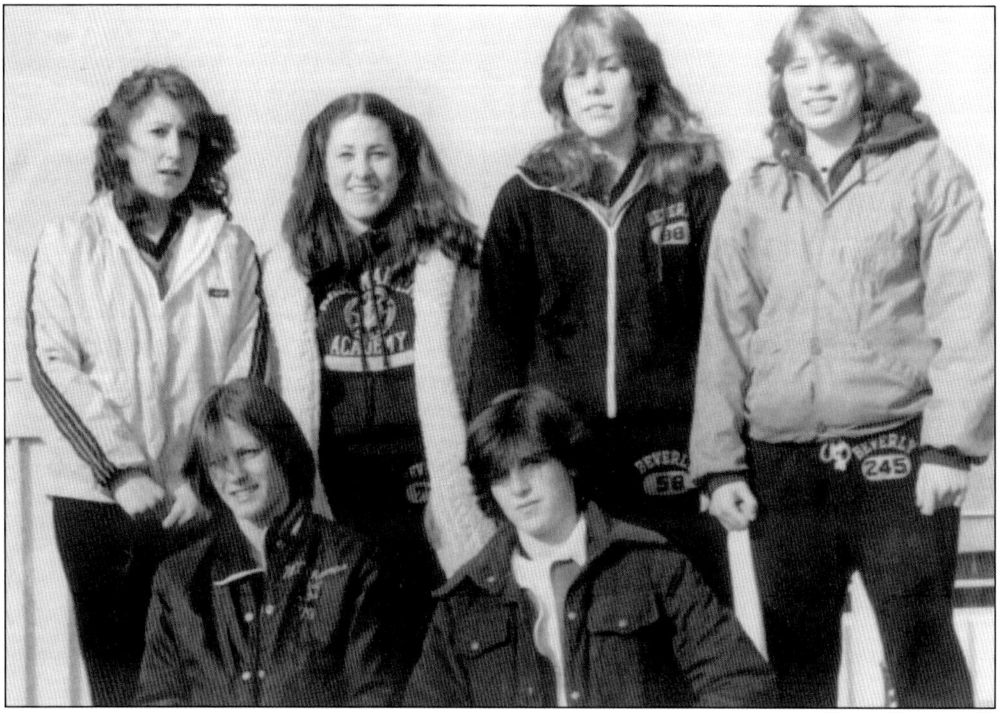

Female athletes have made their mark over the years at Beverly High School. Among them are these track competitors from the 1980s. The six girls in the photograph above qualified for the 1982 state meet. Pictured from left to right are (first row) Lauree Reinhold and Maureen O'Reilly; (second row) Carrie Guarino, Jennifer Parisella, Johanna O'Gorman, and Betty Barr. The photograph below shows the girls of the 1981 winter indoor squad. Shown from left to right are (first row) Deb Wells, Joyce LeClaire, Judy Cass, Sue Rose, Sharon Billings, Kathy Rivard, Ellen Mangan, Betty Barr, Johanna O'Gorman, Sue German, Laura Toothaker, and Lisa Slabacheski; (second row) Brenda Kline, Darlene Solimeno, Della Parisi, Amy Lyons, Alana Connelly, Beth Accomando, Chris Soucy, and Sheila O'Reilly; (third row) Donna Chouinard, Joanna Pietrini, coach Dan Geary, Maureen O'Reilly, and Wendy James.

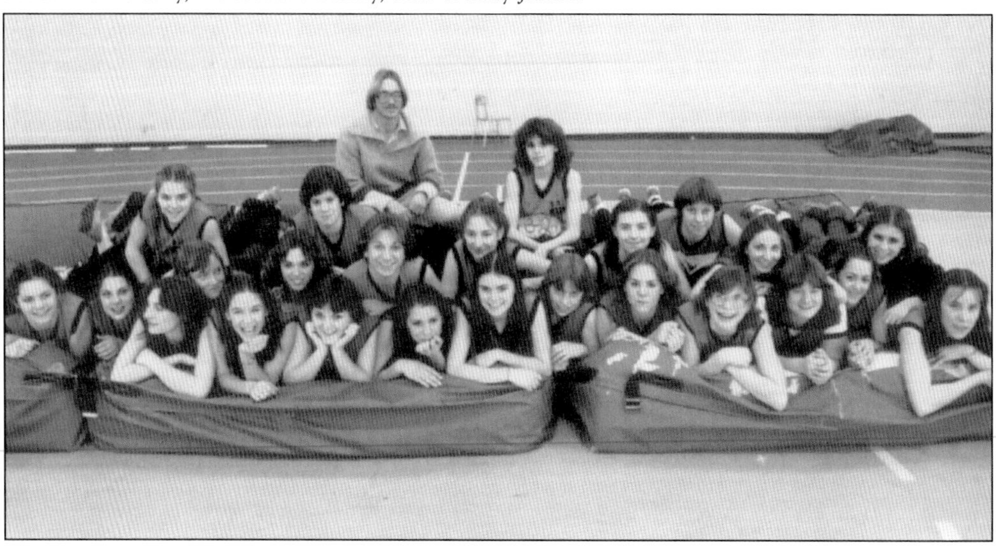

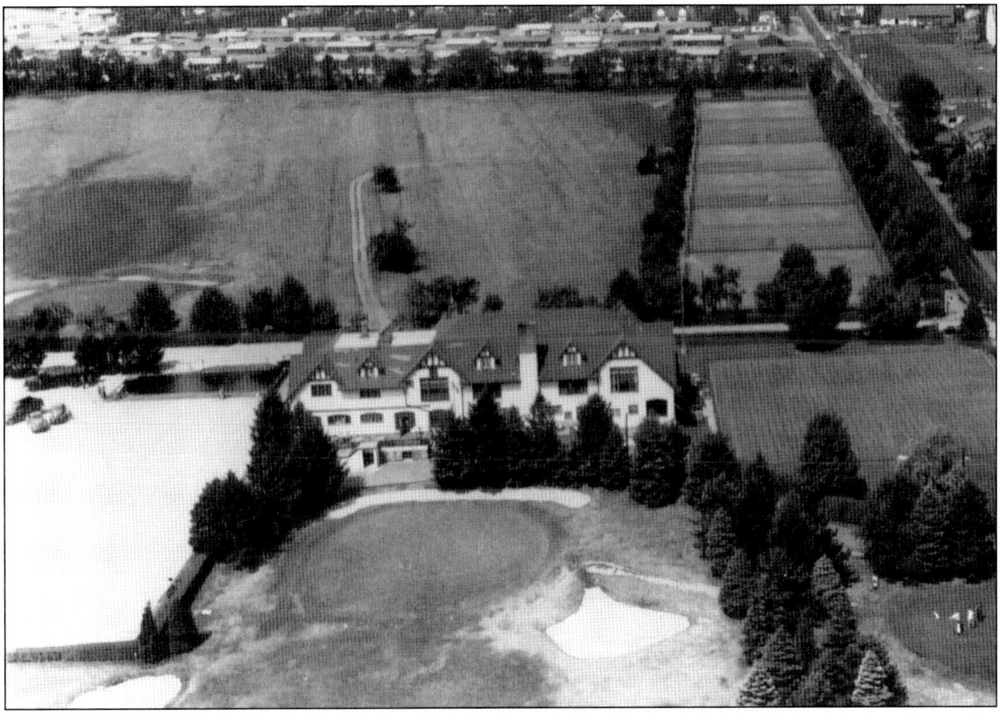

Employees of the Shoe and their families enjoyed many recreational opportunities thanks to the company's athletic association. Activities included an 18-hole golf course, tennis, swimming, cricket, soccer, boating on Shoe Pond, and baseball. Other activities were vegetable gardening, band and chorus, and a gun club. The center of activity was this magnificent Scottish Tudor–style clubhouse, designed by Henry Bailey Alden and built in 1910. The club is now owned by the city.

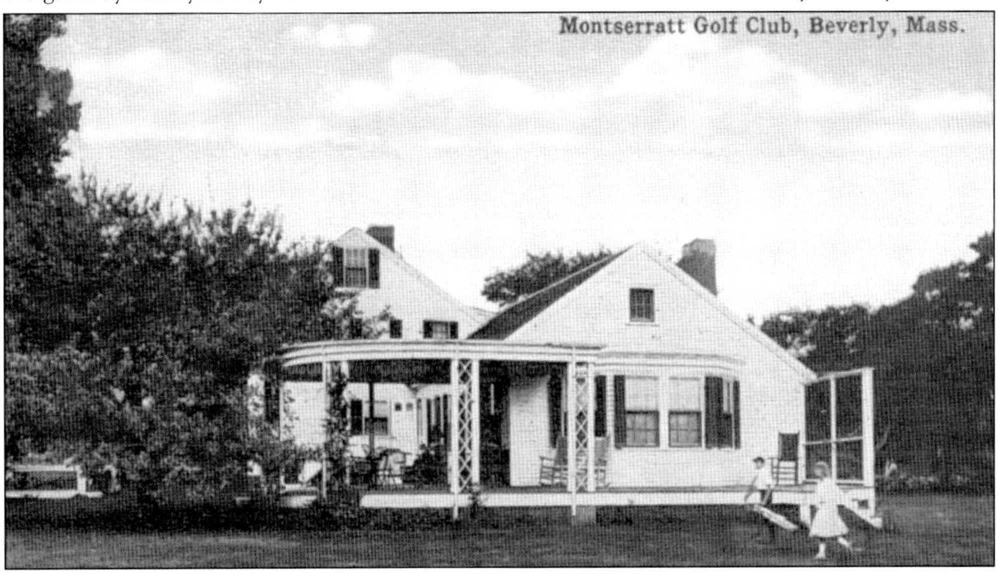

Montserrat Golf Club was built in 1902 on Boyles Street. There were tennis courts (probably grass) in addition to a nine-hole golf course. Membership was exclusive, and members of President Taft's family are known to have played the course. By 1935, the address was listed as a private residence. Perhaps the financial fallout from the Depression took a toll on the membership.

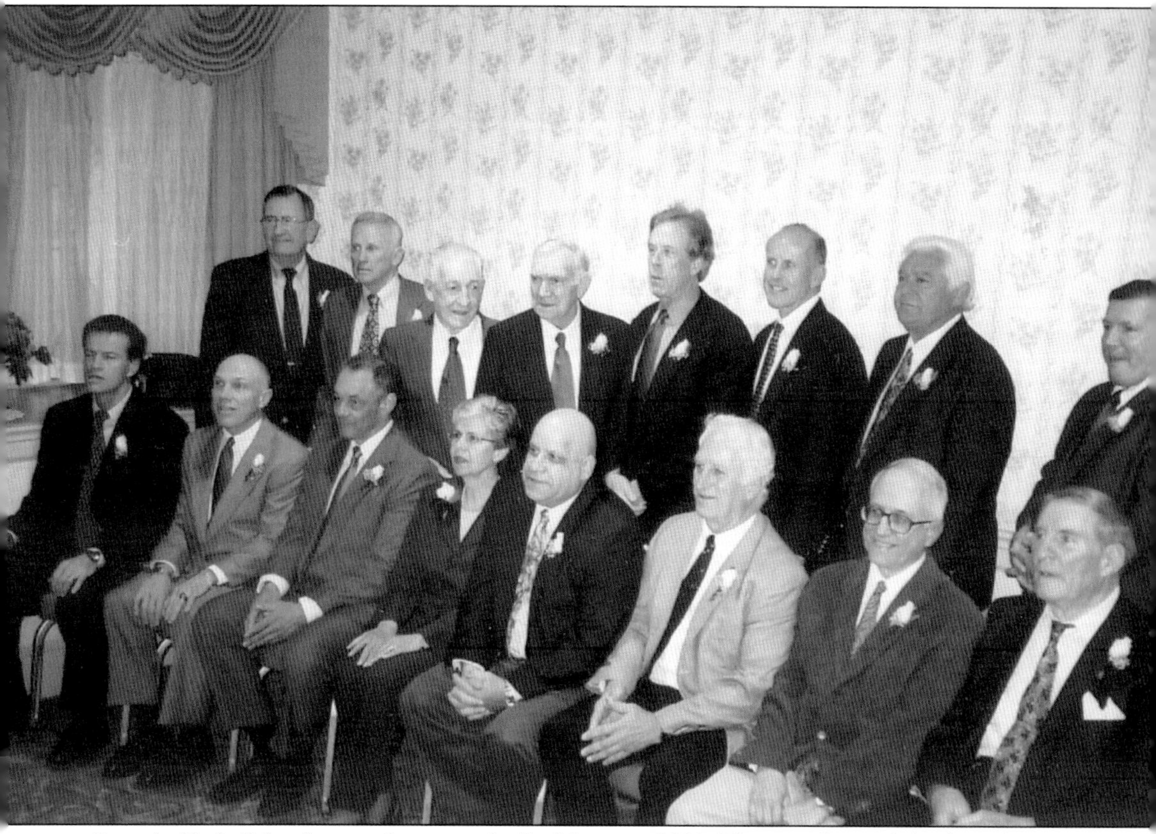

Beverly High School created a sports hall of fame in 2003. The members of the first class are, from left to right, (first row) Bill Gilligan (hockey), Stu Irving (hockey, 1972 Winter Olympics silver medalist with the U.S. hockey team), Bob Ellis (football, track), Emily Witwicki Morency (basketball), Dave "Bippy" Manuel (football, basketball, baseball), Bill Hamor (football coach), Fred Hammond (track coach), and Roy Norden (coach, athletic director); (second row) Robby Robinson (football, baseball), Bill Ransom (football, baseball, track), Mel Deveau (Beverly's greatest football fan), Hugh Nelson (football, baseball), Bill Norris (track, alternate on U.S. Olympic Team), Wally Grant (football, baseball, track), Kenneth "Sandy" Kessaris (football, baseball, basketball), and Dave Tomeo (football). Since 2003, annual inductions have added to the hall of fame roster as the school continues to recognize those who have contributed to its athletic success over the years.

Eight

Events

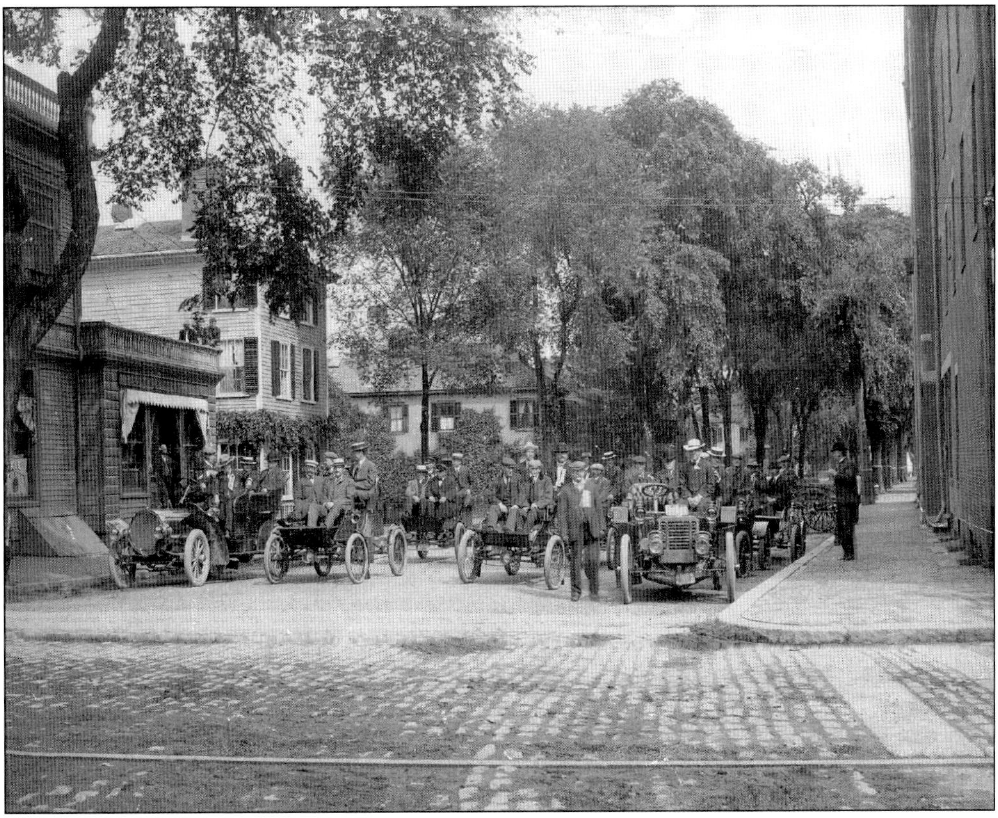

One of many Beverly community events was the carnival known as "Sam Sam," sponsored by the Shoe. Sam Sam was reportedly named for physician Sam Torrey and funeral director Sam Gentlee, who were members of the group that first organized the fair in 1905. As a part of the festivities, the Union Club of Beverly held an automobile rally. Cars are lined up at the intersection of Cabot and Washington Streets.

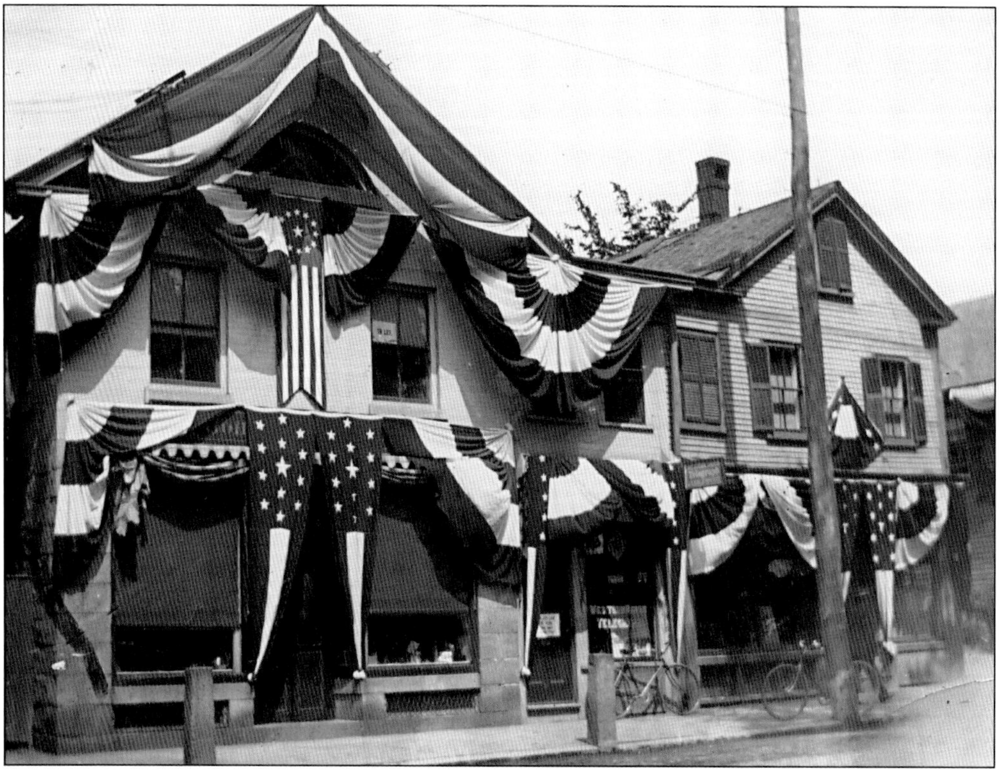

All decked out in bunting for Old Home Week in 1902, the historic building at 160 Cabot Street was once the home of Israel Trask's pewter shop. Founded by 1812, this innovative company manufactured goods that made Beverly famous as a center of pewter making. In recent years, the building has become the home of the Abbott Yarn Shop.

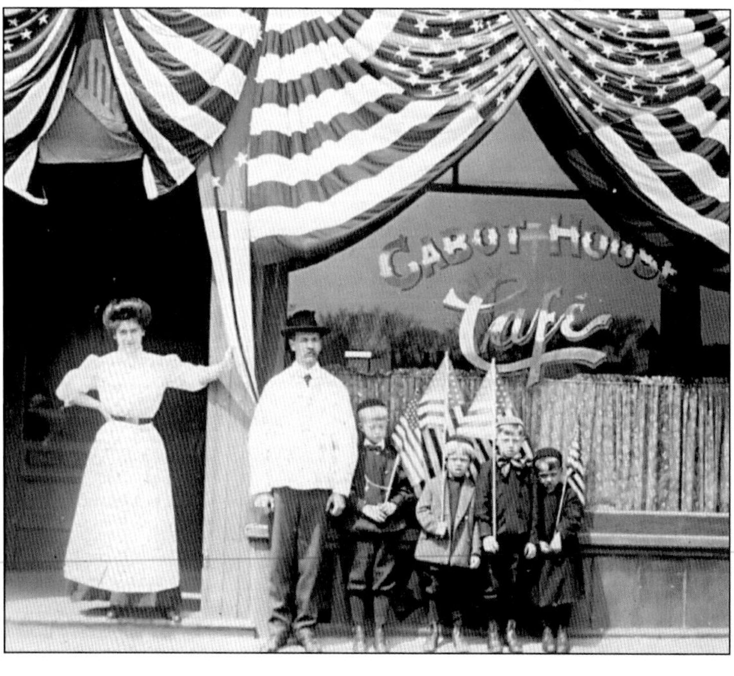

The Cabot House Café, located at 92 Cabot Street, sports banners for Old Home Week in 1902. All four children have come equipped with American flags in preparation for the parade. In addition to the café on the first floor, the Cabot House was described in the Beverly City Directory as a "First Class Transient and Family Hotel"; cost for lodging was $1.50 per day.

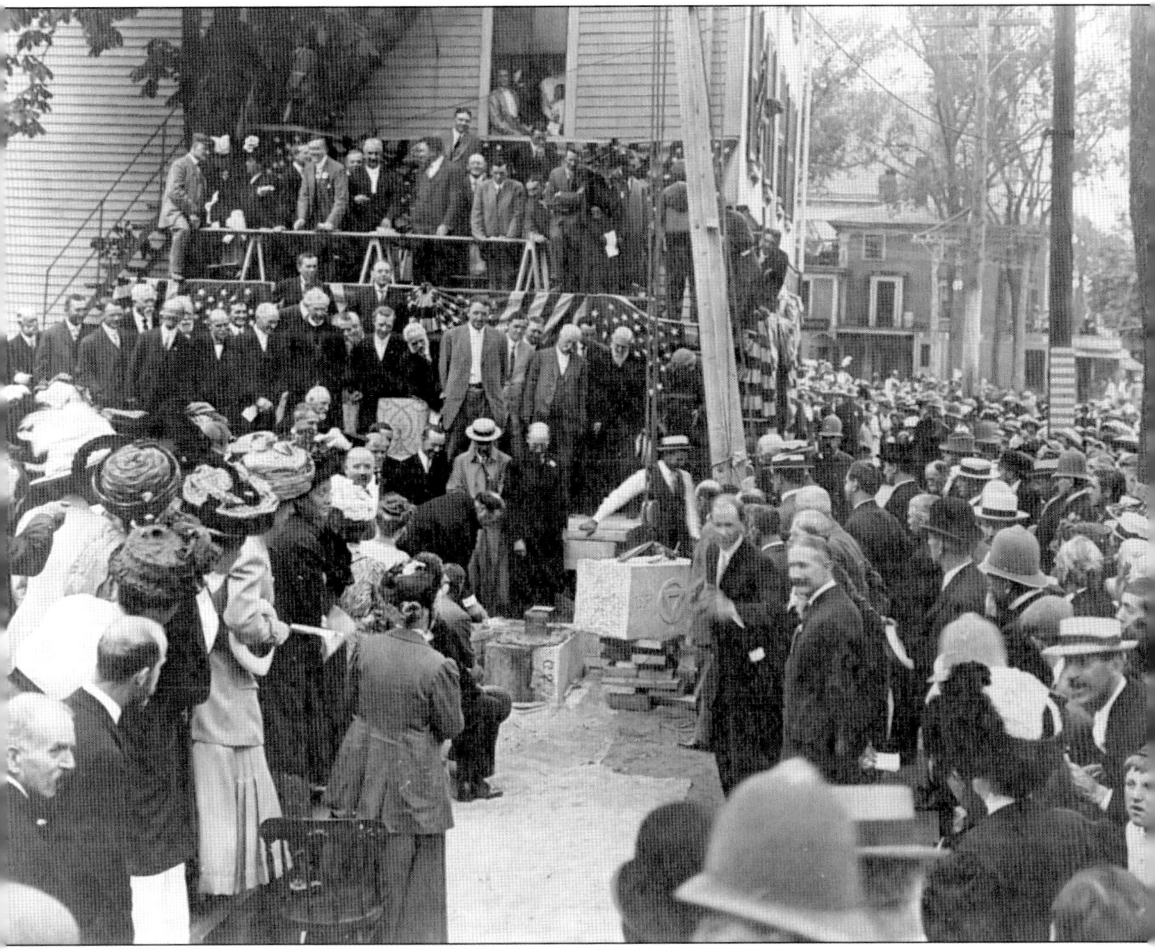

The Young Men's Christian Association (YMCA) movement began in 1844 in London as a response to the terrible living conditions of young working men. The need for a YMCA in Beverly was realized in the late 19th century, and in 1892, a group of businessmen stepped forward to begin a local chapter. The new organization originally leased rooms in the Sinclair Building before outgrowing that space and moving to the Lunt Block on Cabot Street. These new quarters were quickly deemed inadequate for the demands of the YMCA, and fund-raising began to construct a new home along Cabot Street. The community's most recognized summer resident, Pres. William Howard Taft, was asked to lay the cornerstone on August 31, 1910. The *Beverly Saturday Morning Citizen* noted three days later that "Beverly had another record breaking crowd Wednesday afternoon when President Taft laid the cornerstone of the new YMCA building on Cabot and Essex Street."

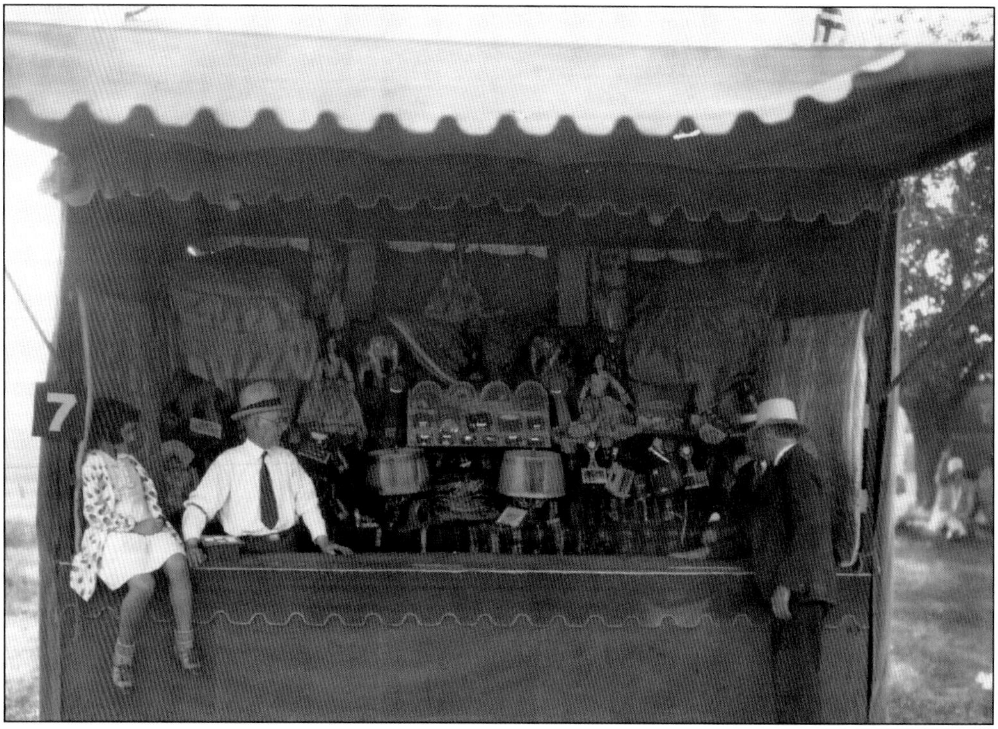

The Sam Sam was an annual Beverly event for many years. It was first sponsored by the Union Club in 1905 as a benefit for Beverly Hospital and was held at Peabody's Field. Within a decade, the Shoe played an active role as host, and the event took place on its grounds adjoining the clubhouse, attracting more than 20,000 attendees. Among the most popular booths at the Sam Sam were these two photographed in 1930: the chance booth (above), which offered tickets for a number of prizes, and the tent (below) occupied by "Kelly the Candy Man," who, for many years, made the circuit of carnivals and fairs to peddle his treats to young and old.

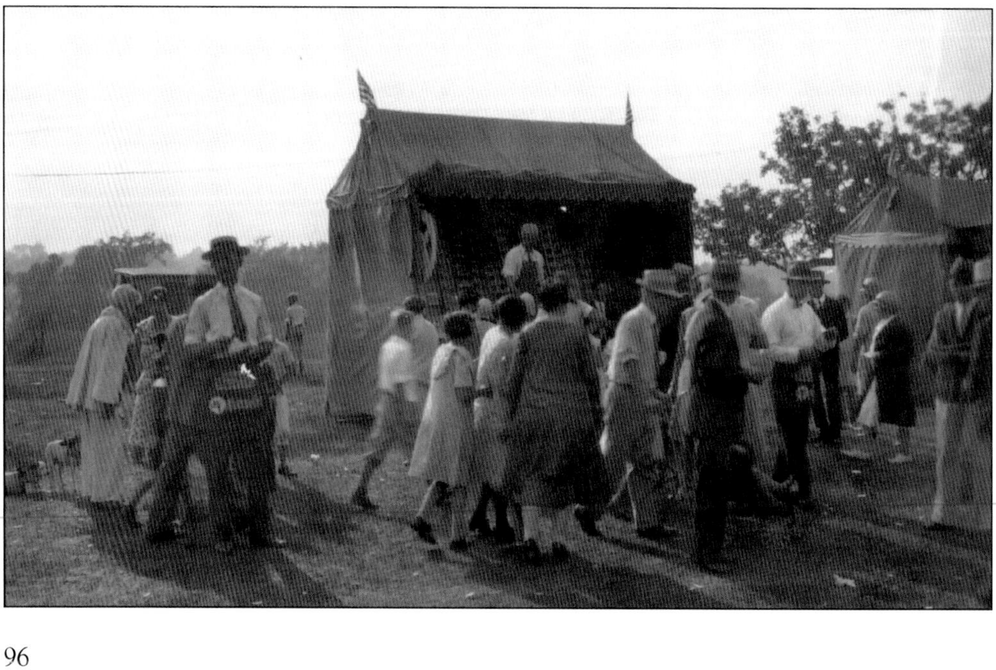

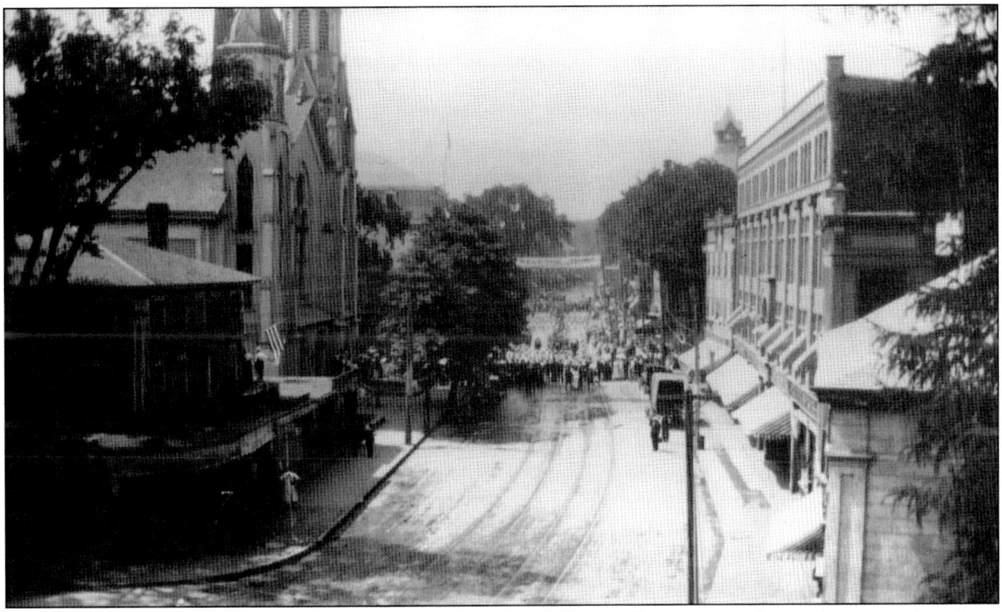

Following World War I, Beverly held a parade to celebrate the return of its soldiers and sailors. First Baptist Church is at left with the Rogers Block at right. The Rogers Block housed several of the local social clubs, benevolent groups, and labor organizations. There were groups dedicated to gardening, husbandry, temperance, science, and literature, among others. A few survive today, like the Masons and the Beverly Female Charitable Society.

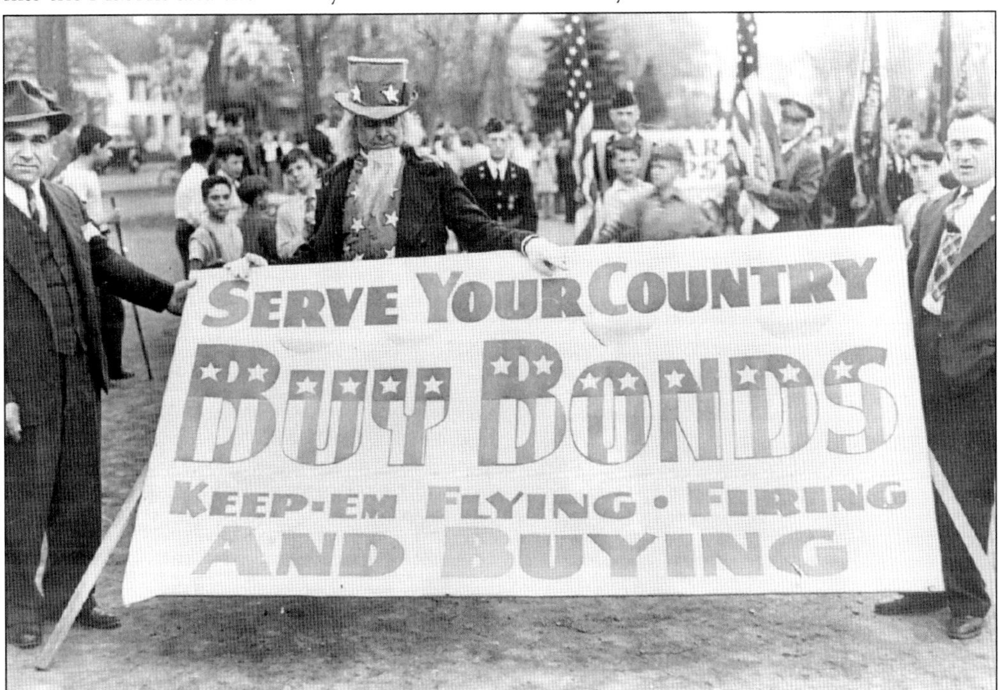

Patriotic Beverly citizens joined with the rest of the nation during World War II to help finance the war effort by purchasing war bonds during rallies, such as this one on Beverly Common. In addition to rallies, advertising and radio appeals were used to encourage Americans to buy bonds.

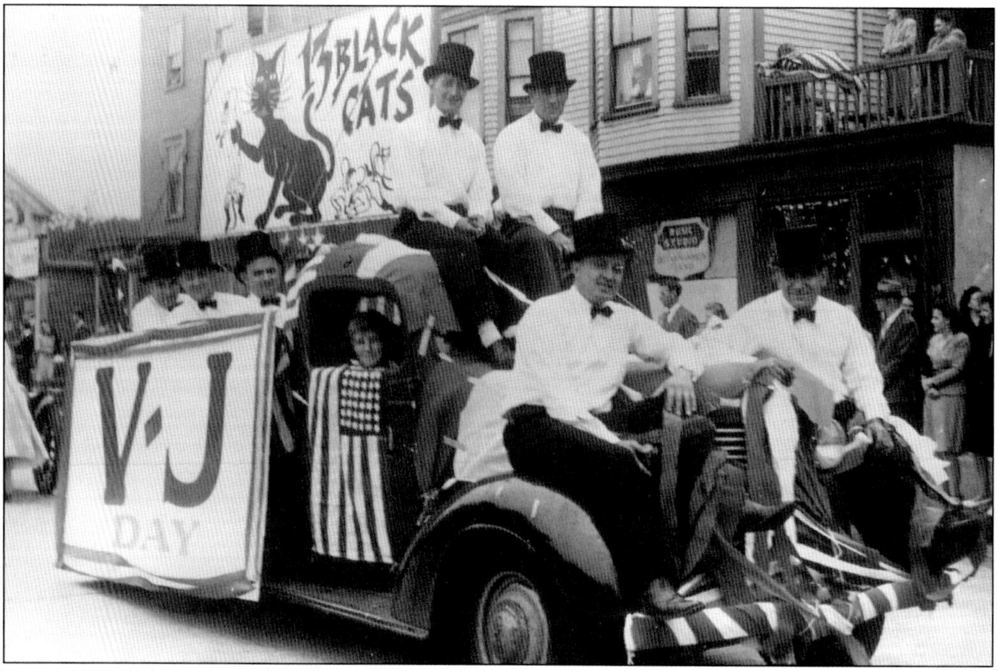

The 13 Black Cats was an organization founded around 1940 by Charlie Bucci to provide support and comfort to Beverly residents. More than a social club, the members provided aid and raised money for the Red Cross, the Community Fund, and war bond drives. Two of its more well-known projects included a Christmas raffle to help families during the holidays and a scholarship for a Beverly High School outstanding athlete.

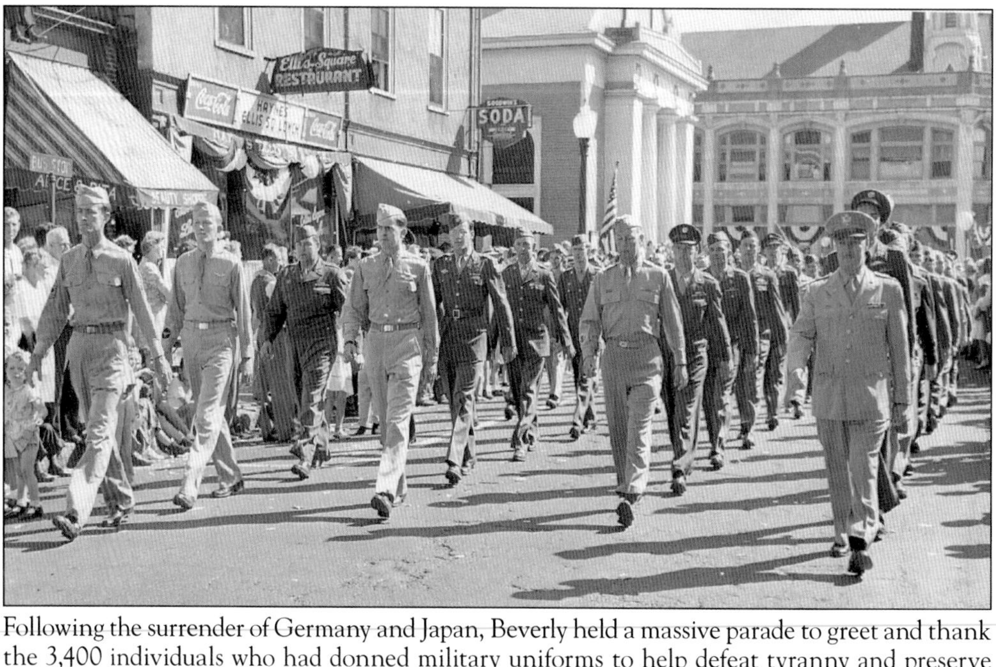

Following the surrender of Germany and Japan, Beverly held a massive parade to greet and thank the 3,400 individuals who had donned military uniforms to help defeat tyranny and preserve freedom. On August 16, 1946, approximately 5,000 marchers, six divisions, and an estimated 50,000 spectators lined the 2-mile route. Here the veterans march through Ellis Square.

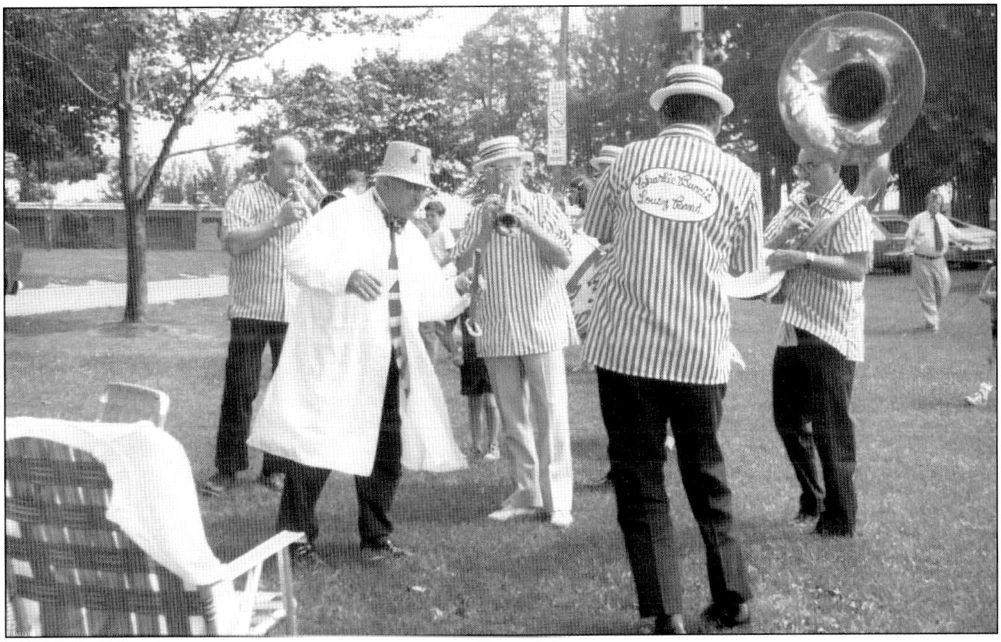

Charlie Bucci formed his brass band by recruiting his friends. Although *Bucci's Lousy Band* was best known for playing at local events and marching in parades, the group's talents were also employed as protestors in 1964. When it became known that the Boston and Maine Railroad was planning to reduce passenger service to the North Shore, the Bucci musicians donned conductor hats and played sing-along tunes in North Station for the protesters.

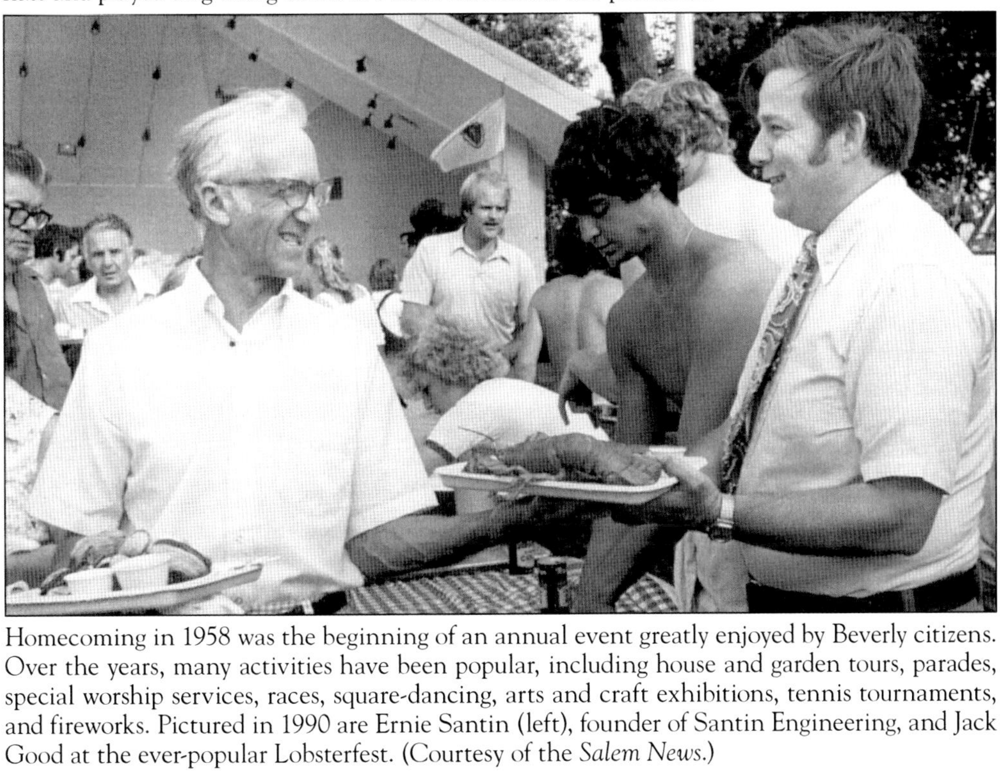

Homecoming in 1958 was the beginning of an annual event greatly enjoyed by Beverly citizens. Over the years, many activities have been popular, including house and garden tours, parades, special worship services, races, square-dancing, arts and craft exhibitions, tennis tournaments, and fireworks. Pictured in 1990 are Ernie Santin (left), founder of Santin Engineering, and Jack Good at the ever-popular Lobsterfest. (Courtesy of the *Salem News*.)

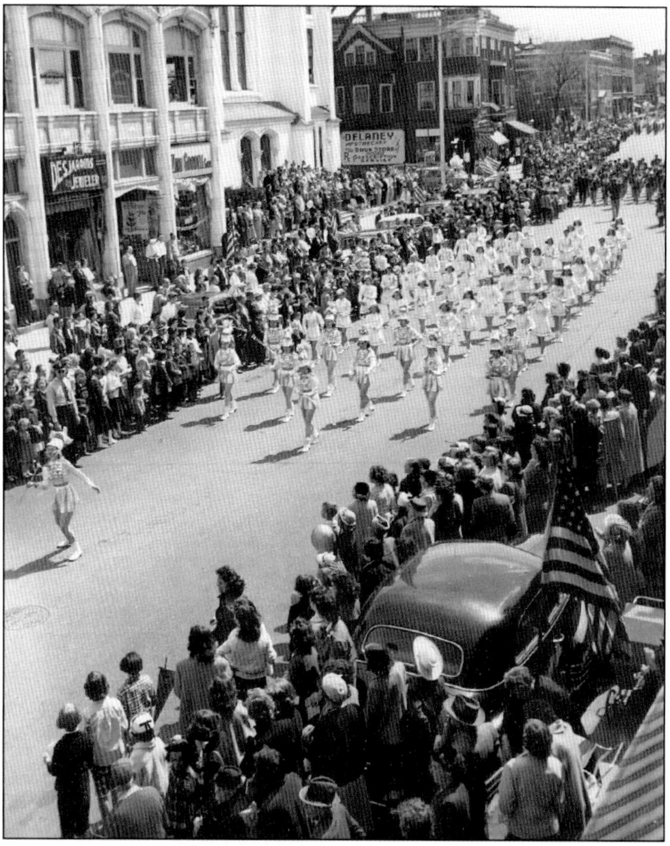

Beverly High School band director John Finnegan promoted the music program by hosting a series of concerts performed by bands from all over Massachusetts. Finnegan led the instrumental music program through 1962. A highlight of the festival was the parade, seen here in 1955 with the Beverly High School marching band.

Over the years, the music department at Beverly High School has staged many wonderful programs, both musicals and plays. In 1994, under the direction of Carolyn Pilanen, the production of *Oklahoma* was a rousing success. Pictured from left to right performing the show's signature number are Billy Anderson, Rachael Arvilla, and Molly Benson.

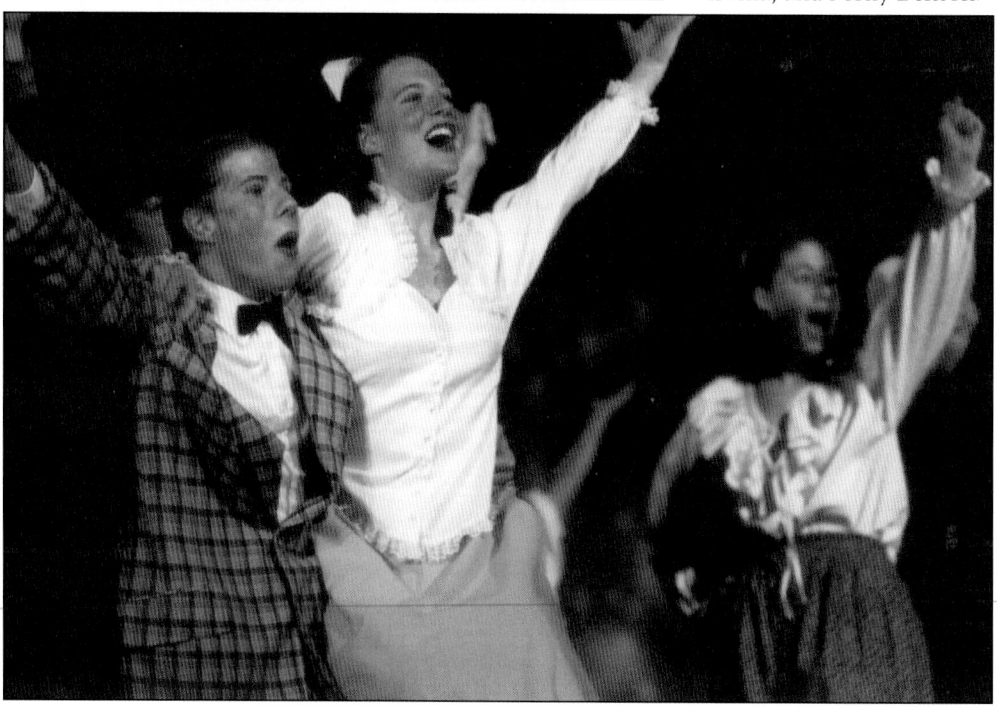

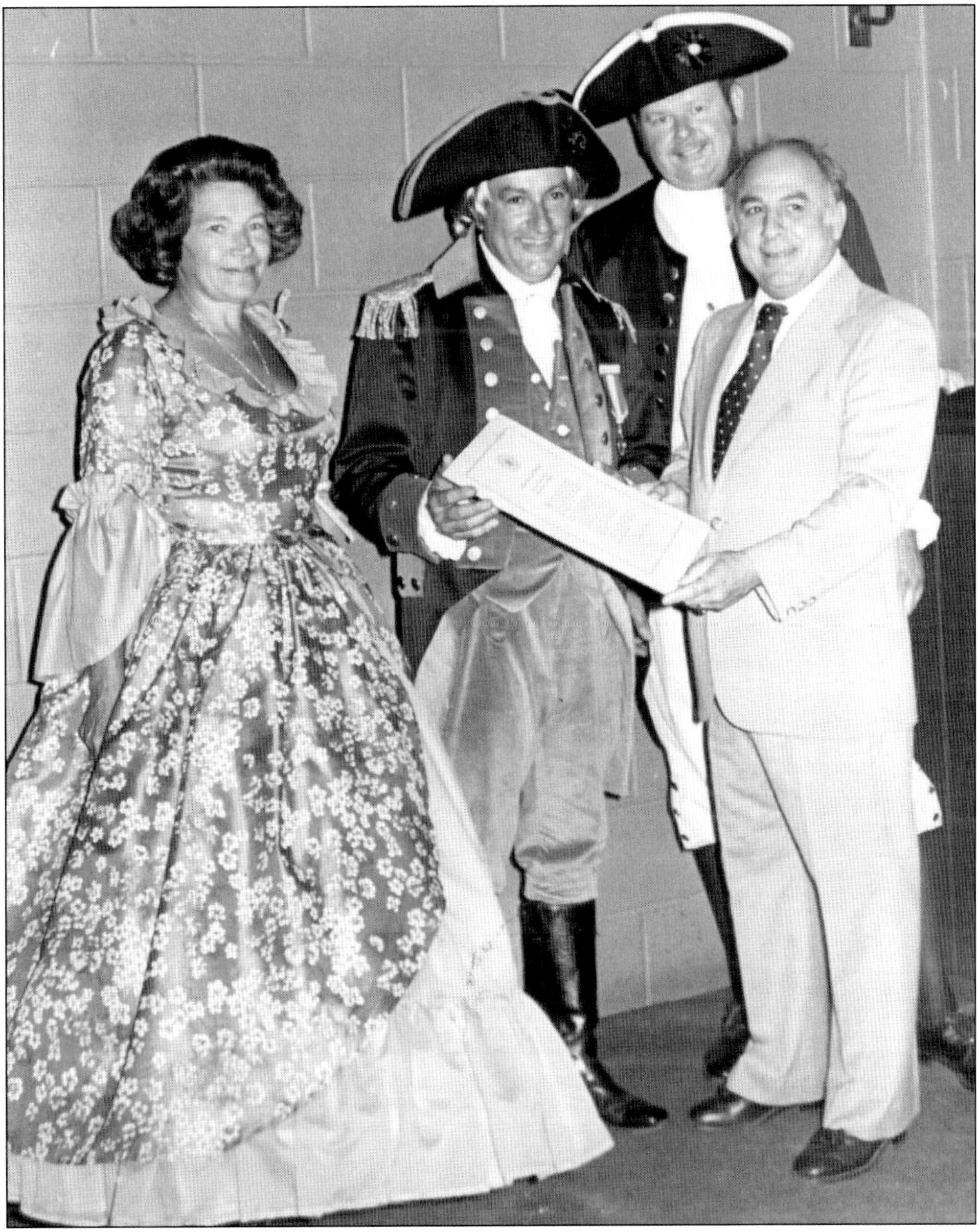

Beverly began planning for the 200th birthday of the United States early in 1972, with the goal of celebrating Beverly's role in the fight for independence. Among the events of 1976 was a Beverly Militia march to the grave site of Reuben Kennison, who died at the Battle of Menotomy in April 1775. New cannons, flags, and flagpoles were installed at Independence Park, and a book, *Beverly and the American Revolution*, by Thomas and Jean Askew was published. Pictured from left to right are Beverly Carlman, Joseph Manzi (bicentennial chair), Doug Henderson (organizer of the Kennison Road Race), and Mayor James Vitale, who were all involved in making the celebration a special one. Carlman, who came to Beverly from the South and embraced local history, wrote a novel about Beverly titled *Fish Flake Hill*. She also wrote extensively about the vessels, owners, and masters along Beverly's waterfront.

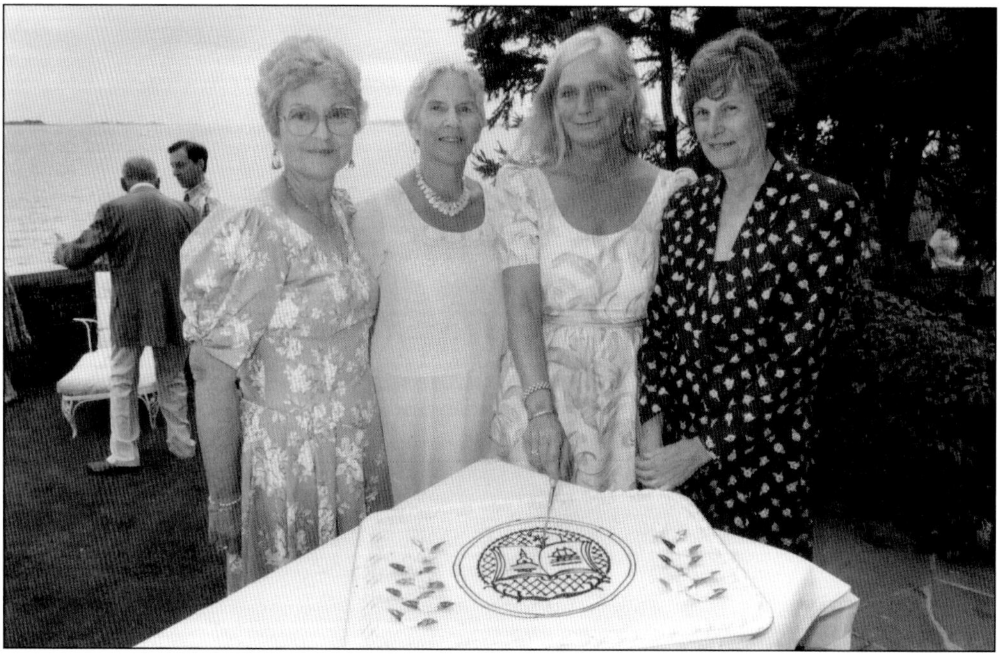

In August 1991, to celebrate the 100th anniversary of its founding, the Beverly Historical Society held a festive garden party by the sea at the home of John and Nancy Benevento. From left to right cutting the cake are Nancy Benevento, the party's hostess; Mary Perron, centennial chairperson; Madilyn Coluntino, refreshment chairperson; and Mimi Batchelder, society president.

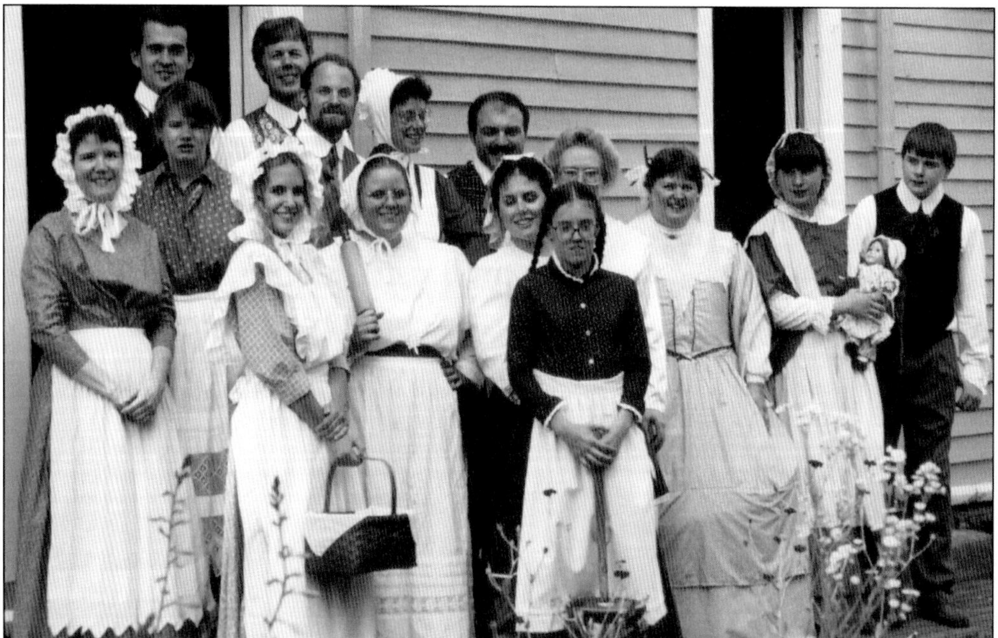

In July 1992, living history tours were given at Hale Farm by reenactors who portrayed members of the Bancroft family (descendants of John Hale), who used the home as a summer residence for many years. Shown standing in front of the house are Kate Pinkham (far left), Lisa McFadden (fourth from left), Larry Ralph (fifth from left), and Christine Tremblay (third from right).

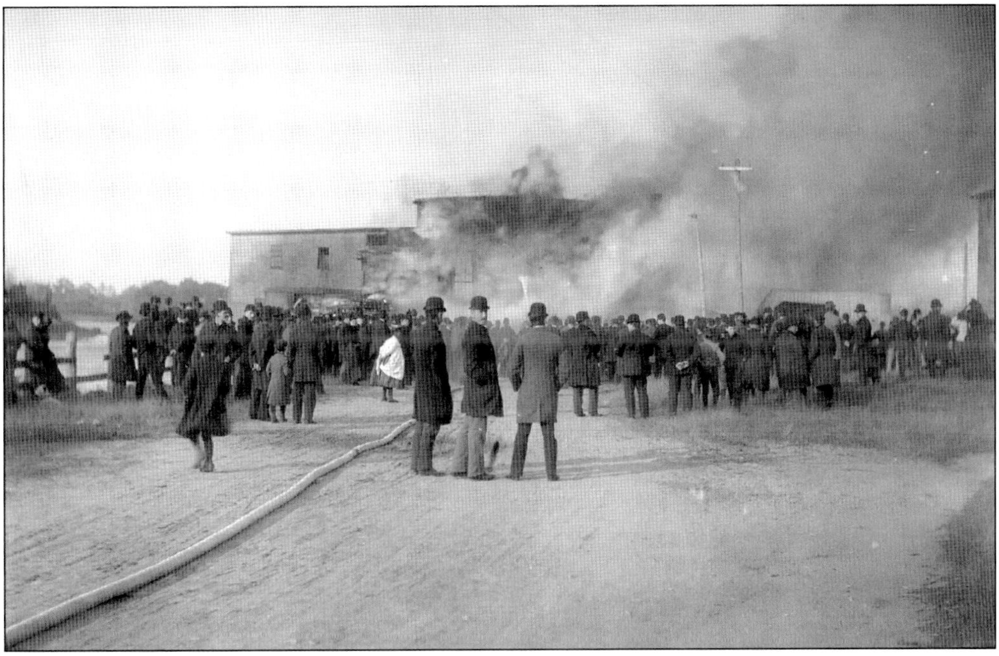

The quiet of a Sunday afternoon on November 1, 1891, was broken when a huge fire was discovered at the George H. Allen Box Factory on Federal Street. The largest shoe factory in town, Woodbury Brothers, also caught and burned, along with a railroad freight house. Many other buildings suffered damage. The final cost was assessed at $200,000.

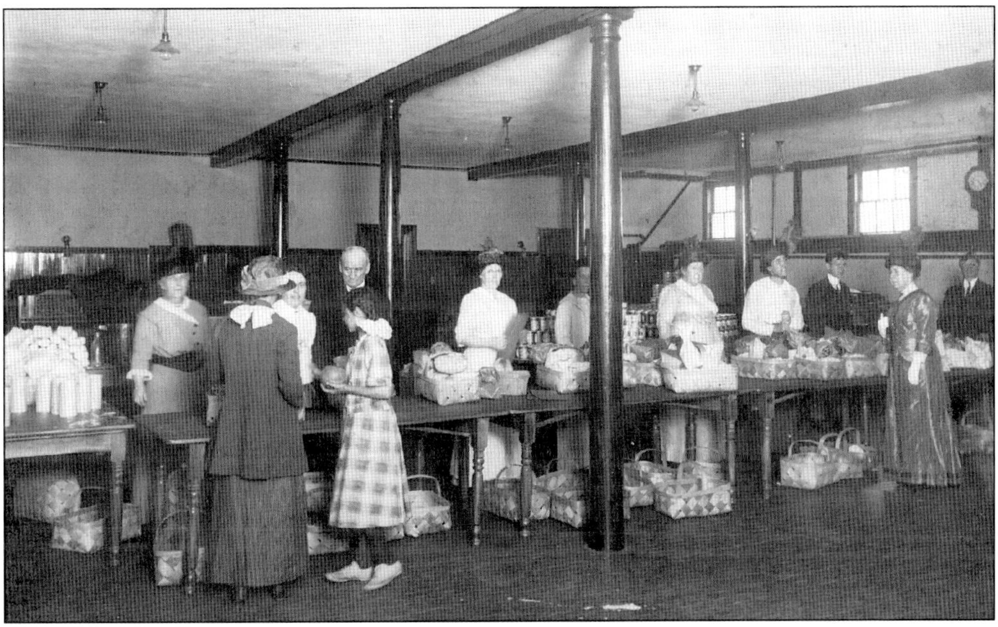

The Great Fire of Salem in June 1914 followed a period of severe drought and warnings by concerned citizens that the city had inadequate fire protection. After the alarm was sounded, Salem sent out calls to 21 cities to help fight the enormous blaze. In the days and weeks that followed, the 20,000 people who lost their homes required assistance. Beverly, like many communities, organized and sent relief packages.

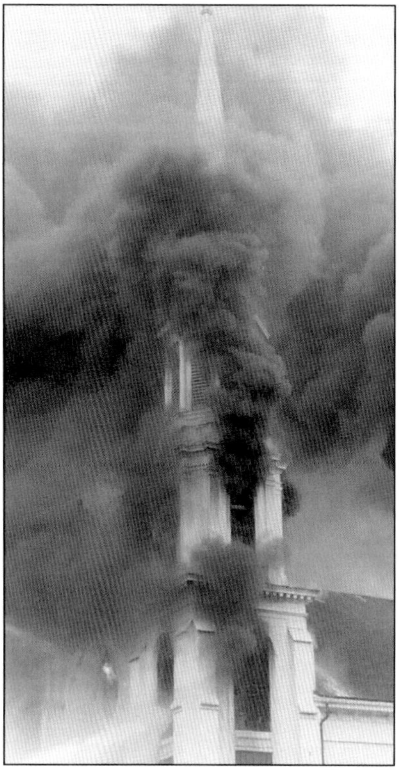

By the time smoke was spotted pouring from the roof on August 26, 1975, the interior of the 105-year-old First Baptist Church was already aflame. Within seconds, the roof collapsed. Seventeen other communities responded to the five-alarm blaze, and firefighters concentrated their efforts on saving the 160-foot steeple. The steeple, which housed a coast guard light, became a symbol of rebirth for the congregation.

On the afternoon of November 16, 1984, the wooden railroad drawbridge connecting Beverly and Salem caught fire and was destroyed in a two-alarm blaze. Passenger service on the Rockport and Ipswich lines was out for a year until the bridge could be rebuilt, forcing commuters and other riders to take buses to Salem and ending freight service north of Salem. Two sets of train cars were trapped by the fire.

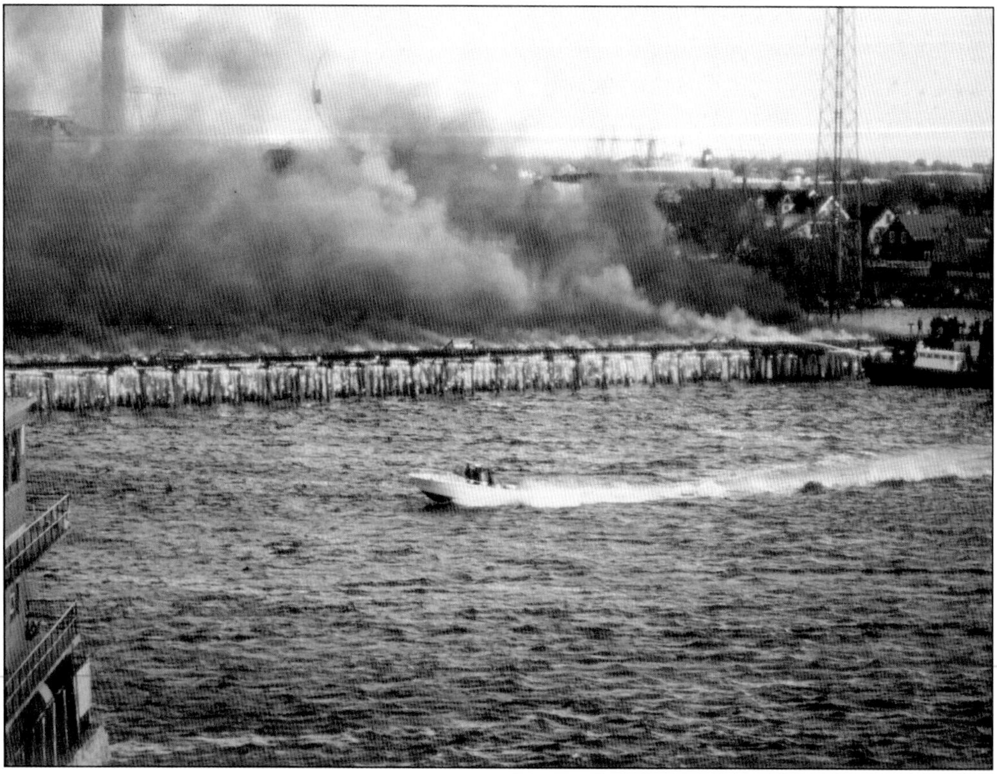

Nine

Community

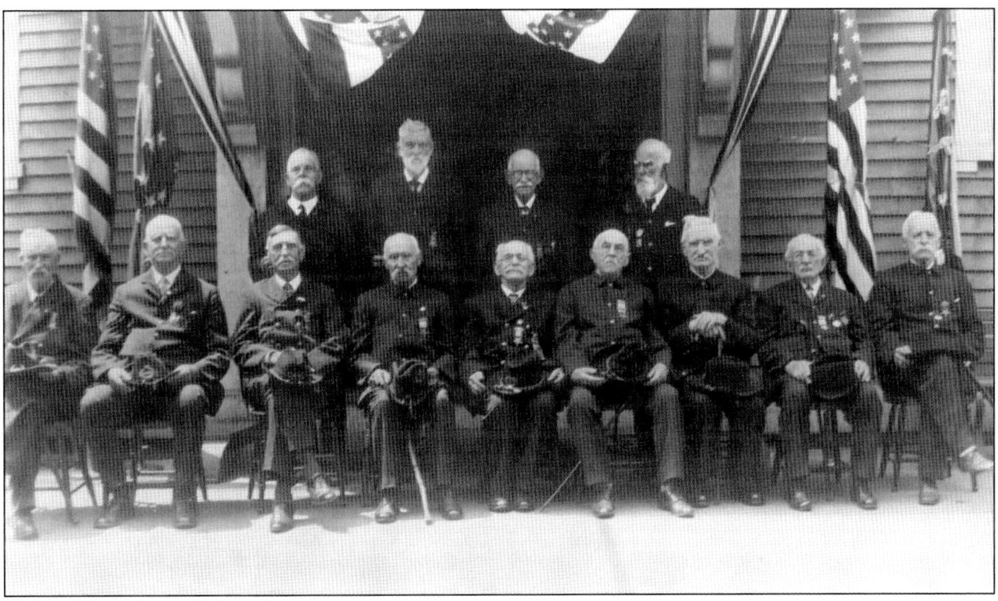

The Grand Army of the Republic (GAR) was the largest Civil War veterans' organization and an early political advocacy group. The GAR played an active role in pension legislation, established retirement homes for soldiers, and created Decoration Day, now called Memorial Day. Beverly's Chipman Post No. 89 provided assistance to comrades and their families. The GAR hall was moved from Cabot Street to Dane Street in the 1940s.

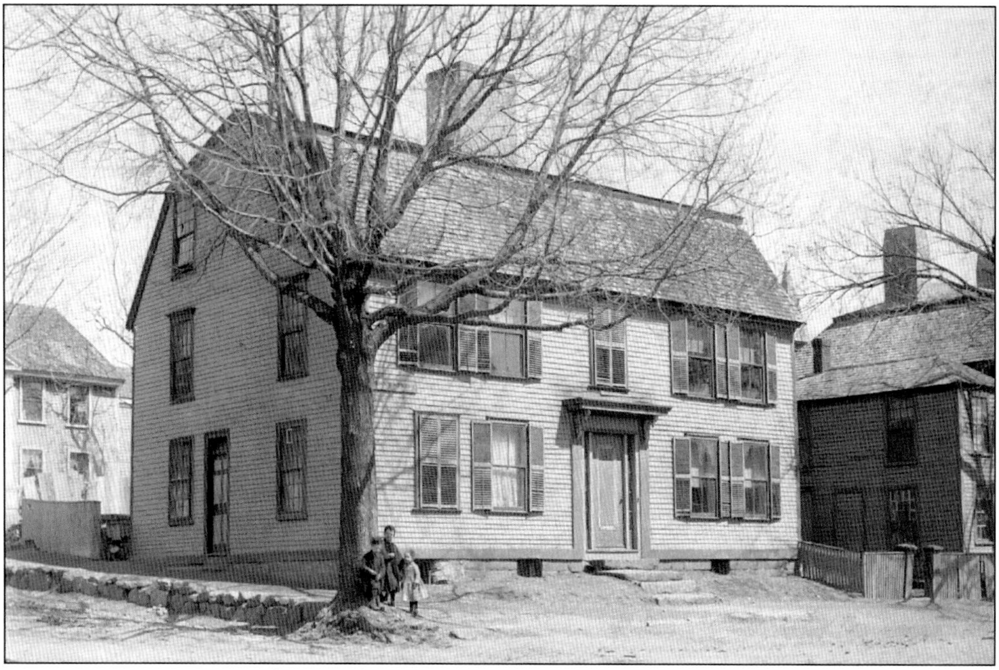

In 1810, Joanna Prince and Hannah Hill became concerned about the many young people living on Beverly's waterfront who did not attend church. The two women established a Sunday school program dedicated to "the moral improvement of the rising generation." This idea led several churches in town to form their own Sabbath schools. The first Sunday school building still stands on Water Street.

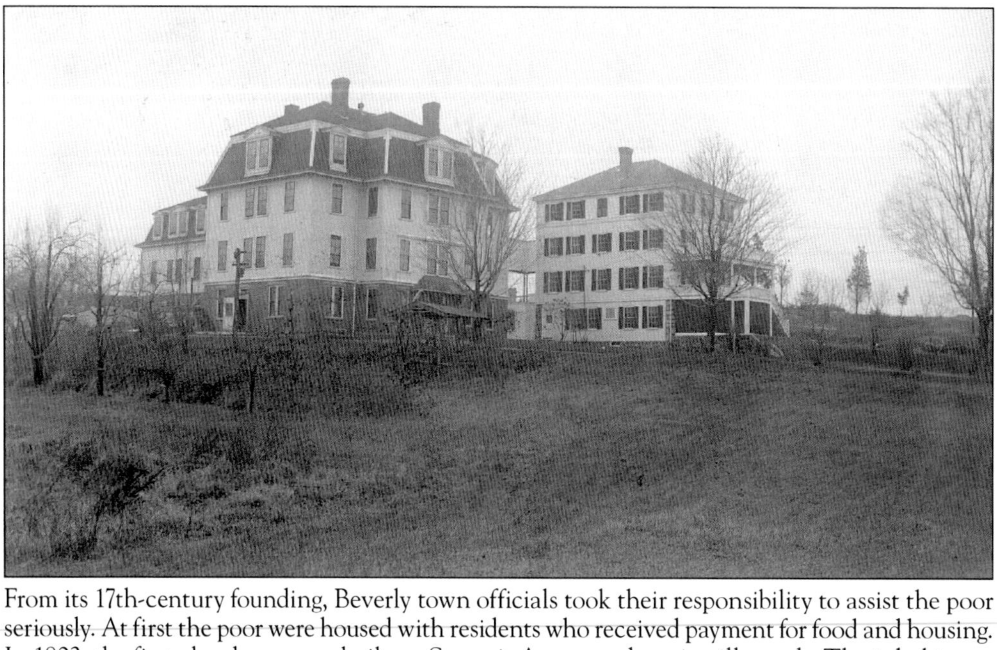

From its 17th-century founding, Beverly town officials took their responsibility to assist the poor seriously. At first the poor were housed with residents who received payment for food and housing. In 1803, the first alms house was built on Summit Avenue, where it still stands. The inhabitants grew vegetables and kept two cows. The photograph shows the larger alms house, which was built at 18 Cedar Street.

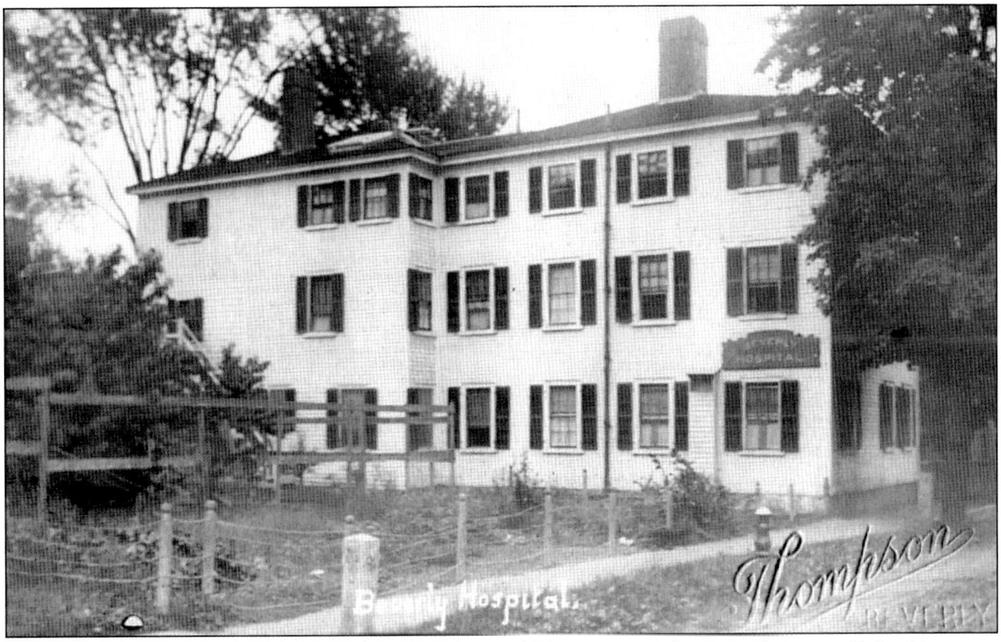

Beverly Hospital began in 1888 when Dr. Samuel Torrey rented rooms for a small facility near his home on Cabot Street, where his father and grandfather had both practiced medicine. The hospital opened its first official site in 1892 at 14 Central Street, seen in the above photograph, and incorporated a year later. The first board of directors included both descendants of Beverly's earliest families (Trask and Woodbury) and those who had originally come to the community as summer residents (Endicott and Loring). The hospital included a nursing school from 1893 until 1972. As Beverly's population escalated in the early 20th century, an expanded hospital was urgently needed, and a facility opened on Herrick Street in 1908. The new complex (seen below) contained five buildings, including wards, private rooms, operating facilities, and accommodations for doctors, nurses, and staff, and cost less than $150,000.

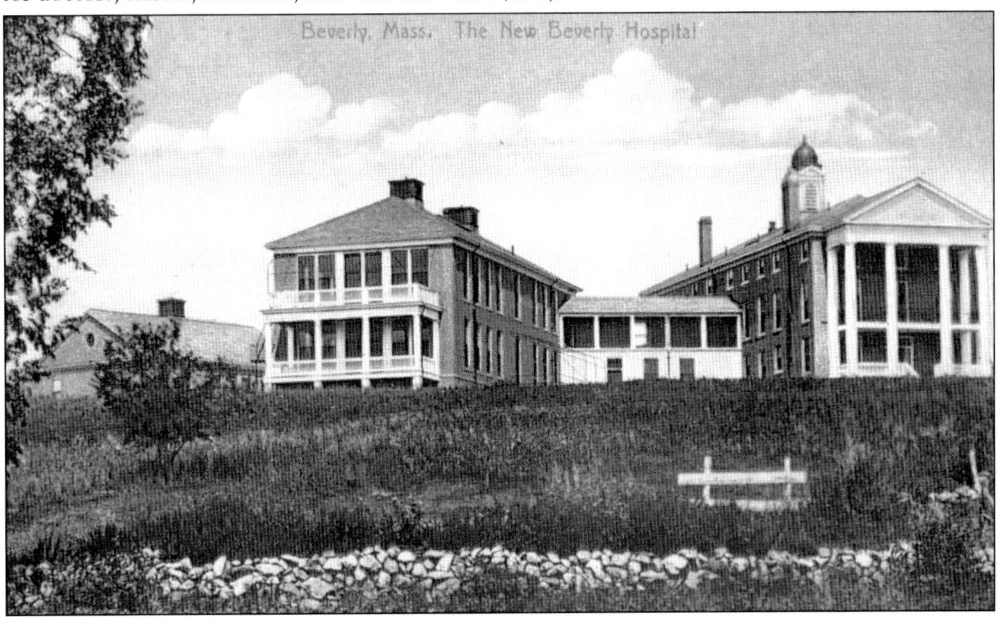

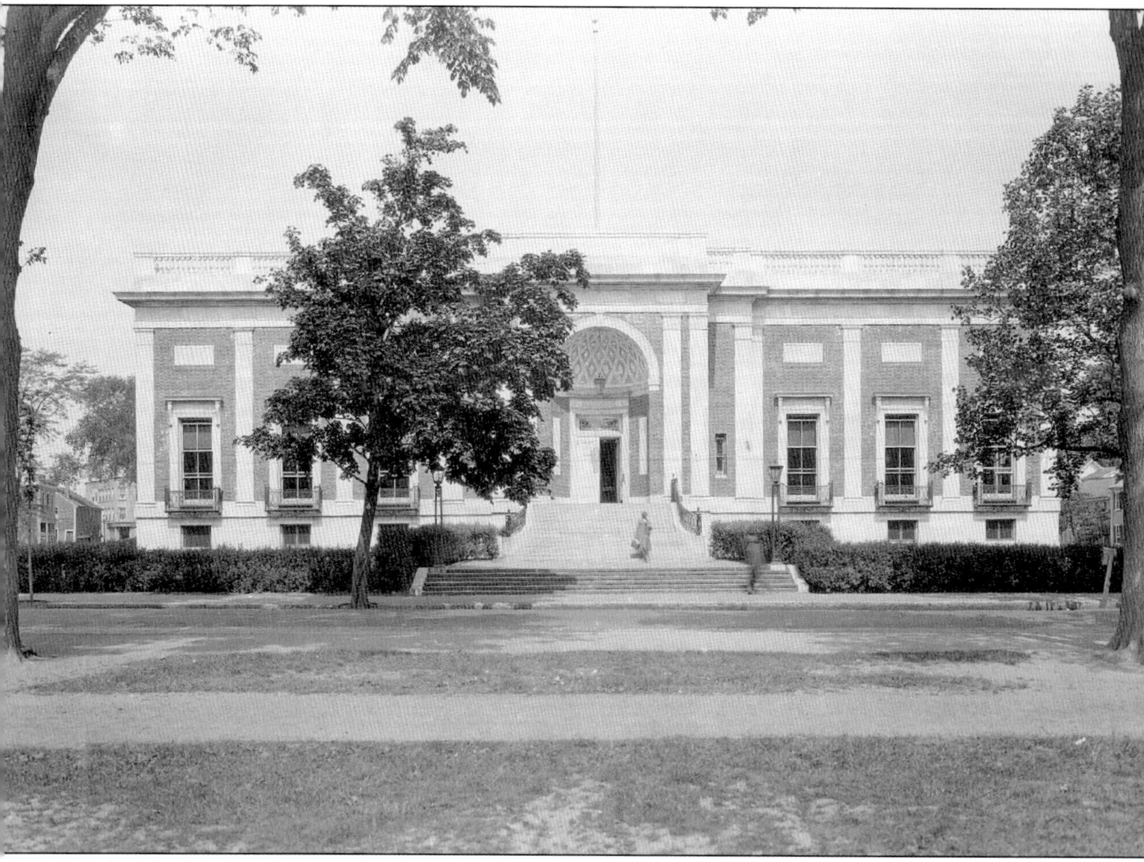

The Beverly Public Library at 32 Essex Street was designed by architect Cass Gilbert (1859–1934) and was built in 1913. Gilbert was a prominent architect of the Beaux-Arts style, and his other projects included the U.S. Supreme Court Building; state capitol buildings in Arkansas, Minnesota, and West Virginia; and the Woolworth Building in New York. The Beverly Social Library, a private institution, turned its collection over to the newly organized Beverly Public Library, which opened in 1855. When the need for a larger building became critical, the community raised the entire amount from taxes and contributions. The library has a Georgian-style brick and marble exterior, with an ornamental terra-cotta half dome over the entrance and skylights to illuminate the interior. The library was expanded in 1993. A branch in Beverly Farms opened in 1886, funded by the Loring family.

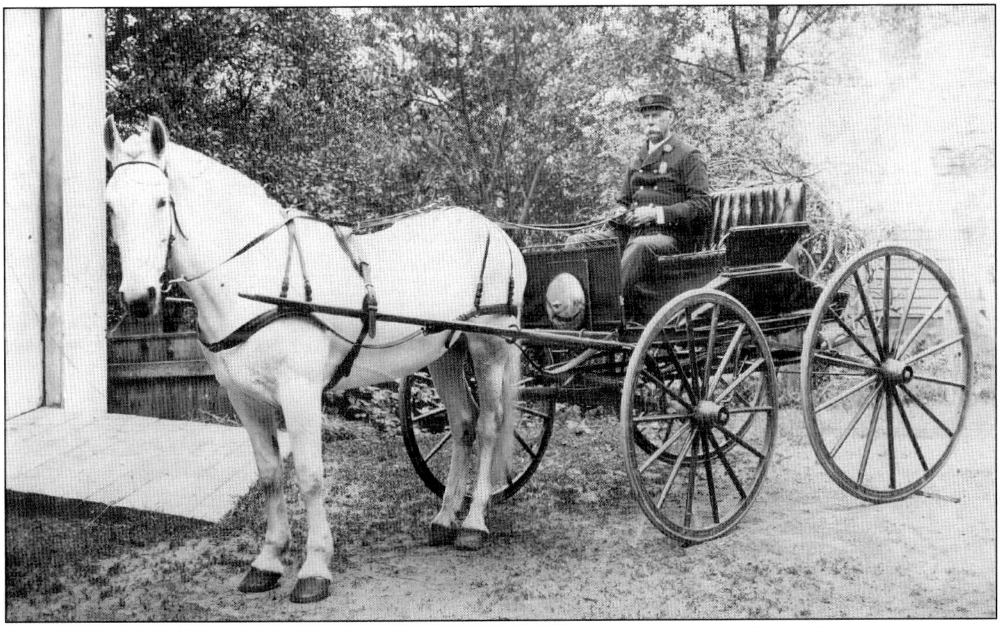

Levi K. Goodhue, who served as Beverly's fire chief at the beginning of the 20th century, used a horse and wagon to get to fires and to perform his other department duties. Goodhue was a part-time chief since he also owned L. K. Goodhue and Company on Federal Street, which made boot heels. Goodhue died unexpectedly on November 19, 1908, and was replaced as chief the next month by Robert H. Grant. The photograph below shows the Central Fire Station as it looked before it was remodeled. Its predecessor was the new structure, built in 1866, in the rear of the town hall to house Beverly's first steam-powered pumper. The new Central Station was dedicated on November 20, 1885, and a year later, a telephone line was installed. The fire alarm office was added in 1949.

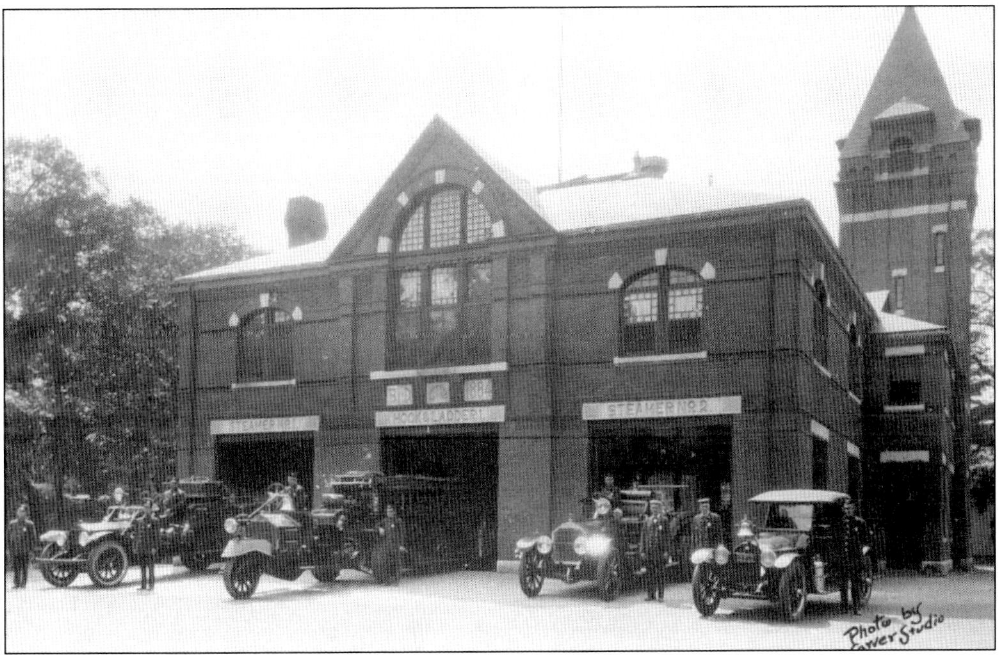

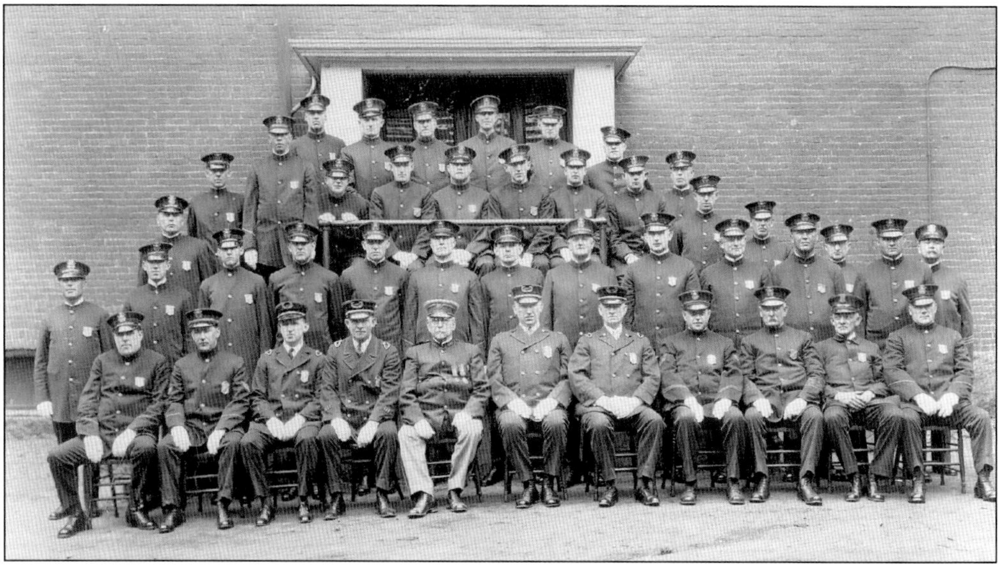

The Beverly Police Department poses in 1925. Pictured from left to right are (first row) Maurice Foley, Sgt. Joseph Murney, Lt. Francis Minton, Chief Joseph Welch, Mayor William Stopford, Capt. Dominick Tahaney, Lt. William Tobin, Sgt. William Pickett, Calvin Williams, Constable Frederick Beckford, and Dan Regan; (second row) Albert Savenelli, Ed Lynch, Fred Steele, Ken Mills, William Cowles, Dan Murphy, Jim Dennis, Ferdinand Bray, Jim McCarthy, Harold Stone, Clifford Standley, and Arthur Wilson; (third row) Clyde Smith, Bill Davidson, Bill Brown, Jack Barry, Warren Adam, Fred Fortin, Henry Slattery, Harold Marley, Ed Egan, Bill Campbell, Eugene Marley, John Norwood, and Harry Monies; (fourth row) Emery Hooper, James Walsh, Ed Glidden, Jim Doliver, John Hanson, Bill Terry, and Louis Shaw. The below photograph shows the Beverly police's color guard in Central Cemetery following the Memorial Day Parade May 1978. (Courtesy of the *Salem News*.)

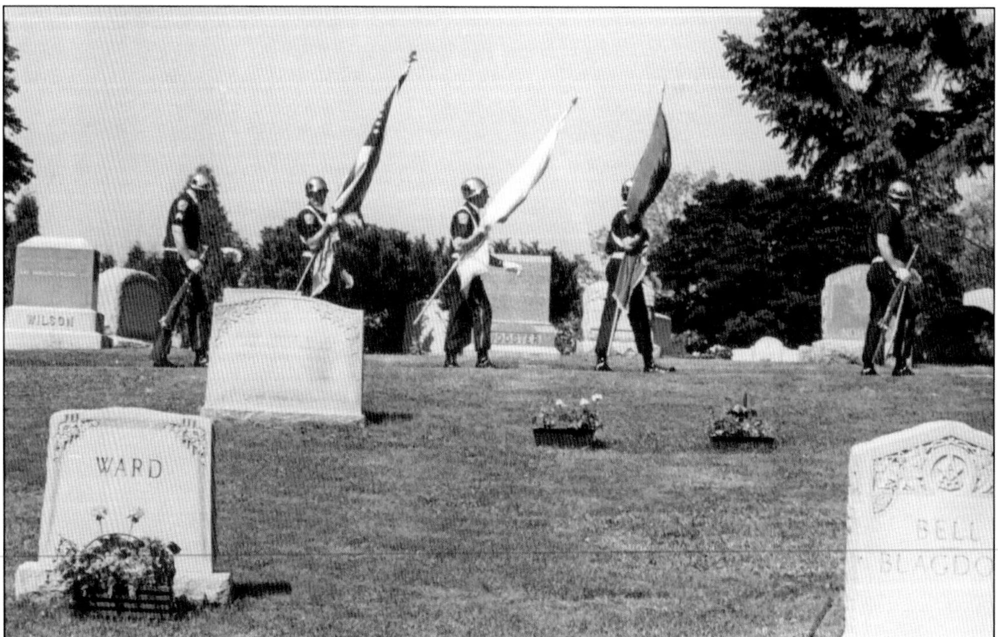

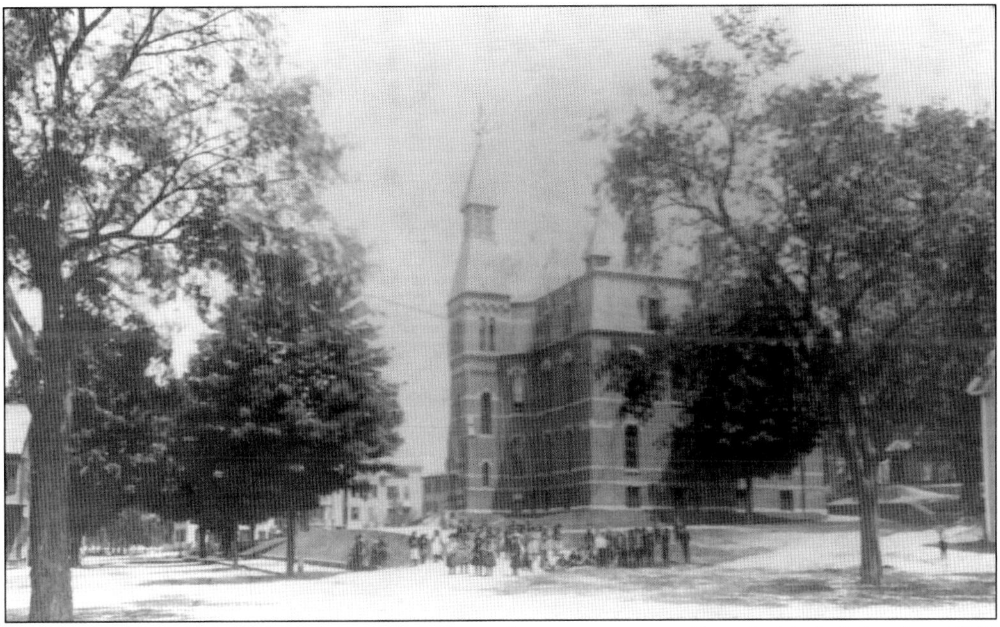

The Victorian Briscoe building on Essex Street began serving as Beverly High School in 1874. The cost of construction was about $75,000. In the 1920s, community leaders determined that it was no longer adequate, and a new school at Colon Street and Sohier Road opened in 1925. The cost was just over $1 million. The new high school under construction in 2010, replacing the 1965 building, was budgeted at $80 million.

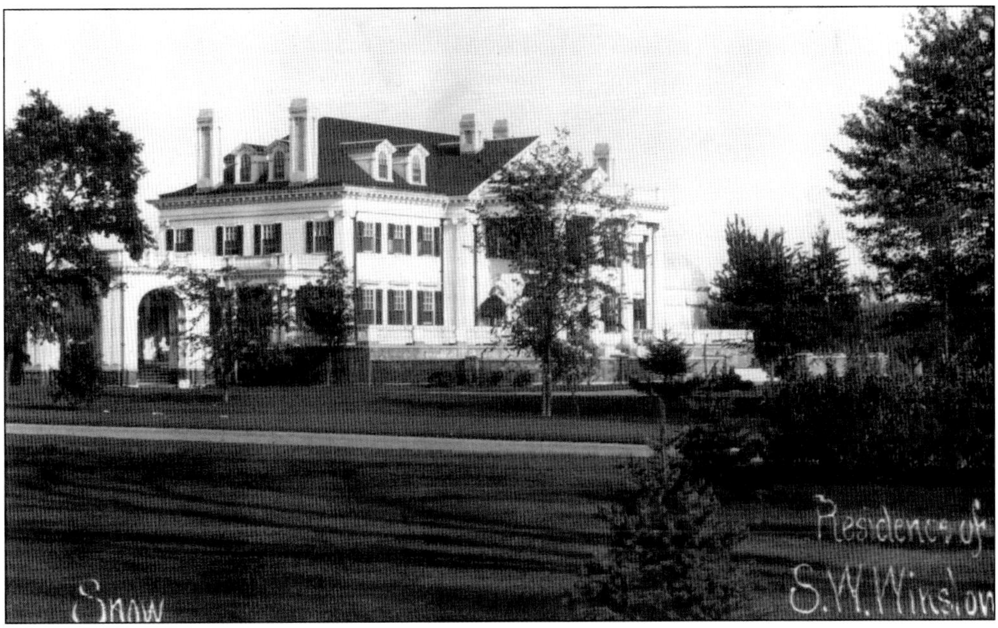

The Shore School of Beverly Farms and the North Shore Country Day School (NSCDS), originally from Medford, merged to form Shore Country Day School in 1936. The NSCDS had purchased the building above in 1931 from United Shoe Machinery Corporation president Sidney Winslow. Since then, the school has expanded its facilities and services, and it now serves more than 400 students on a 17-acre campus.

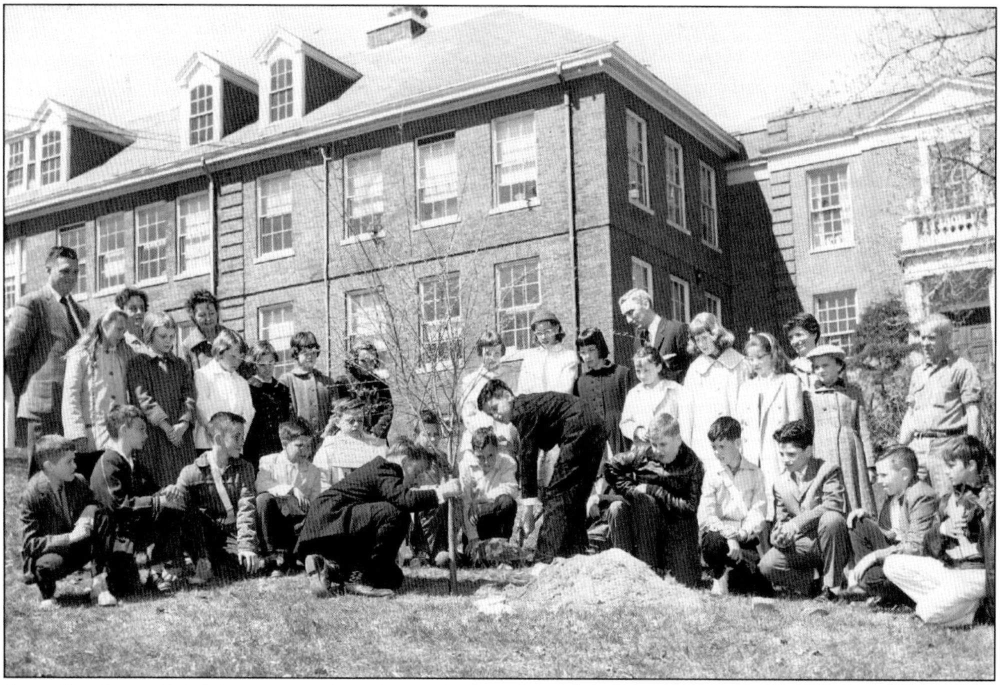

Priscilla Peabody's fifth-grade class from the Upton School is shown planting a tree for Arbor Day in April 1960. Principal Charles E. Rogers is standing at left. Planting the tree are Richard Howard (left) and Dana Dube. In the 1980s, the building on Bridge Street was converted into affordable housing.

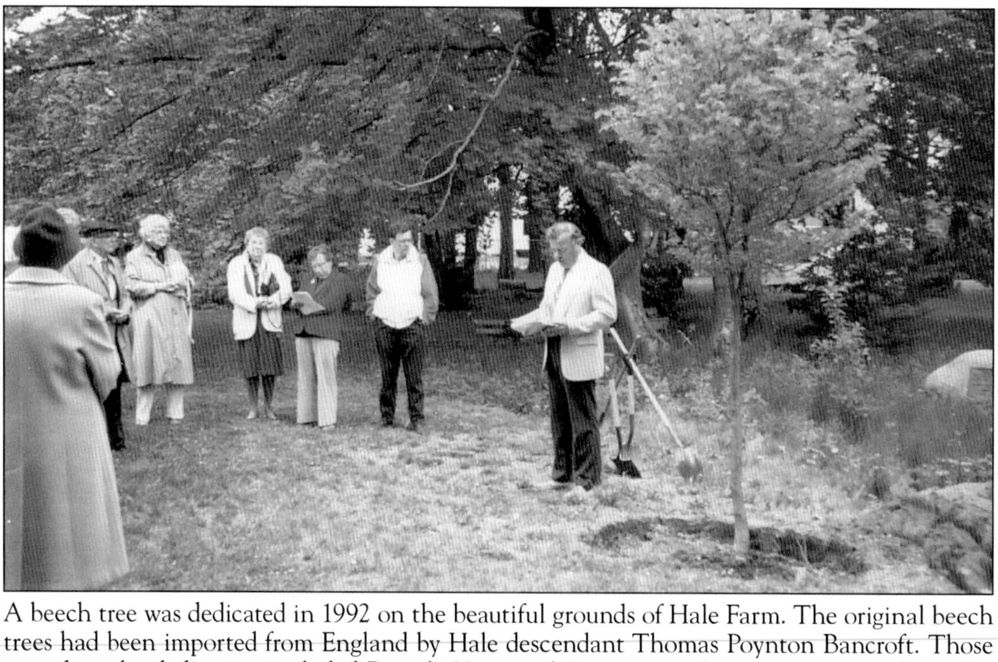

A beech tree was dedicated in 1992 on the beautiful grounds of Hale Farm. The original beech trees had been imported from England by Hale descendant Thomas Poynton Bancroft. Those attending the dedication included Beverly Historical Society members, in no particular order, Robert Lovett, Marguerite Harris (author of *John Hale: A Man Beset by Witches*), Dan Lohnes, and society president Jack Murray (speaking at right).

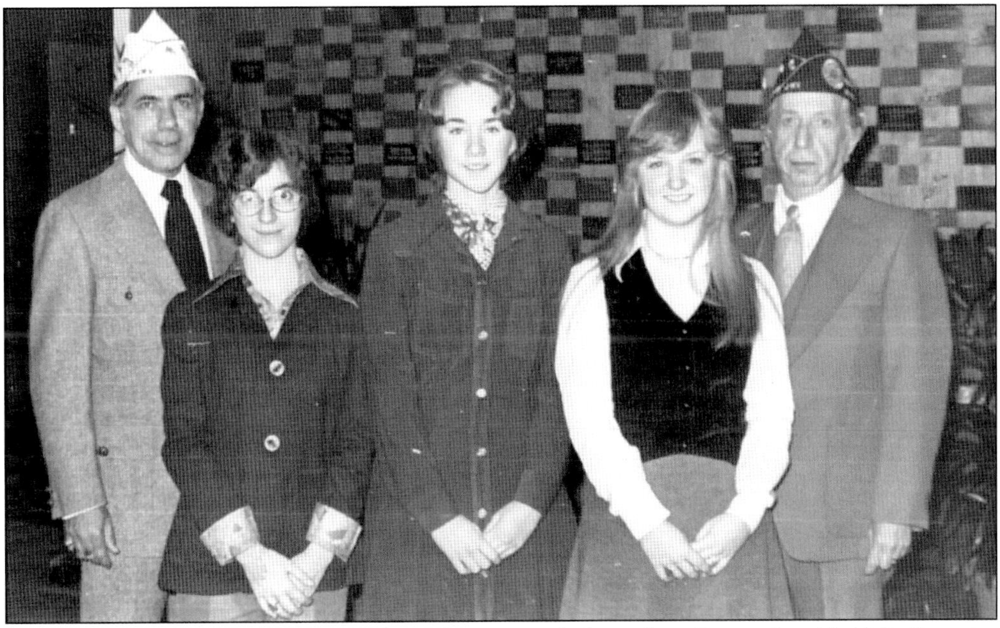

Temple B'Nai Abraham on East Lothrop Street was dedicated on September 14, 1962. Superior Court Justice Jennie Loitman Barron delivered the dedication address. This image shows the presentation of the Temple Citizenship Award on February 14, 1977. From left to right are Albert Ferman, Sandra Yoffa, Elizabeth Callanan, Dawn Meehan, and Edward Goren. (Courtesy of the *Salem News.*)

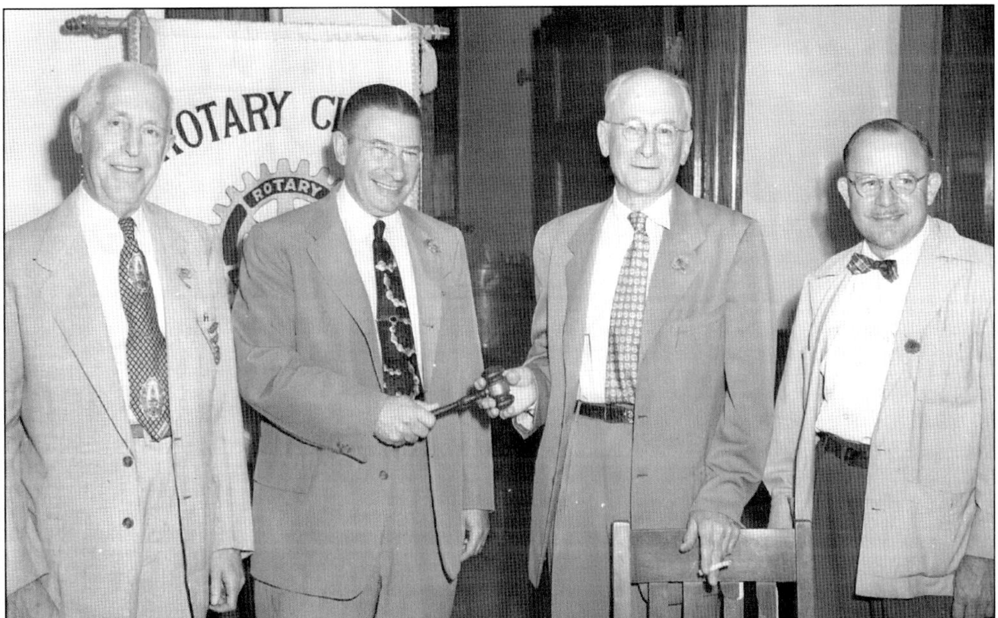

In Beverly, as elsewhere, the Rotary Club provides vital contributions and support to the city, and it counts many community leaders among its members. Pictured at the induction ceremony in 1952 are, from left to right, Bill Parker, inducting officer; Thomas Bott Jr., incoming president; Bill Tannebring, retiring president; and Henry Desjardins, incoming vice chairman.

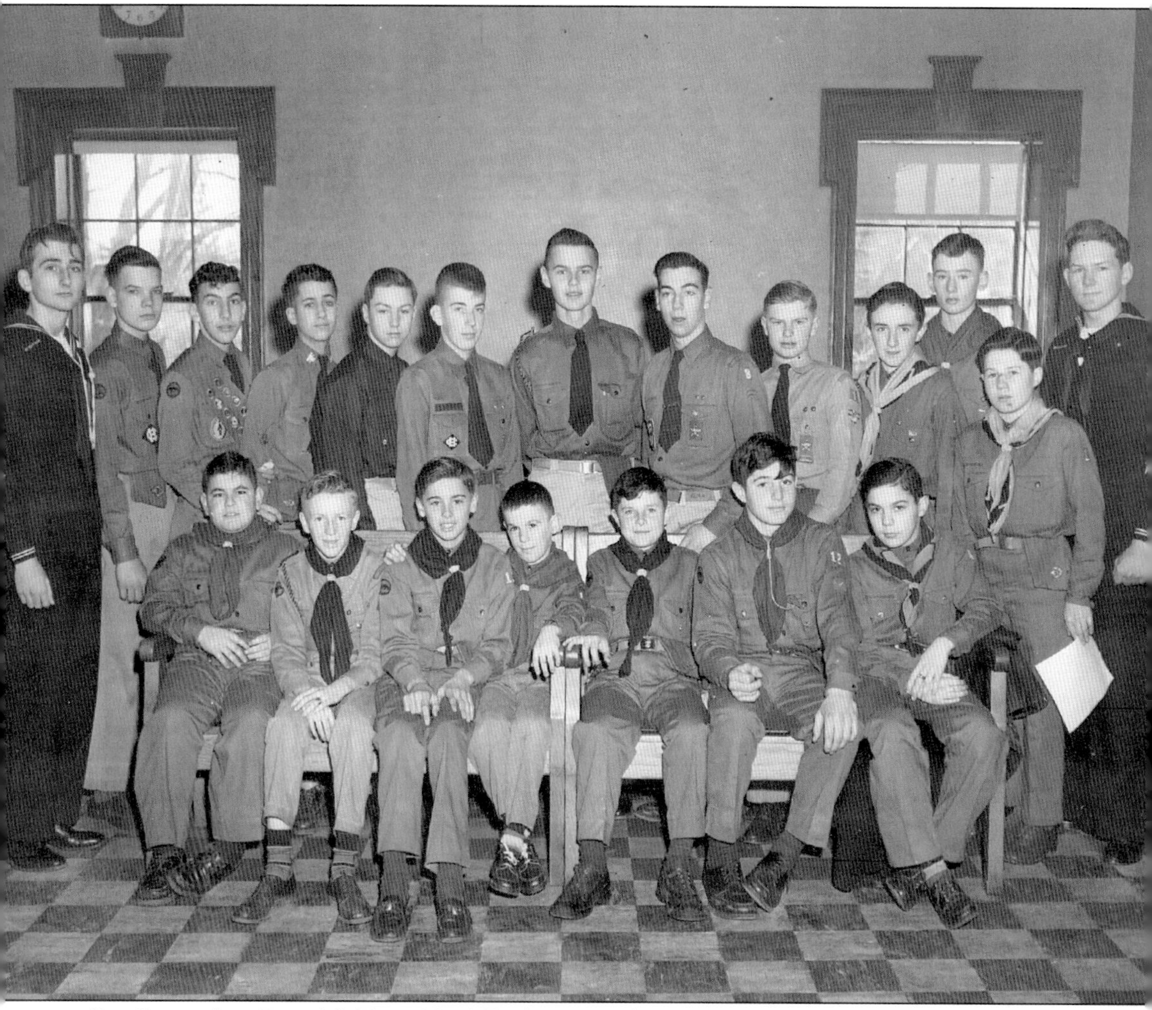

Boy Scouts from Beverly's Troop No. 2 Explorers are shown about 1950. From left to right are (first row) Alfred Daluzzi, Richard Barker, Robert Wightman, Douglas Conrad, Richard McCarthy, Harrison Ball Jr., and Daniel Hefferman; (second row) Peter Tappan, Arthur Channel, Robert Gustafson, Fred Hammond, Richard Woodberry, Paul Larcom, Robert Rasche, Kenneth April, Donald Hannable, Brooks Smith, Clifford Caverly, Joseph Reilly, and Richard Hiltonen. Paul Larcom, who provided the information for this photograph, is a longtime volunteer and contributor to the Beverly Historical Society's Walker Transportation Collection. His specialty is aviation and the Beverly Airport. Fred Hammond became a history teacher and track coach at Beverly High School. He was elected to the school's hall of fame in 2003. He continues to research and teach local history through lectures and walking tours, and he was the recipient of the 2010 Beverly History Award.

Excitement was at a peak when Old Home Week kicked off in August 1902. Buildings up and down Cabot Street were decorated with red, white, and blue bunting. The illuminated water parade in the harbor was a great event that week and, along with the bonfire pictured here, was seen by thousands of people.

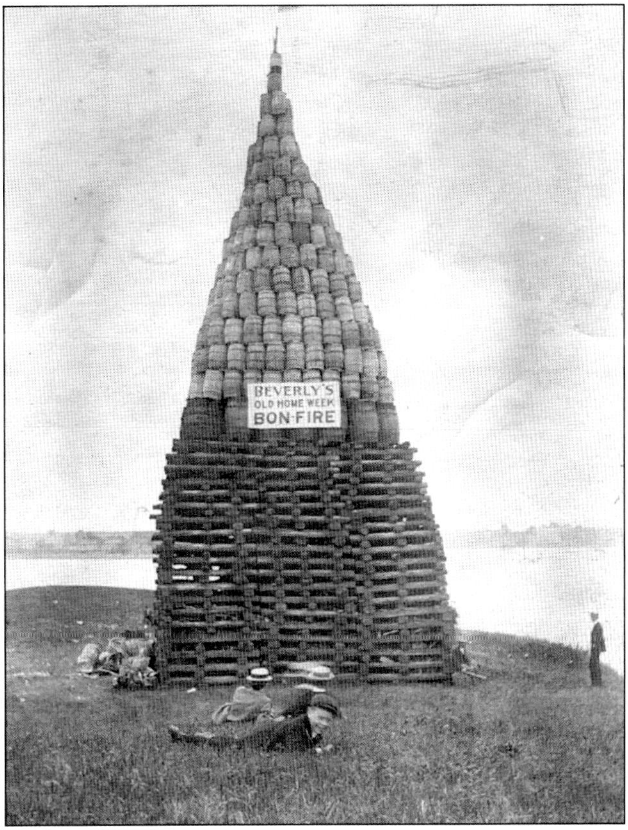

The year-long celebration of Beverly's 300th anniversary started on September 20, 1967, with a concert at First Parish Church. Dozens of events throughout the year were capped with a parade on October 13, 1968. Here Gov. Francis Sargent can be seen greeting Eve Johnson. Arthur Appleton and Edith Roberts are standing on the steps of the Beverly Historical Society at 117 Cabot Street.

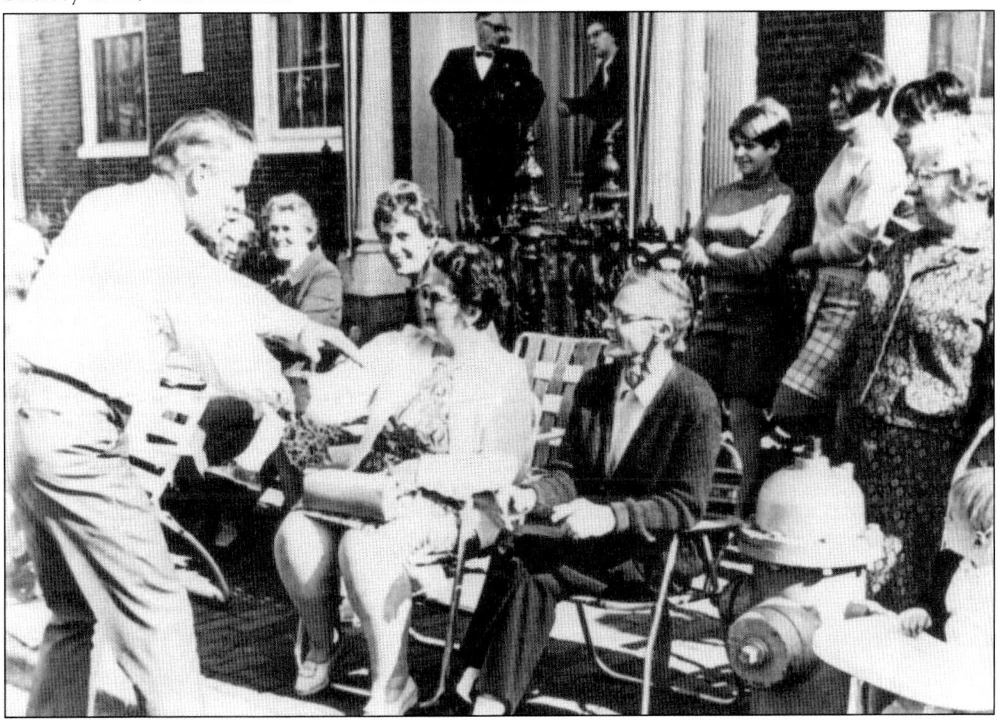

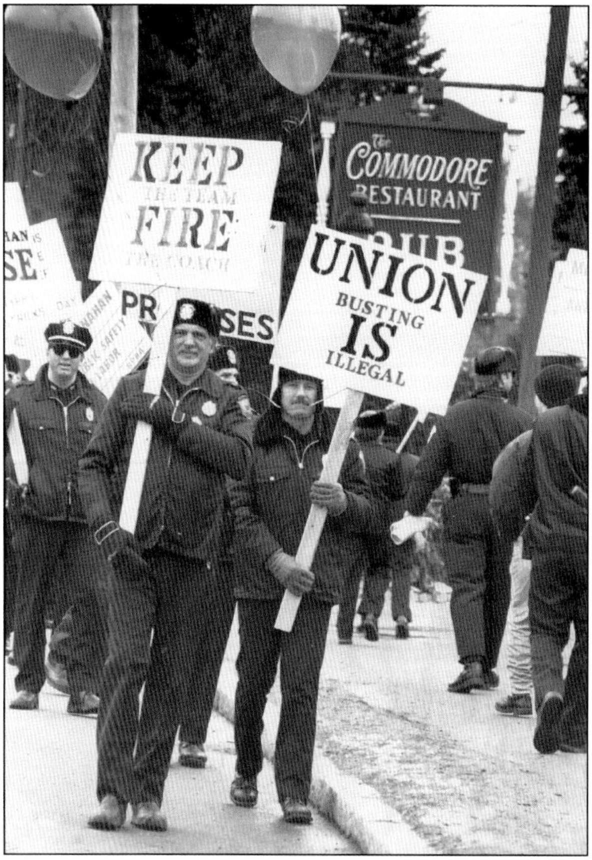

In 1990–1991, Beverly police and the city engaged in a bitter long-term dispute over union contracts. The photograph to the left shows officers picketing at the Commodore Restaurant in March 1990, seeking to embarrass Mayor F. John Monahan during the annual St. Patrick's Day party, which attracted area and state politicians. The Commodore Restaurant, perhaps the most popular of Beverly's full-service dining spots, was owned and operated by the Frangos brothers—John, Mike, and Charles. In the mid-1950s, the brothers took over an Enon Street ice cream stand and built a restaurant that featured function rooms, a pub, and a huge waterwheel. After the restaurant closed, the site became the Commodore Plaza. In September 1991, police showed up again (below) to picket outside a city election candidates' night hosted by the Centerville Improvement Society. (Both courtesy of the *Salem News*.)

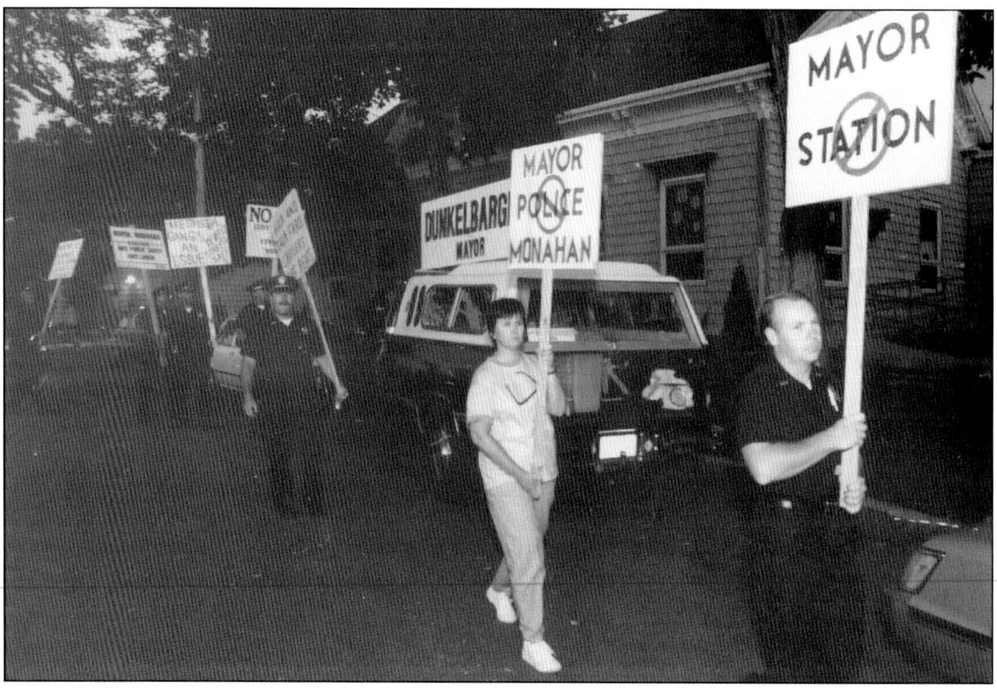

Ten

ARTS AND CULTURE

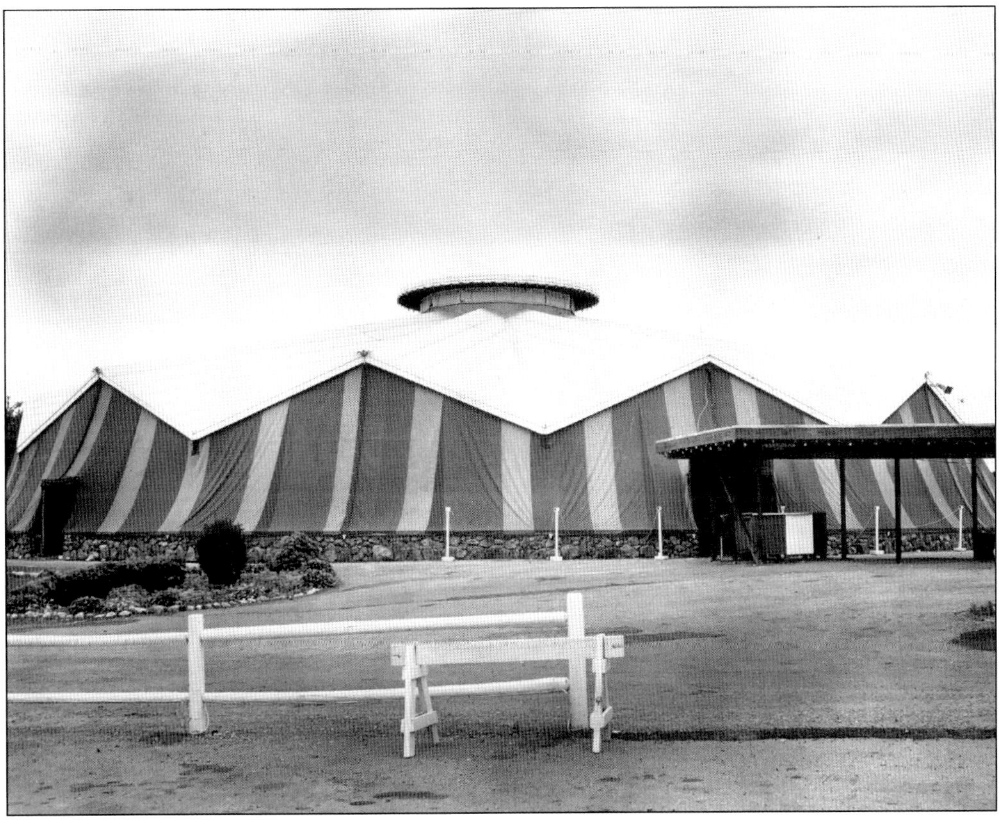

The North Shore Music Theater (NSMT) opened for business in Beverly in 1955 with a performance of *Kiss Me Kate*, and it has been one of Beverly's most cherished cultural institutions since then. Beverly residents care about all forms of culture, including music, theater, magic, art, writing, and history. These traditions began early with theatricals by summer residents and activities sponsored by the Shoe.

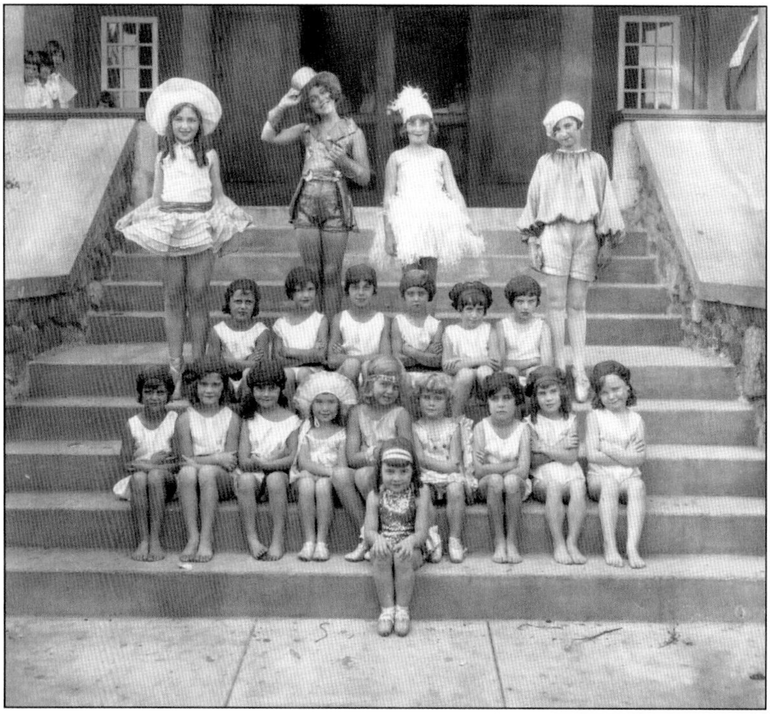

The Shoe offered a variety of activities for its employees and their families and urged them to "work hard, play hard." The right atmosphere was provided by a company clubhouse, which had a theater, an auditorium, a library, locker rooms, and bowling alleys. The children of the workers were also involved in group activities. These little girls performed a dance routine at the 1930 Sam Sam carnival.

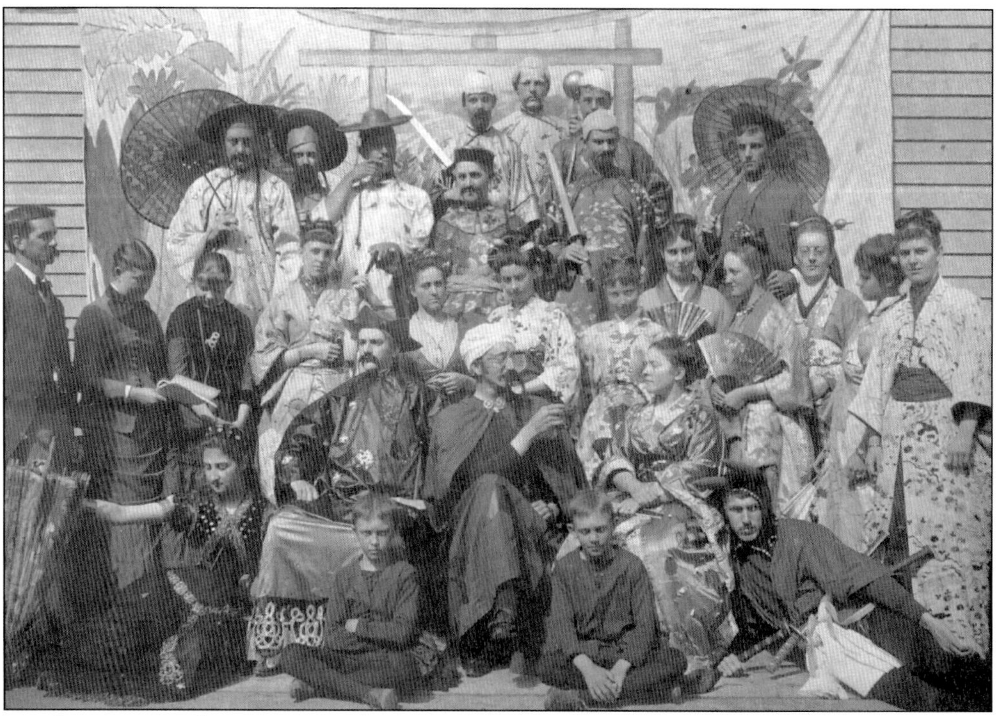

Popular events in the 1880s were the operettas performed by the people of First Parish Church. The musical *Aladdin's Lamp* was written, as were other plays, by Augustus P. Loring and was produced in 1883. In newspaper publicity it was described as "wholesome and innocent." A later production was entitled *Waiwonaissa*. The author described it as "plagiarized from everyone."

The Guild of Beverly Artists was founded in 1935. It does several shows annually and also offers demonstrations, education, and scholarships. Shown is the guild's 1954 fall festival at the Monastery at Lynch Park, which was originally owned by the Sohier family and later by the Hunt sisters. Its name came from the choice of decor, including heavy wooden doors with images of monks. The building was destroyed by fire in 1966.

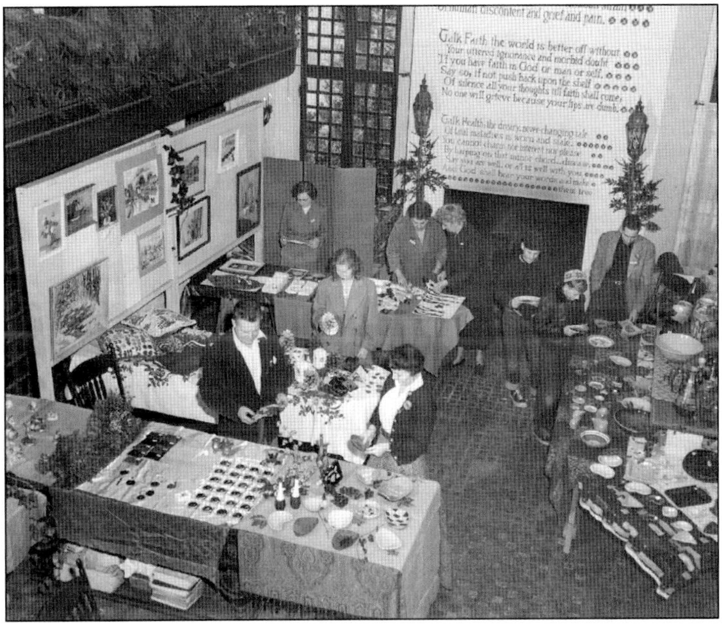

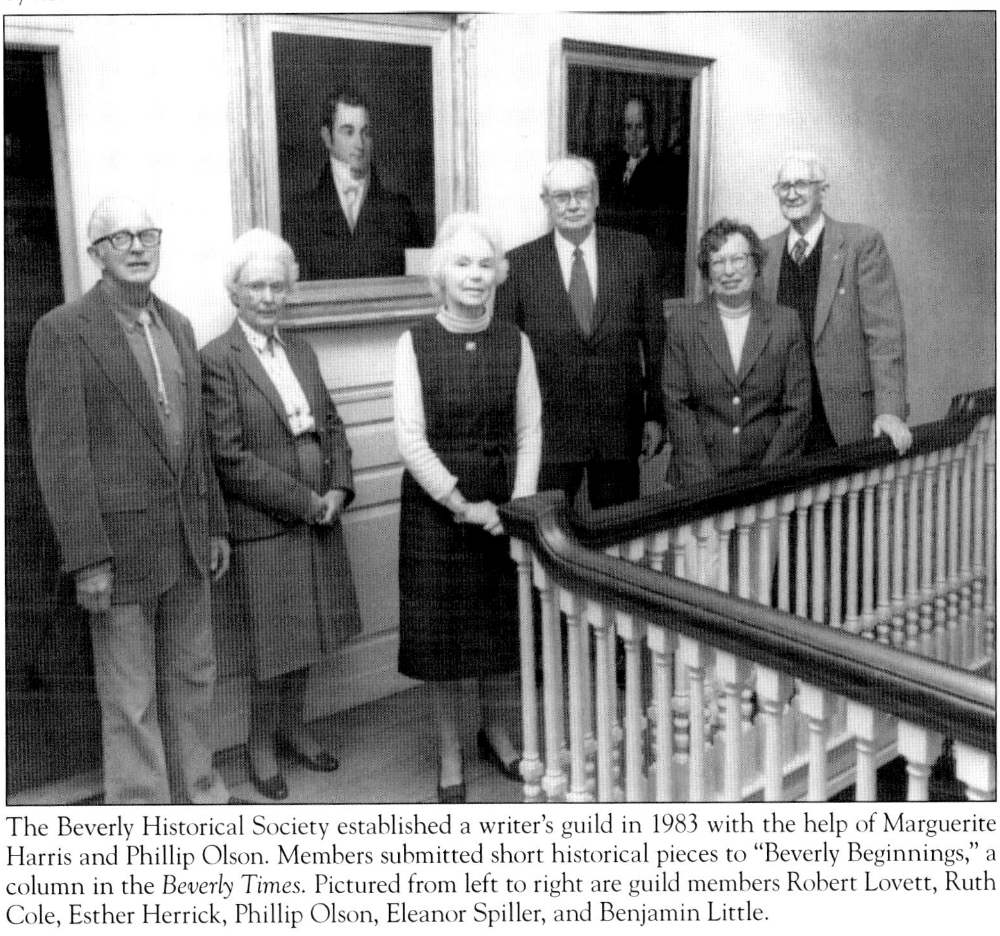

The Beverly Historical Society established a writer's guild in 1983 with the help of Marguerite Harris and Phillip Olson. Members submitted short historical pieces to "Beverly Beginnings," a column in the *Beverly Times*. Pictured from left to right are guild members Robert Lovett, Ruth Cole, Esther Herrick, Phillip Olson, Eleanor Spiller, and Benjamin Little.

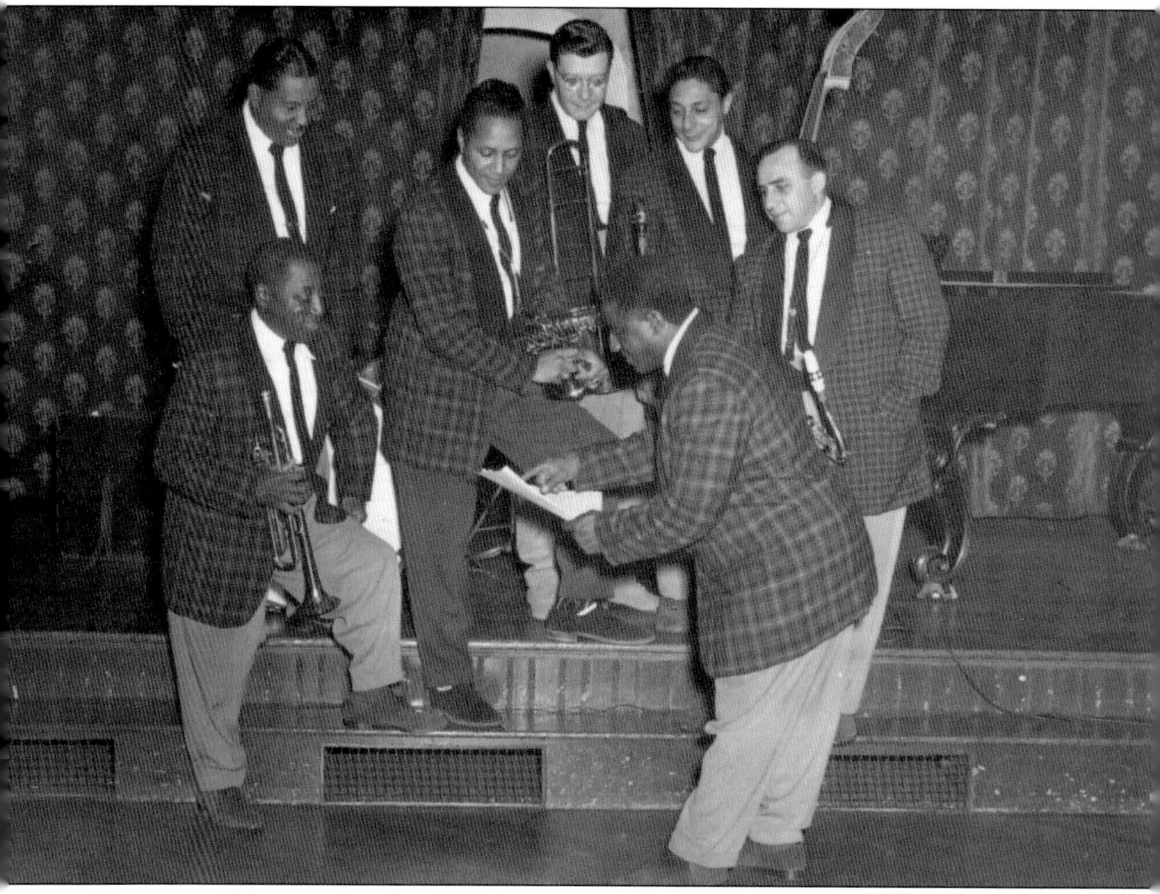

No one would have predicted in 1916 that a group of high school musicians who offered to play for a graduation dance would have lasted as a band for nearly a century. Manuel's Black and White was formed in 1916 by David and Otis Manuel when many musicians were away in Europe fighting World War I. The Manuel brothers, who were of black, Portuguese, and Native American descent, wanted the name of their band to reflect the varied ethnicity of its members. Seven original members were later joined by Al Mitchell, and they spent the 1930s and 1940s touring. Another member, Joe Boccia, reported that the mixed-race group had no problems with bookings or housing while on the road. The people just enjoyed the music. Eventually Manuel's Black and White returned home and, for many years, entertained at local events.

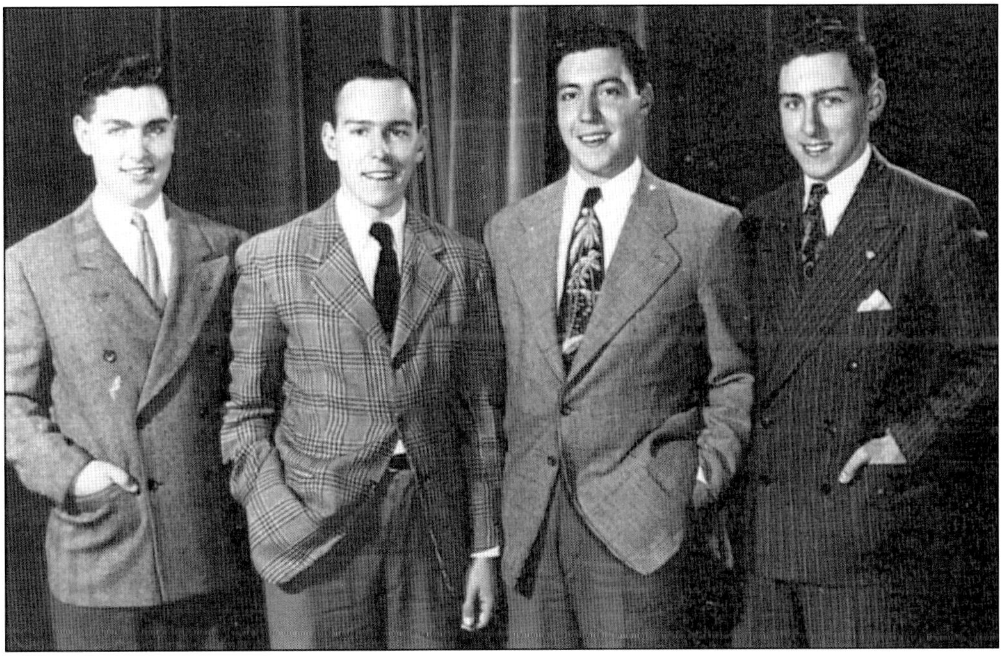

The Nuccio Quartet was a group of four Beverly brothers whose specialty was barbershop music. The men were part of a local family whose love of music was well known on the North Shore. Following World War II, the quartet sang for WESX radio, in various Boston locations, and at many local functions in Beverly.

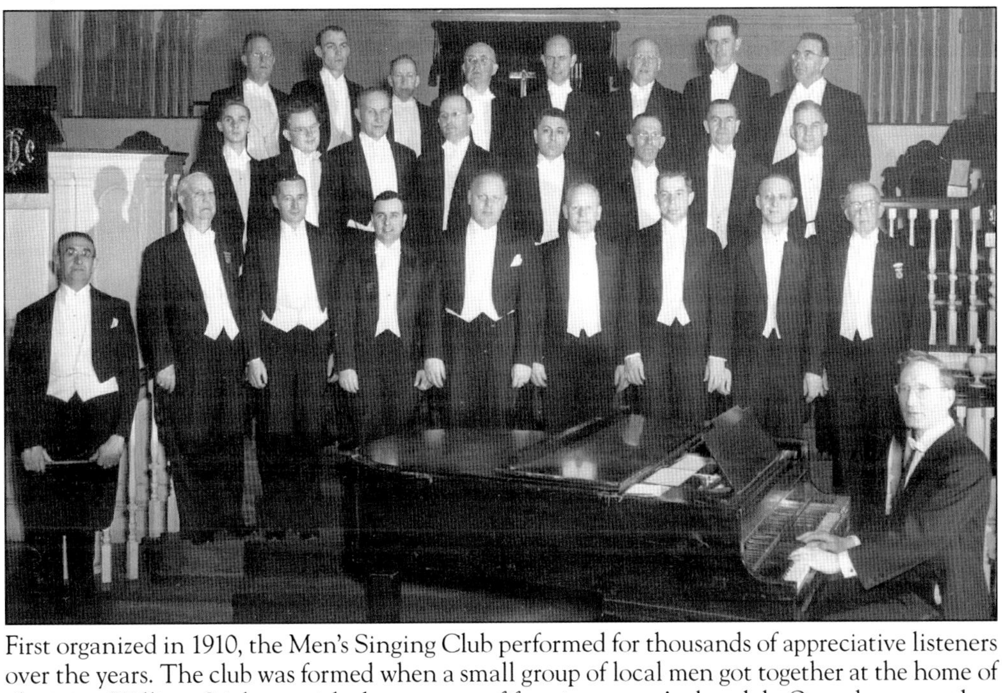

First organized in 1910, the Men's Singing Club performed for thousands of appreciative listeners over the years. The club was formed when a small group of local men got together at the home of physician William Stickney with the purpose of forming a men's glee club. Over the years, they sang at concerts in New York City, Philadelphia, and at venues all over New England, where they won many trophies.

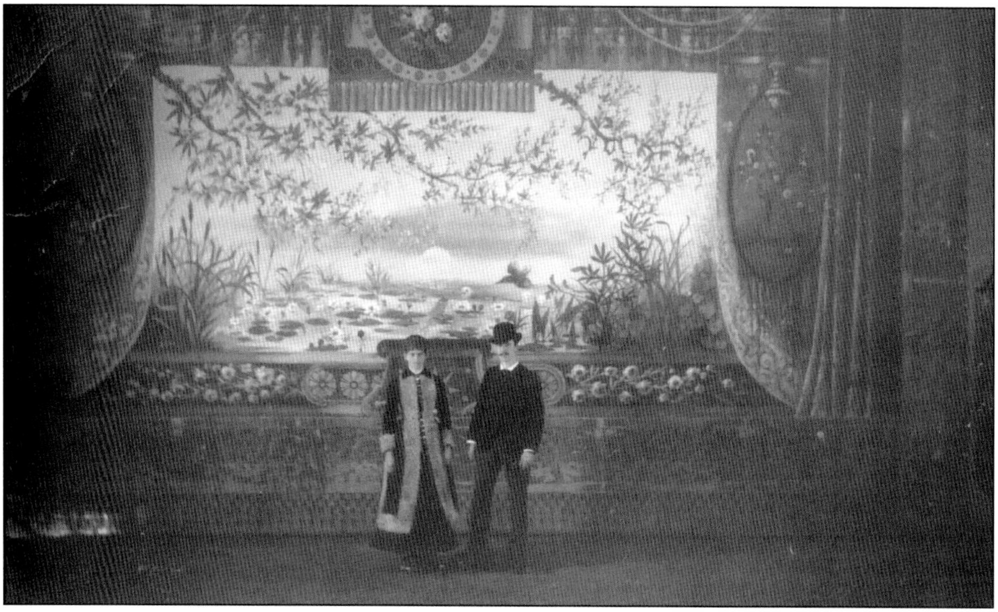

The LeFavour Opera House, which was located between Railroad and Vestry Streets, was built in 1883 by Israel LeFavour. With a seating capacity of between 600 and 800 in the orchestra and 200 in the balcony, the opera house offered a wide range of entertainment, which the *Beverly Citizen* noted "has always been of a high and meritorious order." The building burned in 1927.

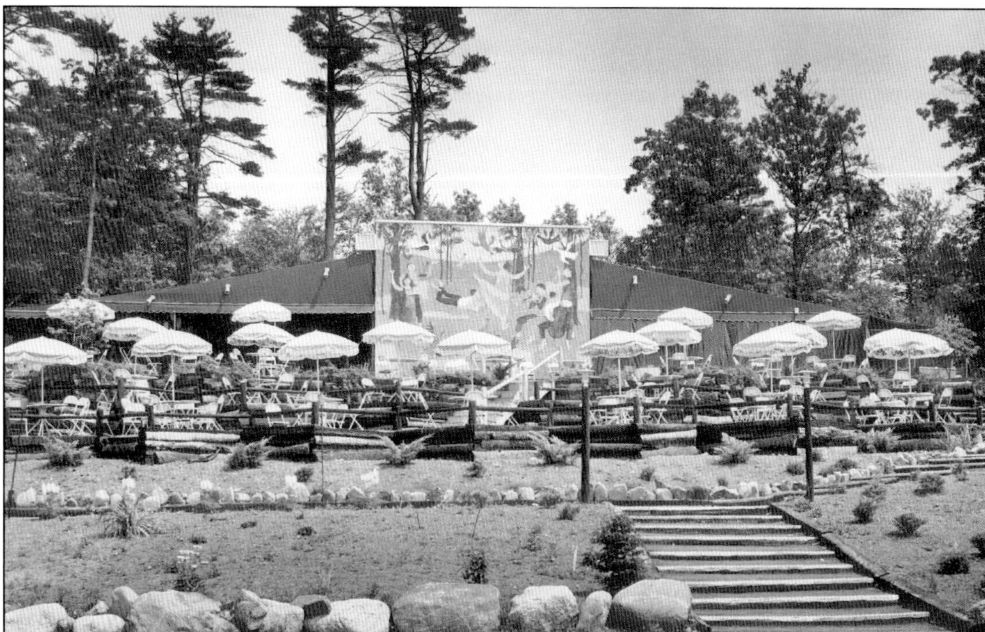

The North Shore Music Theater (NSMT) was designed by the Boston architectural firm of Salzberg and LeBlanc, which created the 12-gabled theater-in-the-round. It was designed to have the feeling of a tent, but would be a permanent building. This theater was the first in the country to feature an arena-style design that offered visitors unobstructed views. The old dinner patio was a popular destination for before-show meals.

From its earliest days, the NSMT designed programs and productions for children. For many young people this was their first experience of live theater. In the 1980s, the Montserrat School of Art (now Montserrat College of Art) first opened on the campus of NSMT. In the first decade of the 21st century, NSMT shows were seen by approximately 300,000 patrons each year. A devastating fire and a series of financial problems forced the management to close NSMT in 2009. Bill Hanney purchased the property in 2010, and area residents look forward to revisiting this local treasure.

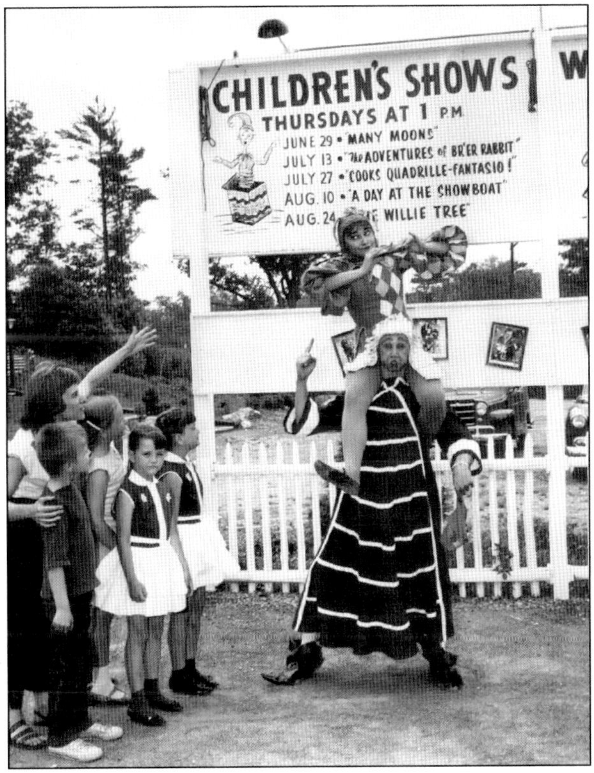

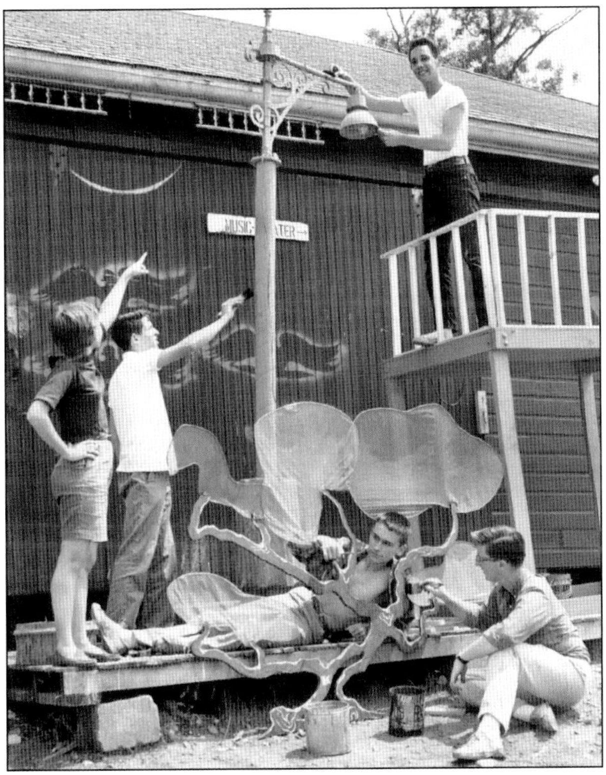

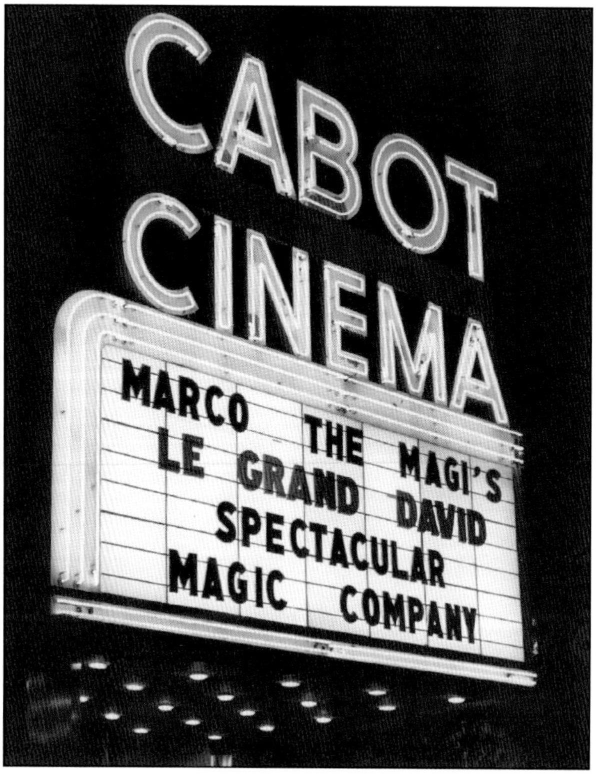

The Ware Theatre was built in 1920. Live variety shows were held there at first, with music provided by an Austin pipe organ. E. M. Loew purchased the theater in the 1930s, making the building a movie house. Restored in 1976 to much of its former glory and renamed the Cabot Street Cinema Theatre, it became the home of Le Grand David and his own Spectacular Magic Company in 1977. Much of the spectacular original interior remains, including ornate plasterwork. Today the Cabot is an elegant reminder of the way moviegoing used to be, with ushers in tuxedos, music, and a café.

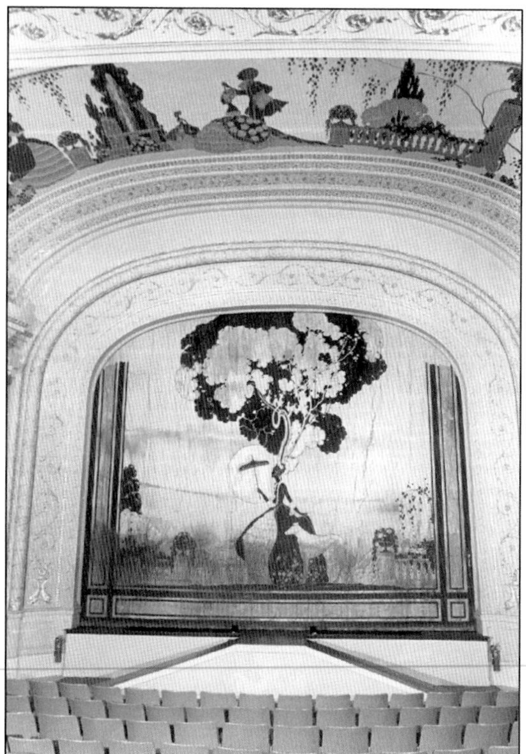

The excitement, opulence, mystery, and comedy of Beverly's own stage magic show have received attention from around the country. Founder Cesareo Pelaez, better known as Marco the Magi, had a dream to start his own major magic show. In February 1977, Marco and Le Grand David (David Bull) opened their first production. At its peak, the enthusiastic troupe had as many as 75 people involved on stage or behind the scenes. Le Grand David is shown by himself at right and below in the cabinet, with Marco at left. The show is performed at both the Cabot Street Cinema Theatre and the Larcom Theatre on Wallis Street.

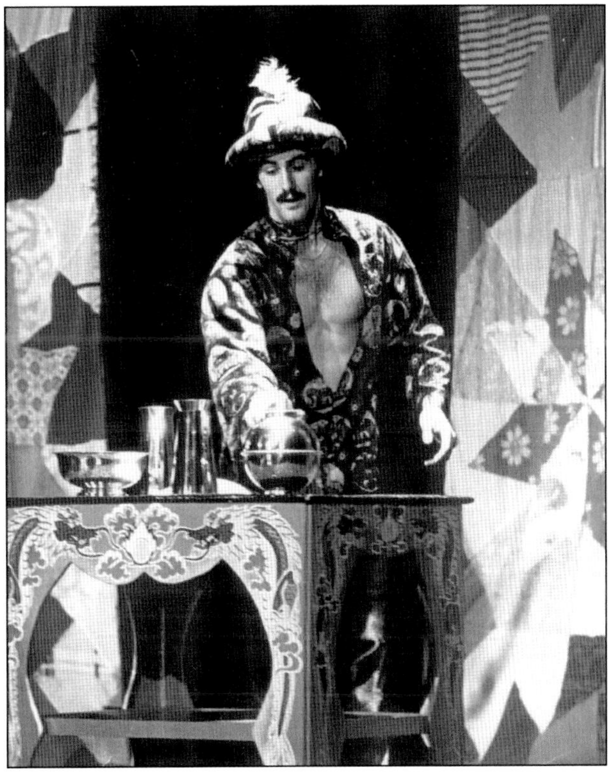

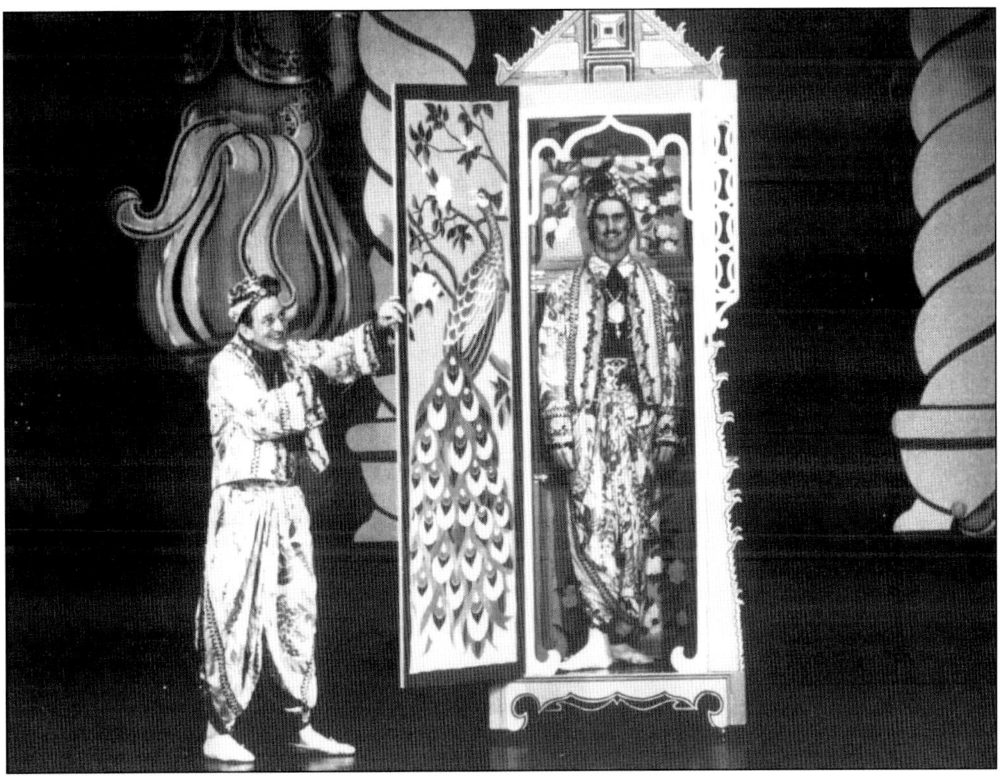

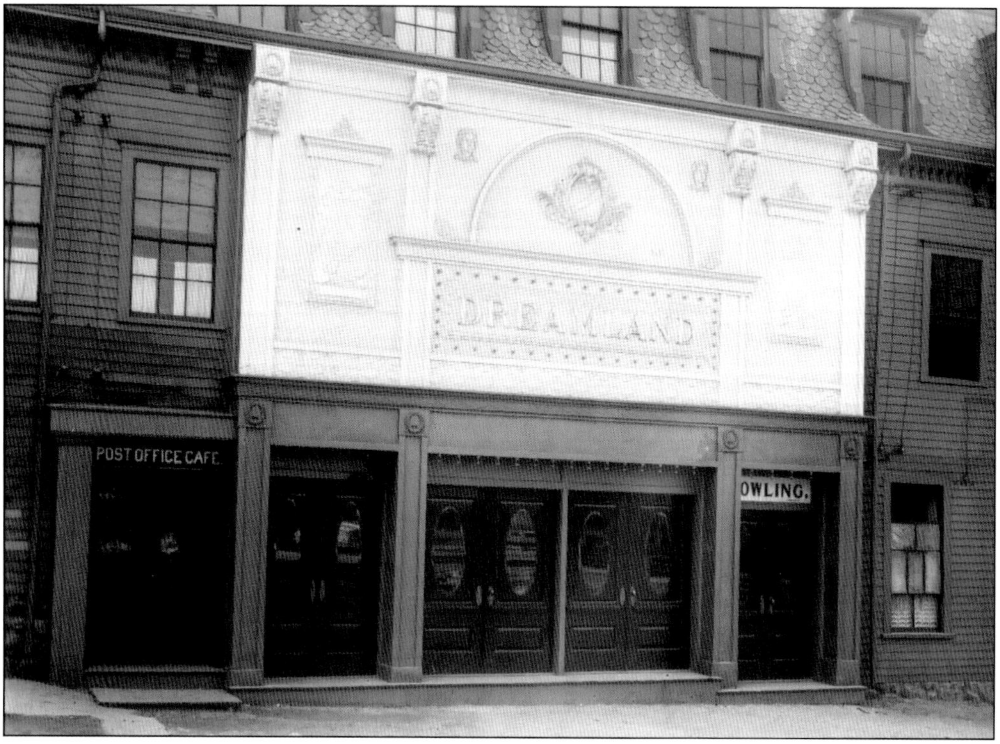

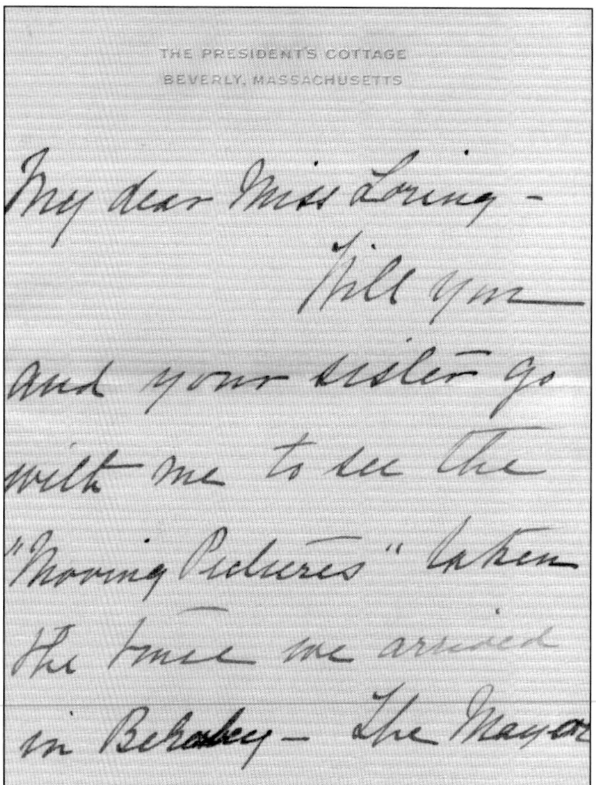

THE PRESIDENT'S COTTAGE
BEVERLY, MASSACHUSETTS

My dear Miss Loring -
Will you
and your sister go
with me to see the
"Moving Pictures" taken
the time we arrived
in Beverly - The Mayor

The Dreamland Theatre, located in the former Seth Norwood Shoe Factory at 66–68 Railroad Avenue, was the first theater in Beverly to show movies, with the first on Labor Day 1909. Pres. Taft and his wife, Nellie, enjoyed the theater and were frequent visitors at the Dreamland. In this letter written to Katharine and Louisa Loring dated July 7, 1910, Nellie Taft wrote, "My dear Miss Loring – Will you and your sister go with me to see the 'Moving Pictures.' Taking the train we arrived in Beverly. The mayor came over and wanted me to go. I will send after you if you will go. It is in 'Dreamland' opposite the railway station at 5 o'clock. Hoping to have the pleasure of having you with me. Sincerely yours, Helen H. Taft. Telephone if you can come."

About the Beverly Historical Society

In 1891, men representative of Beverly's early families founded the Beverly Historical Society. Soon after, Edward Burley willed his home, the 1781 John Cabot House, to the society for its headquarters, and it remains so today, with two floors of exhibits and a research library. The house was built by merchant John Cabot after he moved from Salem. It became the first home of the Beverly Bank in 1802, with vaults in the basement and first floor, which can be seen today. The bank moved in 1868, and the John Cabot House remained a residence until the society acquired the property from Burley.

Notable early officers of the society include poet Lucy Larcom, preservationist Arthur Appleton, and Katharine Peabody Loring. The society's collection has nearly 1 million objects and documents, including manuscripts, books, photographs, paintings, furniture, decorative arts, and other artifacts related to the history of Beverly and the North Shore.

In 1932, the society acquired the Balch House, an important first-period structure. John Balch was one of Beverly's first settlers and was on the site as early as 1636. Balch descendants remain important contributors to the society and gather periodically at the house. The society preserves the house and opens it to visitors and has developed school programming based on the results of a 1998 archaeological dig.

The society acquired the 1694 Hale Farm in 1937. Built for John Hale, Beverly's first minister, the property originally extended to the water and is still spacious enough for a variety of events and programming.

The society received the Walker Transportation Collection in 1969 from Laurence Breed Walker. Encompassing all modes of transportation, it is primarily a document and image collection and has significantly increased in size since the original gift.

The society collects, preserves, and interprets Beverly history, offering a variety of programming, and now digitizes its collections, offering more services online. Members and volunteers, who are critically important to the society, also write for publication, including *John Hale: A Man Beset by Witches*, *North Beverly Remembered*, *Reflections of Mid-20th Century Beverly*, and *Thieves, Cowbeaters and Other True Tales of Colonial Beverly*.